GERMAN
20TH CENTURY
PHILOSOPHY

GERMAN
20TH CENTURY
PHILOSOPHY
The Frankfurt School

Edited by Wolfgang Schirmacher

CONTINUUM

NEW YORK

2000
The Continuum International Publishing Group Inc
370 Lexington Avenue, New York, NY 10017

The German Library
is published in cooperation with Deutsches Haus,
New York University.
This volume has been supported by Inter Nationes,
and a grant from the funds of
Stifterverband für die Deutsche Wissenschaft.

Printed in the United States of America

Library of Congress Cataloging-in-Publication Data

German 20th century philosophy : the Frankfurt school / edited by
Wolfgang Schirmacher.
        p.   cm. — (The German library : v. 78)
    Includes bibliographical references.
    ISBN 0-8264-0966-0. — ISBN 0-8264-0967-9 (paperback)
    1. Critical theory.   I. Schirmacher, Wolfgang.   II. Series.
B3183.5.G47   2000
142—dc21   98-22507
                                                            CIP

Acknowledgments will be found on page 245,
which constitutes an extension of the copyright page.

Contents

Introduction

There is no right way of living a damaged life. We may have more reason today than ever to heed this warning. And the words with which Max Horkheimer and Theodor W. Adorno ended the first chapter of their jointly written *Dialectic of Enlightenment* in 1947 strike us now, on the threshold of the twenty-first century, as prophetic: "Yet the fully enlightened earth radiates disaster triumphant."[1] For all their differences in philosophical temperament and individual scientific interests, the theorists associated with the Frankfurt Institute for Social Research were in complete agreement on one thing—their relentless refusal to make peace with the prevailing conditions. They worked "in opposition to existing conditions" (Leo Löwenthal) to determine anew how we, as individuals, can live humanly with our fellow human beings. The Critical Theory of the Frankfurt School, as it became widely known, never withdrew into an ivory tower; it combined an expressly materialistic theory with the goal of changing social praxis. Critical Theory's defiant and undogmatic Marxism allowed for sociological macro- and microanalyses, a social philosophy in touch with social reality, yet at the same time a darkly primed anthropology borrowed from Arthur Schopenhauer protected it from falling prey to the belief in a linear progress. It is not without irony that the dark side of the Enlightenment, its ambiguous dialectic, has been described so revealingly by the same advocates of the Enlightenment: "In the most general sense of progressive thought, the Enlightenment has always aimed at liberating men from fear and establishing their sovereignty."[2] How was it possible then that "humanity, instead of entering into a truly human condition, lapsed into a new kind of barbarism?" Adorno, a German Jew as were most members of the Frankfurt School, forced to emigrate in 1934, gave a bitter characterization of the utter madness of the self-proclaimed members of the "master race" (*Herrenmenschen*), in "Meditations on Metaphysics," the last section of his *Negative Dialectics* from 1964:

> Auschwitz demonstrated irrefutably that culture has failed. That this could happen in the midst of the traditions of philosophy, of art, and of the enlightening sciences says more than that these traditions and their spirit lacked the power to take hold of men and work a change in them. There is untruth in those fields themselves, in the autarky that is emphatically claimed for them. All post–Auschwitz culture, including its urgent critique, is garbage.[3]

All that could be achieved under such conditions that were "rotten to the very core" (Adorno) was "solidarity with those who suffer" (Horkheimer) and radical counterthinking. The sustained vantage to Critical Theory is due not lastly to that existential gesture with which each new generation spontaneously and vulnerably reacts to the outrageous injustice of life. All attempts at appeasement are defied; something must be done. Much to the disapproval of dogmatic Marxists, the Frankfurt School was little concerned with class struggle and the redistribution of economic resources: instead, the causes were addressed. Theirs was a fundamental rejection of conditions degrading to human dignity and spirit, conditions with which the individual must not be reconciled. Society, economics, technology, science, and culture all stood accused. Essentially, Critical Theory grew out of analysis as discerning as it was unsparing, conducted with the resources of philosophy, sociology, psychoanalysis, and literary criticism. No real improvement in existing conditions was truly expected of any party claiming to be the "vanguard of the working class," as none had gone through the "Great Refusal" of which Herbert Marcuse believed the rebellious students of Berkeley and Paris capable, for one optimistic moment, in the late 1960s.

The most noted philosopher of the Frankfurt School was unquestionably Theodor Adorno,[4] and his "negative dialectics" is to be regarded as a philosophy resolute "in the face of despair."[5] In contradiction to Hegel, the founder of modern dialectics and advocate of all-embracing synthesis, Adorno vehemently insisted that the whole is the untrue.[6] Initially drawn to the phenomenology of Edmund Husserl, Adorno became evermore Marxist-oriented under the influence of Walter Benjamin, and beginning in 1931 he built up the Frankfurt Institute for Social Research together with his close friend and collaborator Max Horkheimer. Yet with respect to the philosophy of history, Adorno remained a skeptic. Not only does his dialectics reject a positive end, it demands of identity-seeking thought its own refutation. Conceding that "to think is to identify," he went on to stress: "dialectics is the consistent sense of nonidentity."[7] Adorno shares this adamant denial of communicative consent as well as the resistance to the total incorporation of things—inherent to subject and thought—with the postmodern thinkers of difference, such as Jacques Derrida and Jean-François Lyotard, who are not always endorsed by today's members of the Frankfurt School—Jürgen Habermas for one. Adorno aimed to protect the particular, the nonidentical and incommensurate from the totalitarian grip of ontological thinking in identities without severing the link to social praxis. The world as it is, the suffering occurring in it every day dare not leave thinking unmoved. On the contrary:

> If negative dialectics calls for the self-reflection of thinking, the tangible implication is that if thinking is to be true—if it is to be true today, in any case—it must also be a thinking against itself. If thought is not measured by the extremity that eludes the concept, it is from the outset in the nature of the musical accompaniment with which the SS liked to drown out the screams of its victims.[8]

From art, Adorno learned to seek out the moment of the true within the havoc and dread of reality, taking it to heart and bringing it to bear in his philosophy: "It lies in the definition of negative dialectics that it will not come to rest in itself, as if it were total. That is its form of hope."[9] The son of an opera singer, Adorno came to appreciate early on the power of aesthetic experience. This familial predisposition and his own inclinations nurtured the decision to take up music. He studied in Vienna with the composer Alban Berg and trained to become a concert pianist. The *wunderkind* lost none of his intensity as he matured; at eighteen he excelled as music critic. But Adorno then switched to philosophy. He received his doctorate at twenty, and in 1933 he produced his first major work, *Kierkegaard: Construction of the Aesthetic.* In art, the mirror-image of an entirely different world can be glimpsed as "sensual appearance of a sense scattered throughout experience." Unlike the postmodernists, Adorno adhered to the difference between art and life whose interplay of appropriation and repulsion cannot be stayed. "Art reaches in gesture for reality only to shrink back from it in the very moment of contact," Adorno tells us in the unfinished, posthumous work *Aesthetic Theory:* "By rejecting reality—and this is not a form of escapism but an inherent quality of art—art vindicates reality."[10] He conceived of the hope that avant-garde art might be the last refuge of truth. Aesthete and music expert, Adorno couldn't find much redeeming value in popular art, and his devastatingly unfair judgment on jazz was used against him often enough. He rejected as philistine the notion of art as functioning in service to life. Nor did he consciously trouble to write in an easily understandable, consumable manner. His philosophical style resembles more the music of Arnold Schönberg, which he loved. Adorno's writings become transparent and even enjoyable only for those who make an effort to learn difficult basic concepts and to read to a different rhythm. Yet despite his harsh critique of culture and civilization in *Dialectic of Enlightenment* and *Minima Moralia*, Adorno was no elitist Mandarin professing to be a Marxist, he possessed rather the sensitivity of a seismograph, registering precisely, as early as the 1940s, the problematic nature of mass culture. Adorno emigrated with the Institute for Social Research to New York, settling there for a time but then landed in Hollywood of all places, where he saw the newest films being made and was able to observe the practices of the culture industry close up.

> The rarified talk about film as an art doubtless befits hacks wishing to recommend themselves; but the conscious appeal to naivete, to the servants' obtuseness that has long since permeated the thoughts of the masters, is equally worthless. Film, which today attaches itself inescapably to men as if it were a part of them, is at the same time remotest of all from their human destiny, which might be realized from one day to the next; and apologetics for it are sustained by resistance to thinking this antinomy. That the people who make films are in no way schemers is no counterargument. The objective spirit of manipulation asserts itself in experiential rules, appraisals of the situation, technical criteria, economically inevitable calculations, the whole specific weight of the industrial apparatus, without any special censorship being needed, and even if the masses were asked they would reflect back the ubiquity of the system. The producers no more function as subjects than do their workers and consumers, but merely as components in a self-regulating machinery. The Hegelian-sounding precept, however, that mass-art should reflect the real taste of the masses and not that of carping intellectuals, is usurpation. The film's opposition, as an all-encompassing ideology, to the objective interests of humankind, its interlacement with the status quo of profit-motivation, bad conscience, and deceit can be conclusively demonstrated. No appeal to an actually existent state of consciousness could ever have the right to veto insight which transcended this state of consciousness by discerning its contradiction to itself and to objective conditions.[11]

In 1949, Adorno returned to Germany. In addition to writing *Dialectic of Enlightenment* during his American exile, he also worked on the innovative study *The Authoritarian Personality*, which firmly established his reputation as empirical sociologist. The intellectual-political climate in the former Federal Republic of Germany was not favorable to the proponents of Critical Theory, and it was not until 1956 that Adorno received tenure as professor at the University of Frankfurt after his friend Horkheimer had been Rector from 1951 to 1953. When the student movement in America, decisively influenced by Marcuse, a former member of the Institute, spread to West Germany, the rebels rediscovered the writings of the other members of the Frankfurt School. The nearly forgotten *Dialectic of Enlightenment* was printed in a pirated edition, Walter Benjamin's works enjoyed an unexpected renaissance, and Adorno's young assistant, Jürgen Habermas, gained prominence as ally to the students' cause, but of a definitely critical bent. Adorno's students could be found in the front lines of the barricades. And for a few years the Frankfurt School became what it had never wanted to be, a ruling ideology that tolerated no strange gods beside it. In the "positivism debate" Adorno won out against the German followers of the critical rationalist Karl Popper, and the once-dominant school that formed around Martin Heidegger disappeared. But the antiauthoritarian disposition soon changed to persecution of dissenters in the universities. Adorno shuddered at those who believed that they had been called by him and justified their activism with quotes from his writings. It was especially infuriating to the freethinker when bare-breasted female students disrupted his lecture in protest of the patriarchate. Deeply offended, the philosopher fled to Wallis, in Switzerland, for the summer holidays and during the summer of 1969 he died there, only sixty-five-years old. Adorno's enduring impact is due above all to a sensibility, rare among philosophers, through which he combines the eternal questions of philosophy and the artist's love of the particular. Adorno is a postmetaphysical thinker not because he presented modest philosophical proposals, as does the Frankfurt School of today, but because he knew how to protect the uniqueness of the particular from every theoretical assimilation and dominion. "There is solidarity between such thinking and metaphysics and the time of its fall,"[12] the closing words of *Negative Dialectics* remind us. The leading philosopher of the Frankfurt School left behind no doctrine as legacy, despite the wealth of writings collected in the thirty-three-volume edition of the *Complete Works*. This was not his weakness, but his strength. He showed us, by example, "negation" as the enlightened path to truly critical thinking.

If Theodor Adorno was the brain, then fellow combatant Max Horkheimer, eight years Adorno's senior, was the uncontested control center and shrewd manager of the Frankfurt School. The son of a textile manufacturer, Horkheimer first joined his father's business, but then completed his secondary education and went on to study philosophy in Frankfurt and Freiburg. The phenomenology of Husserl and neo-Kantianism were an integral part of Horkheimer's academic education, but the decisive impetus toward critical theory came from two nineteenth-century philosophers who could not have been more different: Karl Marx and Arthur Schopenhauer. In his key essay "Traditional and Critical Theory" from 1937, Horkheimer dissociates himself from a theory that will not fight for the abolishment of entrenched injustice. In 1930, Horkheimer, newly appointed philosophy professor at the University of Frankfurt, was also named Director of the Institute for Social Research, founded in 1924, the core members of which included Herbert Marcuse, Leo Löwenthal, Friedrich Pollock, and Erich Fromm (until 1939). After the National Socialists seized power in 1933, the Institute, which was financed through grants and donations, had to relocate—first to Geneva, then on to Columbia University in New York and later California. The Institute became a safe haven for a great many German emigrants in the United States, helping them survive. Even Benjamin, in Paris, and Norbert Elias, in Zurich, counted on the support coming through Horkheimer. The five-volume *Studies in Prejudice*, to which all the Institute members contributed, was published after the war (1949–50) and dealt with the psychological and sociological dynamics of the authoritarian personality, of anti-Semitism, as well as of propaganda.

In their *Dialectic of Enlightenment*, Adorno and Horkheimer had persuasively demonstrated how destructive the effects of the domination of nature are, specifically a domination addicted to nature, itself in thrall to an enlightenment which restricts reason to scientific rationality. Horkheimer intensified his bold critique of instrumental reason in his *Eclipse of Reason* (1947), based on his lectures at Columbia University. He saw in store for us in the transition to a regulated world and a fully automated society the "decline of the individual" and the subjugation of human beings through technology. Scientific mania for progress and totalitarian politics destroy Western civilization. "Where theory does not serve man, we have estrangement, meanness, narrow-mindedness," the contentious philosopher declared, and countered with a philosophy of history that needs no firm belief in salvation yet strives to redeem the utopia of a life in solidarity. A skeptical moralist who sought to correct Marx with Schopenhauer, Horkheimer recognized that at the end of progress of a self-annulling reason nothing is left but the regression to barbarism or the beginning of history. Harboring no illusions, Horkheimer sums up: "The Enlightenment set out to destroy lies and myths and to help truth and freedom triumph. But after its work of destruction had been done, it was compelled to recognize that freedom and truth themselves were part of those myths." The later Horkheimer recommended a return to creative dreams and voluntarily imposed prohibitions, putting his faith in a "corporeal reason" (Nietzsche), which had escaped the coercion toward a system. But he did not shrug off the nightmare of our existence, and in the posthumously published *Notes* (1974) we read the harsh words: "The radically evil in the world exercises its dominion over all creatures the world over and up to the sun."

The thinkers committed to Critical Theory fluctuated constantly between hope and desperation, and when Horkheimer and Adorno painted the gloomiest of pictures, Walter Benjamin responded with his messianic philosophy of history. He greeted Paul Klee's *Angelus Novus* as the "angel of history" who shows us that what we await in the future has already arrived. The "aura" of art has decayed and the new barbarians wear Mickey Mouse smiles. Destruction rejuvenates, commented Benjamin, and his critique of culture denied itself all anachronistic lamentation. Photography and film changed our perception and shattered the aura which was no match for even the Dadaist "Shock." In view of the poverty of experience, the modern individual evolves into a designer who manages with a minimum and makes a fresh start. The philosophical flaneur, whose *Arcades Project* resembles more an unending tale with every new manuscript find, cannot be reduced to a "theological incandescence" (Adorno). As literary theorist and philosopher, Benjamin toiled in the quarry of the past and brought forth saving images of resistance. His "materialistic theology" (Gershom Scholem) conceived of retrieving "forgotten humanness" for a fulfilled time of the present. His "micrological eye" (a quality for which Norbert Elias also was known) discovered the sign of the time in the hidden, the ephemeral, the peripheral. Benjamin's work necessarily remained a fragment, for the aesthetician sought to read the traces of the world, not erect philosophical systems. Benjamin's relevance for literary criticism, media theory, and philosophy lies in his ability to flush out what is still alive and holds potential within the gigantic heap of wreckage we call progress.

Walter Benjamin was born in Berlin, the son of a banker, and enjoyed an upper-middle-class lifestyle. He was a pampered child and retained throughout his life a taste for the finer things, but not the means. The "model of a failed intellectual" (Fritjof Hager), he found it impossible to conform and even his friends considered him quaint and something of a ditherer whose antiquated politeness set him apart. Ernst Bloch, Bertolt Brecht, Adorno, and Hugo von Hofmannsthal held Benjamin in high esteem, but the academic community rejected his most significant writings "Goethe's *Elective Affiunities*" and *The Origins of German Tragic Drama* as being incomprehensible and "obscure." Benjamin's far-reaching essay "The Work of Art in the Age of Mechanical Reproduction" is a scathing assault on bourgeois culture and undisguised praise for the new technologies with which tradition can be outwitted. The emigrant Benjamin spent a brief happy time in 1933 on the Balearic island of Ibiza, where he experienced a sense of being "co-creator of nature." He returned to Paris, for Benjamin the "capital of the nineteenth century," yet, thanks to poets like Baudelaire, at the same time holding the key to the twentieth century. Here, in this magical place, he wrote the *Theses on the Philosophy of History,* which became his legacy. When his flight from the Nazis across the Pyrenees appeared doomed to failure, Benjamin committed suicide in the Spanish port of Bou. He summed up his own life as "defeat in great things, triumph in the small." With the publication in 1955 of a controversial two-volume selection of Benjamin's *Writings,* Adorno ensured that the ideas of his friend who met such a tragic fate would not pass into obscurity. Those disillusioned children of the 1960s discovered in Benjamin someone to identify with, someone whose erudite works resist surrender of a claim to happiness.

One of those who believed to the very end in the utopian ideals of changing the world was Leo Löwenthal, who died in 1993 at a ripe old age, the last of the great thinkers of the Frankfurt School. His family was from Frankfurt, his father a physician, and he completed his doctorate in 1923 with a dissertation on Franz von Baader, philosopher of religion. Löwenthal was also a founding member of the Institute for Social Research and served from 1926 as editor of the Institute's *Journal for Social Research.* A close friend of Marcuse, Löwenthal remained in the United States after the war and taught sociology at Berkeley from 1956. His writings in the sociology of literature and communication studies have become standard texts. Löwenthal turned to a social history of the artist in opposition to the unified front of irrationalist-literature theory of his time. His works on Balzac and Zola, Hamsun and Dostoevsky, are exemplary of the productive cross-disciplinary adventures for which he was famed. His chief interest was in a pronounced ideological-critical text analysis which he expanded to include advertising and mass culture. Commissioned by the American State Department during World War II, Löwenthal analyzed German propaganda. He understood critical theory as "indication and characterization of an opprobrious world." His empirical findings could not prove more vital: "What appears at first glance to be a rather harmless world of entertainment and consumption, proves on closer observation to be a realm of spiritual terror in which the masses must needs recognize the negligibility and insignificance of their daily life. Advertising and terror form an indissoluble unity in the world of the superlative."

Löwenthal's observations on the culture industry continue Adorno's critique, but also display a confidence in the saving power of art set against mass culture. Unable to find anything laudatory in the technological duplication of artistic productions, he was all the more interested in the artist as outsider and his art as socioethical alternative to the morally indifferent forces of the market: "Art is the real message of the socially unredeemed, it is in fact the great reservoir of organized protest against social misery which allows the possibility of social happiness to shine through." Löwenthal sees the theory that history is written by the victors repudiated in the work of art. "In every work of art the voice of the losers in the world process is articulated, of those who will one day hopefully be the winners." With this hope, Löwenthal transformed a critical motive of Benjamin's *Illuminations*. In *Minima Moralia*, Adorno gave his version, pointing out: "If Benjamin said that history had hitherto been written from the standpoint of the victor, and needed to be written from that of the vanquished, we might add that knowledge must indeed present the fatally rectilinear succession of victory and defeat, but should also address itself to those things which were not embraced by this dynamic, which fell by the wayside—what might be called the waste of products and blind spots that have escaped the dialectic."[13]

The most influential thinker worldwide of the Frankfurt School is Herbert Marcuse, of whom Martin Heidegger, his former teacher, once said: "One of my best students, unfortunately corrupted by Freud." Marcuse, co-founder of Critical Theory, hoped for a new sensibility with whose help modern technology could develop into an unfettered art of living. A visionary philosopher of technology and thinker of the revolution of consciousness, he combined Marx with Freud, inner and external liberation. A native Berliner and Jewish antifascist, Marcuse declared the power of negation to be the basis of an aesthetics of freedom. As the intellectual father of the international-student movement, he was more a phenomenologically rather than ideologically oriented student of Marx, and in the 1960s he became known through such cult books as *Eros and Civilization* and *One-Dimensional Man.* The counterculture hailed Marcuse's insistence that Eros should not be repressed nor should culture be built on sublimation. But the political philosopher who had rescued Marx's *Economic-Philosophical Manuscripts* from oblivion strove to complement his hedonism with uncompromising social criticism. With his review of Hegel in the book of the same name, he argued that *Reason and Revolution* are not mutually exclusive. And his *One-Dimensional Man,* an astute forecast of the triumphal advance of the capitalistic system, became the bible of leftist critics of civilization. Since every protest is assimilated by capitalism and transformed into a product of consumption, Marcuse urged us to follow the example of authentic art and its "Great Refusal." The romantic realist could not be won for the class struggle. But he believed in the idealistic students capable of banding together in solidarity with the exploited, the ostracized, and the incapacitated out of disgust with the obscene affluent society. Not in the repressive tolerance of a society out only for a good time, which cheats us out of our autonomy, but in an aesthetic revolution did Marcuse see our chance of liberated consciousness and a radical change in our senses. Works of art cannot take the place of revolutions, but the permanence of art is brought about through its ceaseless rebellion against society. The philosopher emphasized early on the subversive role played here by pop culture.

But Marcuse was not cut out for the part of guru for the believers in the revolution, he knew the classics of philosophical literature all too well for that. Marcuse came from a well-to-do family and studied in Berlin and Freiburg, his strongest formative influence coming from the Freiburg phenomenologists Husserl and Heidegger. After completing his dissertation on the German-artist novel, Marcuse sought unsuccessfully to win Heidegger's support for his habilitation. He became interested in psychoanalysis, developed an enthusiasm for the early Marx, and established close ties with Adorno and Horkheimer, who, like Marcuse, incorporated phenomenology and historical materialism into a critical theory. When the Frankfurt Institute for Social Research was forced to flee Hitler, Marcuse also went into exile, first to Paris, then arriving in New York in 1934. He became an American citizen in 1940, and in 1954 accepted an appointment to Brandeis University. One of the sharpest critics of the Vietnam War, Marcuse was dismissed from his post, but in 1965 he was offered a professorship in San Diego. He had gained fame by then, staunchly supporting the insurgent students as well as scorning fossilized communism, and began a series of extended lecture tours. In Berkeley, Berlin, and Paris, Marcuse encouraged the New Left to uphold the right to liberation in defiance of the doctrine of nonviolence, but without falling into terrorism. Marcuse died in July 1979 during a stay at a sanatorium in Starnberg, near Munich. The two decades since his death have seen postmodernism easily overcome the oedipus complex that had created false authorities. But from Marcuse's viewpoint this liberation must be judged as half-hearted, lacking as it is in the life-enhancing solidarity of a socially fulfilled life.

Norbert Elias was the least known of the key thinkers of the Frankfurt School. He completed his doctoral dissertation "Idea and the Individual" (1924) in Breslau and his postdoctoral studies in Freiburg with Husserl, and Karl Jaspers in Heidelberg. In Frankfurt in 1930, Elias became assistant to Karl Mannheim, founder of the "sociology of knowledge," and joined the discussion circle of the Institute for Social Research. In 1933 he fled from the Nazis, first to Paris and later to England where he taught from 1938. After his retirement, he continued his research in Amsterdam. And then the almost-unknown scholar was thrust into the spotlight when he received the Adorno Award in 1977. His "process sociology of civilization," a descriptive microanalysis in the spirit of critical theory, was suddenly discovered and he became the "new" theorist of the Frankfurt School. Never mind that Elias's main work, *The Civilizing Process*, had been published back in 1939 and went completely unnoticed at the time. In addition to philosophy, Elias had studied medicine, psychology, and sociology and he made use of this broad basis of knowledge for his well-documented cultural history, which redefined civilization. On the whole, the civilizing process takes its normal course unplanned, yet does exhibit a certain order that Elias called "human figurations." This concrete order is neither reasonable nor unreasonable but instead expresses social processes of change. Elias's scientific interest was held by ordinary, everyday phenomena such as the use of knife and fork or the rituals of greeting. In these figurations, the human individual brings his or her modes of behavior in harmony with those of other individuals, and in this way achieves, over time, civilized social intercourse.

More often than not, the reality of the world bears no resemblance to our desires, but becoming civilized means replacing external controls with prudent internal restraints. With his pioneering behavioral research, Elias furnished evidence that from the "Court Society" to the present day, a steadily increasing "affect control" has held sway. So we should really marvel at how peaceful things are in the world, he challenged. Elias is widely recognized today as a "human science researcher" *(Menschenwissenschaftler)*, and he saw himself as a bridge-builder between the disciplines. He died in 1990. "I never belonged," declared Elias, whose *Studies on the German Character* (1989) trenchantly defined the German national character as shaped by historical conflicts. The iconoclast Elias anticipated the "Society of Individuals," emergent today, and bid farewell to general sociology from Marx to Talcott Parsons. "Micrology is the place where metaphysics find a haven from totality,"[14] advised Adorno, whereas the critics of the "master of micrological observation" argue that Elias describes only superficial changes beneath which we are still barbarians. But for all its enlightened optimism, Elias's "historical psychology" remained aware of the danger: that in a well-regulated community, aggressions harbored by the inhabitants are easily directed against oneself. "Compassion for the difficulties of civilization" was his express recommendation.

Jürgen Habermas is the most prominent heir of Critical Theory, but his new "Frankfurt School" differs significantly in its renunciation of all metaphysical claim to truth. Whereas his early works *Theory and Practice, Technology and Science as Ideology,* and *Knowledge and Human Interest,* with their reference to a comprehensive emancipatory reason clearly reveal the influence of Adorno and Marcuse, Habermas's own "Theory of Communicative Action" set itself far more modest goals. Philosophy should function as a "clearing house" for the sciences and initiate communicative action as mutual understanding. "It cannot be the task of philosophy to render meaning." With this precept, Habermas defined the difference to his notable predecessors and insisted on a strict delimitation between science and art. Habermas offers us an ethics of modernity: in the transformation of intersubjective convictions into a social force through the participation of an informed public. Instead of a radical critique of reason, he recommends a reason existing in the unity of diversity of its voices. Habermas freely links together the linguistic practice of individuals oriented toward understanding with a discourse theory of law, as we can follow in his treatise *Between Facts and Norms*. In the United States, Habermas is admired as a master thinker—though against his wishes—for the good reason that his "rationality of communicative action" is considered the last great philosophical system of a leftist theory of society. At the time when Critical Theory was at its influential peak, Habermas worked at the Frankfurt Institute for Social Research, was a colleague of Adorno as well as contact person for the revolutionary-minded students, and he became friends with the much older Marcuse, the "vagabond professor." Thus Habermas's function as communicator of the spirit of the Frankfurt School took on a special quality, as becomes clear through his keen and appreciative articles on Adorno, Benjamin, and Marcuse in this volume.

In his *Negative Dialectics*, Adorno proclaims "to want substance in cognition is to want a utopia" and defines philosophy as "the prism in which its [utopia's] color is caught."[15] It is not necessarily a contradiction that Elias sought to describe the nature of society in realistic terms and considered a "de-ideologizing" advisable for general sociology. We can do one thing without omitting the other, for a "critical humanism" (Elias) is of essence to both: to Horkheimer's skepticism, instructed by negative experience, as well as to Benjamin's historical-philosophical vision. Marcuse pointed to compassion with those who suffer as a central motivation of the Frankfurt School, but this insight, reminiscent of Schopenhauer, is complemented by the hope for paradise on earth, something Marx claimed was realistic. In view of the experience of totalitarianism, Critical Theory explicitly distanced itself from class struggle, for Marx the only path to liberation of the proletariat; but the Frankfurt School clung to the idea of revolution. Marcuse lays the blame for our being deprived of autonomy with the repressive tolerance of the consumer society: goods instead of liberation. Like Adorno and Benjamin, he believed in art, an art that becomes an art of living, capable of a "revolution of the senses," a worldly experience guided by creativity. Opponents argued that such an aestheticization of society made excessive demands of art and was ineffectual politically; but the members of the Frankfurt School were not put off by such pragmatic deliberations. Precisely because they had a deeper understanding of history, economics, and society than any philosophical school before them, they were not inclined to underestimate the "aesthetic dimension," as Marcuse calls it, and its transhistorical truth:

> I see the political potential of art in art itself, in the aesthetic form as such. Furthermore, I argue that by virtue of its aesthetic form, art is largely autonomous vis-a-vis the given social relation. In its autonomy art both protests these relations, and at the same time transcends them. Thereby, art subverts the dominant consciousness, the ordinary experience.[16]

Critical Theory is emphatically self-critical in conceding the necessity of art for counterthinking, for thinking against one's own convictions, without however giving up its philosophical claim to truth.

W. S.
Translated by Virginia Cutrufelli

NOTES

1. T. W. Adorno and M. Horkheimer, *Dialectic of Enlightenment*, J. Cumming, trans. New York, 1995, 3.
2. Ibid.
3. T. W. Adorno, *Negative Dialectics*, E. B. Ashton, trans. New York, 1973, 366ff.
4. Selections from *Minima Moralia, Negative Dialectics*, and *Aesthetic Theory* were planned for inclusion in this collection. But permission to reprint could not be obtained.
5. T. W. Adorno, *Minima Moralia*, E. F. N. Jephcott. London, 1978, 247.
6. Cf. Ibid., 50.
7. Adorno, *Negative Dialectics*, 5.
8. Ibid., 365.
9. Ibid., 406.
10. T. W. Adorno, *Aesthetic Theory*, C. Lenhardt, trans. London, 1984, 2.
11. Adorno, *Minima Moralia*, 205.
12. Adorno, *Negative Dialectics*, 408.
13. Adorno, *Minima Moralia*, 151.
14. Adorno, *Negative Dialectics*, 407.
15. Ibid., 57.
16. H. Marcuse, *The Aesthetic Dimension*. Boston, 1978, ix.

Max Horkheimer

ON THE CONCEPT OF PHILOSOPHY

The formalization of reason leads to a paradoxical cultural situation. On the one hand, the destructive antagonism of self and nature, an antagonism epitomizing the history of our civilization, reaches its peak in this era. We have seen how the totalitarian attempt to subdue nature reduced the ego, the human subject, to a mere tool of repression. All the other functions of the self, as expressed in general concepts and ideas, have been discredited. On the other hand, philosophical thinking, whose task it is to essay a reconciliation, has come to deny or to forget the very existence of the antagonism. What is called philosophy, together with all the other branches of culture, superficially bridges the chasm and thus adds to the dangers. An underlying assumption of the present discussion has been that philosophical awareness of these processes may help to reverse them.

Faith in philosophy means the refusal to permit fear to stunt in any way one's capacity to think. Until recently in Western history, society lacked sufficient cultural and technological resources for forging an understanding between individuals, groups, and nations. Today the material conditions exist. What is lacking are men who understand that they themselves are the subjects or the functionaries of their own oppression. Because all conditions for the development of such understanding exist, it is absurd to expect that the notion of the "immaturity of the masses" is tenable. Moreover, the observer who views the social process even in the most backward parts of Europe will be obliged to admit that those who are led are at least as mature as the wretched, inflated little *Führers* whom they are asked to follow idolatrously. The realization that at this very moment everything depends upon the right use of man's autonomy should rally those who have not been silenced to defend culture against threatened debasement at the hands of its conformist fair-weather friends or annihilation at the hands of the barbarians within the gates.

The process is irreversible. Metaphysical therapies that propose to turn back the wheel of history are, as has been said above in the discussion of neo-Thomism, vitiated by the very pragmatism they profess to abhor.

> The struggle is too late; and every means taken merely makes the disease worse; for the disease has seized the very marrow of spiritual life, viz., consciousness in its ultimate principle [*Begriff*], or its pure inmost nature itself. There is therefore no power left in conscious life to surmount the disease. . . . It is then the memory alone that still preserves the dead form of the spirit's previous state, as a vanished history, vanished men know not how. And the new serpent of wisdom, raised on high before bending worshippers, has in this manner painlessly sloughed merely a shrivelled skin.[1]

Ontological revivals are among the means that aggravate the disease. Conservative thinkers who have described the negative aspects of enlightenment, mechanization, and mass culture have often tried to mitigate the consequences of civilization either by reemphasizing old ideals or by pointing out new aims that could be pursued without the risk of revolution. The philosophy of the French counter-revolution and that of German prefascism are examples of the first-named attitude. Their critique of modern man is romanticist and anti-intellectualist. Other enemies of collectivism advance more progressive ideas, e.g., the idea of the confederation of Europe or that of political unity for the whole of the civilized world, as advocated by Gabriel Tarde[2] at the end of the nineteenth century and Ortega y Gasset[3] in our own time. Although their analyses of the objective mind of our era are most pertinent, their own educational conservatism is certainly one of its elements. Ortega y Gasset likens the masses to spoiled children;[4] the comparison appeals to just those sections of the masses that are most completely deprived of individuality. His reproach that they are ungrateful to the past is

---

1. G. W. F. Hegel, *The Phenomenology of Mind,* J. B. Baillie, trans., New York, 1931, pp. 564–65.

2. Cf. *Les Lois de l'Imitation,* Engl. trans., *The Laws of Imitation,* New York, 1903, particularly pp. 184–88 and pp. 388–93.

3. Cf. *La Rebelión de las Masas,* Engl. trans., *The Revolt of the Masses,* New York, 1932, particularly pp. 196–200.

4. Ibid., pp. 63–64.

one of the elements of mass propaganda and mass ideology. The very fact that his philosophy is slanted for popular availability, i.e., its pedagogical character, nullifies it as philosophy. Theories embodying critical insight into historical processes, when used for panaceas, have often turned into repressive doctrines. As recent history teaches, this holds true for radical as well as for conservative doctrines. Philosophy is neither a tool nor a blueprint. It can only foreshadow the path of progress as it is marked out by logical and factual necessities; in doing so it can anticipate the reaction of horror and resistance that will be evoked by the triumphal march of modern man.

There is no definition of philosophy. Definition of it is identical with the explicit account of what it has to say. However, some remarks on both definitions and philosophy may further elucidate the role that the latter could play. They will also give opportunity to clarify further our use of such abstract terms as nature and spirit, subject and object.

Definitions acquire their full meanings in the course of a historical process. They cannot be used intelligently unless we humbly concede that their penumbrae are not easily penetrated by linguistic short-cuts. If, through fear of possible misunderstandings, we agree to eliminate the historical elements and to offer supposedly atemporal sentences as definitions, we deny ourselves the intellectual heritage bequeathed to philosophy from the beginning of thought and experience. The impossibility of such a complete disavowal is evidenced in the procedure of the most antihistorical "physicalist" philosophy of our times, logical empiricism. Even its protagonists admit some undefinable terms of everyday usage into their dictionary of strictly formalized science, thus paying tribute to the historical nature of language.

Philosophy must become more sensitive to the muted testimonies of language and plumb the layers of experience preserved in it. Each language carries a meaning embodying the thought forms and belief patterns rooted in the evolution of the people who speak it. It is the repository of the variegated perspectives of prince and pauper, poet and peasant. Its forms and content are enriched or impoverished by the native usage of every man. Yet it would be a mistake to assume that we can discover the essential meaning of a word by simply asking the people who use it. Public-opinion polls are of little avail in this search. In the age of formalized reason, even the masses abet the deterioration of concepts and ideas. The man in the street, or, as he is sometimes called today, the man in the fields and factories, is learning to use words almost as schematically and unhistorically as the experts. The philosopher must avoid his example. He cannot talk about man, animal, society, world, mind, thought, as a natural scientist talks about a chemical substance: the philosopher does not have the formula.

There is no formula. Adequate description, unfolding the meaning of any of these concepts, with all its shades and its interconnections with other concepts, is still a main task. Here, the word with its half-forgotten layers of meaning and association is a guiding principle. These implications have to be re-experienced and preserved, as it were, in more enlightened and universal ideas. Today, one is too easily induced to evade complexity by surrendering to the illusion that the basic ideas will be clarified by the march of physics and technology. Industrialism puts pressure even upon the philosophers to conceive their work in terms of the processes of producing standardized cutlery. Some of them seem to feel that concepts and categories should leave their workshops clean-cut and looking brand-new.

> Hence definition renounces, of itself, the concept-terms properly so-called, which would be essentially principles of the subject-matter, and contents itself with *marks*, that is, with determinations in which *essentiality* for the object itself is a matter of indifference, and which are designed merely to be *distinguishing tokens* for an external reflection. A single *external* determinateness of this kind is so entirely inadequate to the concrete totality and the nature of its concept that its exclusive selection is beyond justification, nor could any one suppose that a concrete whole had its true expression and character in it.[5]

Each concept must be seen as a fragment of an inclusive truth in which it finds its meaning. It is precisely the building of truth out of such fragments that is philosophy's prime concern.

There is no royal road to definition. The view that philosophical concepts must be pinned down, identified, and used only when they exactly follow the dictates of the logic of identity is a symptom of the quest for certainty, the all-too-human impulse to trim intellectual needs down to pocket size. It would make it impossible to convert one concept into another without impairing its identity, as we

---

5. *Hegel's Logic of World and Idea (Being a Translation of the Second and Third Parts of the Subjective Logic) with Introduction on Idealism Limited and Absolute*, by Henry S. Macran, Oxford, 1929, p. 153 (sect. 3, ch. 2).

do when we speak of a man or a nation or a social class as remaining identical, although its qualities and all the aspects of its material existence are undergoing change. Thus study of history may prove that the attributes of the idea of freedom have been constantly in process of transformation. The postulates of the political parties who fought for it may have been contradictory even in the same generation, and still there is the identical idea that makes all the difference in the world between these parties or individuals on the one hand and the enemies of freedom on the other. If it is true that we must know what freedom is in order to determine which parties in history have fought for it, it is no less true that we must know the character of these parties in order to determine what freedom is. The answer lies in the concrete outlines of the epochs of history. The definition of freedom is the theory of history, and vice versa.

The pinning-down strategy characteristic of and justified in natural science, and wherever practical use is the goal, manipulates concepts as though they were intellectual atoms. Concepts are pieced together to form statements and propositions, and these in turn are combined to form systems. Throughout, the atomic constituents of the system remain unchanged. They are felt to attract and repel one another everywhere in the mechanism, according to the familiar principles of traditional logic, the laws of identity, contradiction, *tertium non datur,* etc. that we use, almost instinctively, in every act of manipulation. Philosophy pursues a different method. True, it also employs these hallowed principles, but in its procedure this schematism is transcended, not by arbitrary neglect of it, but by acts of cognition in which logical structure coincides with the essential traits of the object. Logic, according to philosophy, is the logic of the object as well as of the subject; it is a comprehensive theory of the basic categories and relations of society, nature, and history.

The formalistic method of definition proves particularly inadequate when applied to the concept of nature. For to define nature and its complement, spirit, is inevitably to pose either their dualism or their unity, and to pose the one or the other as an ultimate, a "fact," while in truth these two fundamental philosophical categories are inextricably interconnected. A concept such as that of "fact" can itself be understood only as a consequence of the alienation of human consciousness from extrahuman and human nature, which is in turn a consequence of civilization. This consequence, it is true, is strictly real: the dualism of nature and spirit can no more be denied in favor of their alleged original unity than the real historical trends reflected in this dualism can be reversed.

To assert the unity of nature and spirit is to attempt to break out of the present situation by an impotent *coup de force,* instead of transcending it intellectually in conformity with the potentialities and tendencies inherent in it.

In actual fact, every philosophy that ends in assertion of the unity of nature and spirit as an allegedly ultimate datum, that is to say, every kind of philosophical monism, serves to intrench the idea of man's domination of nature, the ambivalent character of which we have tried to show. The very tendency to postulate unity represents an attempt to consolidate the claim of spirit to total domination, even when this unity is in the name of the absolute opposite of spirit, nature: for nothing is supposed to remain outside the all-embracing concept. Thus even the assertion of the primacy of nature conceals within itself the assertion of the absolute sovereignty of spirit, because it is spirit that conceives this primacy of nature and subordinates everything to it. In view of this fact, it is a matter of little moment at which of the two extremes the tension between nature and spirit is resolved—whether unity is advocated in the name of absolute spirit, as in idealism, or in the name of absolute nature, as in naturalism.

Historically, these two contradictory types of thinking served the same purposes. Idealism glorified the merely existent by representing it as nevertheless spiritual in essence; it veiled the basic conflicts in society behind the harmony of its conceptual constructions, and in all its forms furthered the lie that elevates the existing to the rank of God, by attributing to it a "meaning" that it has lost in an antagonistic world. Naturalism—as we have seen in the example of Darwinism—tends to a glorification of that blind power over nature which is supposed to have its model in the blind play of the natural forces themselves; it is almost always accompanied by an element of contempt for mankind—softened, it is true, by skeptical gentleness, the attitude of a physician shaking his head—a contempt that is at the bottom of so many forms of semi-enlightened thinking. When man is assured that he is nature and nothing but nature, he is at best pitied. Passive, like everything that is only nature, he is supposed to be an object of "treatment," finally a being dependent on more or less benevolent leadership.

Theories that fail to differentiate spirit from objective nature, and define it quasiscientifically as nature, forget that spirit has also become non-nature, that, even if it were nothing but a reflection of nature, it still, by virtue of its having this character of reflection, transcends the *hic et nunc.* Ruling out of this quality of spirit—that it is simultaneously identical with and different from nature—leads directly to the view that man is essentially nothing but an element and an object of blind natural processes. As an element of nature, he is like the earth of which he is made; as earth, he is of no consequence, by the standards of his own civilization—whose complicated, streamlined artifacts, automatons, and skyscrapers are in a sense evaluated in the circumstance that he is of no greater worth than the raw material of his futile metropolises.

The real difficulty in the problem of the relation between spirit and nature is that hypostatizing the polarity of these two entities is as impermissible as reducing one of them to the other. This difficulty expresses the predicament of all philosophical thinking. It is inevitably driven to abstractions such as "nature" and "spirit," while every such abstraction implies a misrepresentation of concrete existence that ultimately affects the abstraction itself. For this reason, philosophical concepts become inadequate, empty, false, when they are abstracted from the process through which they have been obtained. The assumption of an ultimate duality is inadmissible—not only because the traditional and highly questionable requirement of an ultimate principle is logically incompatible with a dualistic construction, but because of the content of the concepts in question. The two poles cannot be reduced to a monistic principle, yet their duality too must be largely understood as a product.

Since the time of Hegel many philosophical doctrines have gravitated toward insight into the dialectical relation of nature and spirit. Only a few important examples of speculation on this topic may be mentioned here. F. H. Bradley's *One Experience* is supposed to indicate the harmony of the divergent conceptual elements. John Dewey's idea of experience is deeply related to Bradley's theory. Dewey, who in other passages, making the subject a part of nature, subscribes to naturalism *tout court,* calls experience "something which is neither exclusive and isolated subject or object, matter or mind, nor yet one plus the other."[6] Thus he shows that he belongs to the generation that evolved the *Lebensphilosophie.* Bergson, whose whole teaching seems to be an effort to overcome the antinomy, has maintained the unity in such concepts as *durée* and *élan vital,* and the separation in postulating a dualism of science and metaphysics and correspondingly of nonlife and life. Georg Simmel[7] has developed the doctrine of the capacity of life to

---

6. *Experience and Nature,* Chicago, 1925, p. 28.
7. Cf. particularly *Lebensanschauung* and *Der Konflikt der Modernen Kultur,* Munich and Leipzig, 1918.

transcend itself. However, the concept of life that underlies all these philosophies denotes a realm of nature. Even when spirit is defined as the highest stage of life, as in Simmel's metaphysical theory, the philosophical problem is still decided in favor of a refined naturalism against which Simmel's philosophy is at the same time a constant protest.

Naturalism is not altogether in error. Spirit is inseparably related to its object, nature. This is true not only with regard to its origin, the purpose of self-preservation, which is the principle of natural life, and not only logically, in the sense that every spiritual act implies matter of some kind, or "nature"; but the more recklessly spirit is posed as an absolute, the more is it in danger of retrogressing to pure myth and of modeling itself on precisely the mere nature that it claims to absorb in itself or even to create. Thus the most extreme idealistic speculations led to philosophies of nature and of mythology; the more that spirit, released from all restraint, tried to claim as its own product not only the forms of nature, as in Kantianism, but also its substance, the more does spirit lose its own specific substance, and the more do its categories become metaphors of the eternal repetition of natural sequences. The epistemologically insoluble problems of spirit make themselves felt in all forms of idealism. Although it is claimed for spirit that it is the justification or even source of all existence and of nature, its content is always referred to as something outside autonomous reason, even if only in the quite abstract form of the datum—this unavoidable aporia of all theory of knowledge testifies to the fact that the dualism of nature and spirit cannot be posed in the sense of a definition, as the classic Cartesian theory of the two substances would have it. On the one hand, each of the two poles has been torn away from the other by abstraction; on the other, their unity cannot be conceived and ascertained as a given fact.

The fundamental issue discussed in this book, the relation between the subjective and objective concepts of reason, must be treated in the light of the foregoing reflections on spirit and nature, subject and object. What has been referred to in Chapter I as subjective reason is that attitude of consciousness that adjusts itself without reservation to the alienation between subject and object, the social process of reification, out of fear that it may otherwise fall into irresponsibility, arbitrariness, and become a mere game of ideas. The present-day systems of objective reason, on the other hand, represent attempts to avoid the surrender of existence to contingency and blind hazard. But the proponents of objective reason

are in danger of lagging behind industrial and scientific developments, of asserting meaning that proves to be an illusion, and of
creating reactionary ideologies. Just as subjective reason tends to
vulgar materialism, so objective reason displays an inclination to
romanticism, and the greatest philosophical attempt to construe
objective reason, Hegel's, owes its incomparable force to its critical
insight regarding this danger. As vulgar materialism, subjective reason can hardly avoid falling into cynical nihilism; the traditional
affirmative doctrines of objective reason have an affinity with ideology and lies. The two concepts of reason do not represent two separate and independent ways of the mind, although their opposition
expresses a real antinomy.

The task of philosophy is not stubbornly to play the one against
the other, but to foster a mutual critique and thus, if possible, to
prepare in the intellectual realm the reconciliation of the two in
reality. Kant's maxim, "The critical path alone is still open," which
referred to the conflict between the objective reason of rationalistic
dogmatism and the subjective reasoning of English empiricism, applies even more pertinently to the present situation. Since isolated
subjective reason in our time is triumphing everywhere, with fatal
results, the critique must necessarily be carried on with an emphasis
on objective reason rather than on the remnants of subjectivistic
philosophy, whose genuine traditions, in the light of advanced
subjectivization, now in themselves appear as objectivistic and
romantic.

However, this emphasis on objective reason does not mean what
would be called, in the phraseology of the warmed-over theologies
of today, a philosophical decision. For just like the absolute dualism
of spirit and nature, that of subjective and objective reason is
merely an appearance, although a necessary appearance. The two
concepts are interlaced, in the sense that the consequence of each
not only dissolves the other but also leads back to it. The element
of untruth lies not simply in the essence of each of the two concepts,
but in the hypostatization of either one as against the other. Such
hypostatization results from the basic contradiction in the human
condition. On the one hand, the social need of controlling nature
has always conditioned the structure and forms of man's thinking
and thus given primacy to subjective reason. On the other hand,
society could not completely repress the idea of something transcending the subjectivity of self-interest, to which the self could not
help aspiring. Even the divorcing and formal reconstruction of the
two principles as separate rest on an element of necessity and his-

torical truth. By its self-critique, reason must recognize the limitations of the two opposite concepts of reason; it must analyze the development of the cleavage between the two, perpetuated as it is by all the doctrines that tend to triumph ideologically over the philosophical antinomy in an antinomic world.

Both the separateness and the interrelatedness of the two concepts must be understood. The idea of self-preservation, the principle that is driving subjective reason to madness, is the very idea that can save objective reason from the same fate. Applied to concrete reality, this means that only a definition of the objective goals of society that includes the purpose of self-preservation of the subject, the respect for individual life, deserves to be called objective. The conscious or unconscious motive that inspired the formulation of the systems of objective reason was the realization of the impotence of subjective reason with regard to its own goal of self-preservation. These metaphysical systems express in partly mythological form the insight that self-preservation can be achieved only in a supraindividual order, that is to say, through social solidarity.

If one were to speak of a disease affecting reason, this disease should be understood not as having stricken reason at some historical moment, but as being inseparable from the nature of reason in civilization as we have known it so far. The disease of reason is that reason was born from man's urge to dominate nature, and the "recovery" depends on insight into the nature of the original disease, not on a cure of the latest symptoms. The true critique of reason will necessarily uncover the deepest layers of civilization and explore its earliest history. From the time when reason became the instrument for domination of human and extra-human nature by man—that is to say, from its very beginnings—it has been frustrated in its own intention of discovering the truth. This is due to the very fact that it made nature a mere object, and that it failed to discover the trace of itself in such objectivization, in the concepts of matter and things not less than in those of gods and spirit. One might say that the collective madness that ranges today, from the concentration camps to the seemingly most harmless mass-culture reactions, was already present in germ in primitive objectivization, in the first man's calculating contemplation of the world as a prey. Paranoia, the madness that builds logically constructed theories of persecution, is not merely a parody of reason, but is somehow present in any form of reason that consists in the mere pursuit of aims.

Thus the derangement of reason goes far beyond the obvious malformations that characterize it at the present time. Reason can realize its reasonableness only through reflecting on the disease of the world as produced and reproduced by man; in such self-critique, reason will at the same time remain faithful to itself, by preserving and applying for no ulterior motive the principle of truth that we owe to reason alone. The subjugation of nature will revert to subjugation of man, and vice versa, as long as man does not understand his own reason and the basic process by which he has created and is maintaining the antagonism that is about to destroy him. Reason can be more than nature only through concretely realizing its "naturalness"—which consists in its trend to domination—the very trend that paradoxically alienates it from nature. Thus also, by being the instrument of reconciliation, it will be more than an instrument. The changes of direction, the advances and retrogressions of this effort, reflect the development of the definition of philosophy.

The possibility of a self-critique of reason presupposes, first, that the antagonism of reason and nature is in an acute and catastrophic phase, and, second, that at this stage of complete alienation the idea of truth is still accessible.

The shackling of man's thoughts and actions by the forms of extremely developed industrialism, the decline of the idea of the individual under the impact of the all-embracing machinery of mass culture, create the prerequisites of the emancipation of reason. At all times, the good has shown the traces of the oppression in which it originated. Thus the idea of the dignity of man is born from the experience of barbarian forms of domination. During the most ruthless phases of feudalism, dignity was an attribute of might. Emperors and kings wore halos. They demanded and received veneration. Anyone who was negligent in obeisance was punished, anyone who committed *lèse majesté* was put to death. Today, freed from its bloody origin, the notion of the dignity of the individual is one of the ideas defining a humane organization of society.

The concepts of law, order, justice, and individuality have had a similar evolution. Medieval man took refuge from justice by appealing to mercy. Today we fight for justice, a justice universalized and transvaluated, embracing equity and mercy. From the Asiatic despots, the pharaohs, the Greek oligarchs, down to the merchant princes and *condottieri* of the Renaissance and the fascist leaders of our own era, the value of the individual has been extolled by those who had an opportunity of developing their individualities at the expense of others.

Again and again in history, ideas have cast off their swaddling clothes and struck out against the social systems that bore them. The cause, in large degree, is that spirit, language, and all the realms of the mind necessarily stake universal claims. Even ruling groups, intent above all upon defending their particular interests, must stress universal motifs in religion, morality, and science. Thus originates the contradiction between the existent and ideology, a contradiction that spurs all historical progress. While conformism presupposes the basic harmony of the two and includes the minor discrepancies in the ideology itself, philosophy makes men conscious of the contradiction between them. On the one hand it appraises society by the light of the very ideas that it recognizes as its highest values; on the other, it is aware that these ideas reflect the taints of reality.

These values and ideas are inseparable from the words that express them, and philosophy's approach to language is indeed, as has been indicated above, one of its most crucial aspects. The changing contents and stresses of words record the history of our civilization. Language reflects the longings of the oppressed and the plight of nature; it releases the mimetic impulse. The transformation of this impulse into the universal medium of language rather than into destructive action means that potentially nihilistic energies work for reconciliation. This makes the fundamental and intrinsic antagonism between philosophy and fascism. Fascism treated language as a power instrument, as a means of storing knowledge for use in production and destruction in both war and peace. The repressed mimetic tendencies were cut off from adequate linguistic expression and employed as means for wiping out all opposition. Philosophy helps man to allay his fears by helping language to fulfill its genuine mimetic function, its mission of mirroring the natural tendencies. Philosophy is at one with art in reflecting passion through language and thus transferring it to the sphere of experience and memory. If nature is given the opportunity to mirror itself in the realm of spirit, it gains a certain tranquillity by contemplating its own image. This process is at the heart of all culture, particularly of music and the plastic arts. Philosophy is the conscious effort to knot all our knowledge and insight into a linguistic structure in which things are called by their right names. However, it expects to find these names not in isolated words and sentences—the method intended in the doctrines of oriental sects, and which can still be traced in the biblical stories of the baptizing of things and men—but in the continuous theoretical effort of developing philosophical truth.

This concept of truth—the adequation of name and thing—inherent in every genuine philosophy, enables thought to withstand if not to overcome the demoralizing and mutilating effect of formalized reason. The classical systems of objective reason, such as Platonism, seem to be untenable because they are glorifications of an inexorable order of the universe and therefore mythological. But it is to these systems rather than to positivism that we owe gratitude for preserving the idea that truth is the correspondence of language to reality. Their proponents were wrong, however, in thinking that they could achieve this correspondence in eternalistic systems, and in failing to see that the very fact that they were living amidst social injustice prevented the formulation of a true ontology. History has proved all such attempts illusory.

Unlike science, ontology, the heart of traditional philosophy, attempts to derive the essences, substances, and forms of things from some universal ideas that reason imagines it finds in itself. But the structure of the universe cannot be derived from any first principles that we discover in our own minds. There are no grounds for believing that the more abstract qualities of a thing should be considered primary or essential. Perhaps more than any other philosopher, Nietzsche has realized this fundamental weakness of ontology.

> The other idiosyncrasy of philosophers [he says] is no less dangerous; it consists in confusing the last and first things. They place that which makes its appearance last . . . the "highest concept," that is to say, the most general, the emptiest, the last cloudy streak of evaporating reality, at the beginning as the beginning. This again is only their manner of expressing their veneration: the highest thing must not have grown out of the lowest, it must not have grown at all. . . . Thus they attain to their stupendous concept "God." The last, most attenuated and emptiest thing is postulated as the first thing, as the absolute cause, as *ens realissimum*. Fancy humanity having to take the brain diseases of morbid cobweb spinners seriously!—And it has paid dearly for having done so.[8]

Why should the logically prior or the more general quality be accorded ontological precedence? Concepts ranked in the order of their generality mirror man's repression of nature rather than nature's own structure. When Plato or Aristotle arranged concepts

---

8. "The Twilight of the Idols," in *Complete Works of Freidrich Nietzsche*, Oscar Levy, ed. New York, 1925, p. 19.

according to their logical priority, they did not so much derive them from the secret affinities of things as unwittingly from power relations. Plato's depiction of the "great chain of being" barely conceals its dependence on traditional notions of the Olympian polity and thus on the social reality of the city–state. The logically prior is no nearer the core of a thing than the temporally prior; to equate priority either with the essence of nature or of man means to debase humans to the crude state to which the power motive tends to reduce them in reality, to the status of mere "beings." The major argument against ontology is that the principles man discovers in himself by meditation, the emancipating truths that he tries to find, cannot be those of society or of the universe, because neither of these is made in the image of man. Philosophical ontology is inevitably ideological because it tries to obscure the separation between man and nature and to uphold a theoretical harmony that is given the lie on every hand by the cries of the miserable and disinherited.

Distorted though the great ideals of civilization—justice, equality, freedom—may be, they are nature's protestations against her plight, the only formulated testimonies we possess. Toward them philosophy should take a dual attitude. (1) It should deny their claims to being regarded as ultimate and infinite truth. Whenever a metaphysical system presents these testimonies as absolute or eternal principles, it exposes their historical relativity. Philosophy rejects the veneration of the finite, not only of crude political or economic idols, such as the nation, the leader, success, or money, but also of ethical or esthetic values, such as personality, happiness, beauty, or even liberty, so far as they pretend to be independent ultimates. (2) It should be admitted that the basic cultural ideas have truth values, and philosophy should measure them against the social background from which they emanate. It opposes the breach between ideas and reality. Philosophy confronts the existent, in its historical context, with the claim of its conceptual principles, in order to criticize the relation between the two and thus transcend them. Philosophy derives its positive character precisely from the interplay of these two negative procedures.

Negation plays a crucial role in philosophy. The negation is double-edged—a negation of the absolute claims of prevailing ideology and of the brash claims of reality. Philosophy in which negation is an element is not to be equated with skepticism. The latter uses negation in a formalistic and abstract way. Philosophy takes existing values seriously but insists that they become parts of a theoretical whole that reveals their relativity. Inasmuch as subject and object, word and thing, cannot be integrated under present conditions, we are driven, by the principle of negation, to attempt to salvage relative truths from the wreckage of false ultimates. The skeptic and positivist schools of philosophy find no meaning in general concepts that would be worth salvaging. Oblivious to their own partiality, they fall into unresolvable contradictions. On the other hand, objective idealism and rationalism insist, above all, upon the eternal meaning of general concepts and norms, regardless of their historical derivations. Each school is equally confident of its own thesis and hostile to the method of negation inseparably bound up with any philosophical theory that does not arbitrarily stop thinking at some point in its course.

Some cautions against possible misconstruction are in order. To say that the essence or the positive side of philosophical thought consists in understanding the negativity and relativity of the existing culture does not imply that the possession of such knowledge constitutes, in itself, the overcoming of this historical situation. To assume this would be to confound true philosophy with the idealistic interpretation of history, and to lose sight of the core of dialectical theory, namely, the basic difference between the ideal and the real, between theory and practice. The idealistic identification of wisdom, however deep, with fulfillment—by which is meant the reconciliation of spirit and nature—enhances the ego only to rob it of its content by isolating it from the external world. Philosophies that look exclusively to an inner process for the eventual liberation end as empty ideologies. As has been remarked earlier, Hellenistic concentration on pure inwardness allowed society to become a jungle of power interests destructive of all the material conditions prerequisite for the security of the inner principle.

Is activism, then, especially political activism, the sole means of fulfillment, as just defined? I hesitate to say so. This age needs no added stimulus to action. Philosophy must not be turned into propaganda, even for the best possible purpose. The world has more than enough propaganda. Language is assumed to suggest and intend nothing beyond propaganda. Some readers of this book may think that it represents propaganda against propaganda, and conceive each word as a suggestion, slogan, or prescription. Philosophy is not interested in issuing commands. The intellectual situation is so confused that this statement itself may in turn be interpreted as offering foolish advice against obeying any command, even one that might save our lives; indeed, it may even be construed as a command directed against commands. If philosophy is to be put to work, its first task should be to correct this situation. The concentrated energies necessary for reflection must not be prematurely drained into the channels of activistic or non-activistic programs.

Today even outstanding scholars confuse thinking with planning. Shocked by social injustice and by hypocrisy in its traditional religious garb, they propose to wed ideology to reality, or, as they prefer to say, to bring reality closer to our heart's desire, by applying the wisdom of engineering to religion. In the spirit of August Comte, they wish to establish a new social catechism. "American Culture," writes Robert Lynd,

> if it is to be creative in the personality of those who live it, needs to discover and to build prominently into its structure a core of richly evocative common purposes which have meaning in terms of the deep personality needs of the great mass of the people. Needless to say, the theology, eschatology, and other familiar aspects of traditional Christianity need not have any place in such an operating system. It is the responsibility of a science that recognizes human values as a part of its data to help to search out the content and modes of expression of such shared loyalties. In withholding its hand science becomes a partner to those people who maintain outworn religious forms because there is nothing else in sight.[9]

Lynd seems to look at religion in somewhat the manner in which he looks at social science itself—which, in his view, "will stand or fall on the basis of its serviceability to men as they struggle to live."[10] Religion becomes pragmatistic.

Despite the genuine progressive spirit of such thinkers, they miss the core of the problem. The new social catechisms are even more futile than the revivals of Christian movements. Religion, in its traditional form or as a progressive social cult, is regarded, if not by the great masses, at least by its authorized spokesmen, as an instrument. It cannot regain status by propagating new cults of the present or future community, of the state, or of the leader. The truth it seeks to convey is compromised by its pragmatic end. Once men come to speak of religious hope and despair in terms of "deep personality needs," emotionally rich common sentiments, or scientifically tested human values, religion is meaningless for them. Even Hobbes's prescription that religious doctrines be swallowed like

---

9. *Knowledge for What*, Princeton, 1939, p. 239.
10. Ibid., p. 177.

pills will be of little avail. The language of the recommendation disavows what it means to recommend.

Philosophical theory itself cannot bring it about that either the barbarizing tendency or the humanistic outlook should prevail in the future. However, by doing justice to those images and ideas that at given times dominated reality in the role of absolutes—e.g., the idea of the individual as it dominated the bourgeois era—and that have been relegated in the course of history, philosophy can function as a corrective of history, so to speak. Thus ideological stages of the past would not be equated simply with stupidity and fraud—the verdict brought against medieval thought by the philosophy of the French Enlightenment. Sociological and psychological explanation of earlier beliefs would be distinct from philosophical condemnation and suppression of them. Though divested of the power they had in their contemporary setting, they would serve to cast light upon the current course of humanity. In this function, philosophy would be mankind's memory and conscience, and thereby help to keep the course of humanity from resembling the meaningless round of the asylum inmate's recreation hour.

Today, progress toward utopia is blocked primarily by the complete disproportion between the weight of the overwhelming machinery of social power and that of the atomized masses. Everything else—the widespread hypocrisy, the belief in false theories, the discouragement of speculative thought, the debilitation of will, or its premature diversion into endless activities under the pressure of fear—is a symptom of this disproportion. If philosophy succeeds in helping people to recognize these factors, it will have rendered a great service to humanity. The method of negation, the denunciation of everything that mutilates mankind and impedes its free development, rests on confidence in man. The so-called constructive philosophies may be shown truly to lack this conviction and thus to be unable to face the cultural debacle. In their view, actions seems to represent the fulfillment of our eternal destiny. Now that science has helped us to overcome the awe of the unknown in nature, we are the slaves of social pressures of our own making. When called upon to act independently, we cry for patterns, systems, and authorities. If by enlightenment and intellectual progress we mean the freeing of man from superstitious belief in evil forces, in demons and fairies, in blind fate—in short, the emancipation from fear—then denunciation of what is currently called reason is the greatest service reason can render.

On Theodor W. Adorno

NO RIGHT TO BE A SELF: COUNTERTHINKING
by Martin Hielscher

In the passage entitled "Warning: not to be misused" from *Minima Moralia*, Adorno discusses the dialectic "method" that constitutes his thought and that of critical theory in general, as well as the dialectic inherent in turn in this very method. While he calls it "a refuge for all the thoughts of the oppressed, even those unthought by them," he also describes it as a "formal technique of apologetics": "Its truth or untruth, therefore, is not inherent in the method itself, but in its intention in the historical process."[1]

Working from a succession of approaches and focusing on the history of dialectics and on Hegel's system in particular, Adorno frames the immanent problem of dialectics, as the mediation of the particular and the whole, in such a way that this mediation is shown to be discontinuous, transitory, and questionable per se. This mediation becomes a mode of thought and expression that must perpetually be carried out anew, a mode in which the "false," the thought brought to bear in opposition to it, and the experience that motivates this thought are formulated in such a way that the interwovenness of truth and untruth always remains apparent. The gesture of privileged knowledge, of insight, the viewpoint that fancies itself lofty and shrewd, in confident awareness of its opposition to a sea of ignorance and blindness, is still a viewpoint that has not broken with the self-misjudgment upon which the false world rests, a viewpoint that is not even aware of its self-misjudgment.

The power of the subject, ever mindful of the whole, to burst asunder the merely particular and at the same time to sublate it into

---

1. Theodor W. Adorno, *Minima Moralia. Refections from Damaged Life*, trans. E. F. N. Jephcott (London: Verso, 1978) 244.

the struggle for the restitution of that which has been cut off from the whole, that which within itself reveals the movement of the whole to be oppression and mere self-preservation, this power becomes itself a form of falseness when it is exercised in falseness. This is the misuse against which Adorno warns.

"The new form" into which the negative philosophy strives to suspend and preserve that which is dissolved, i.e., the apologistic ideology of the badly established order, and the dissolvent, i.e. the critical apparatus, can never "emerge in a pure state . . . [a]s long as domination reproduces itself . . ." The critical philosophy that strives to sublate its very self becomes, taking into account the characteristic determination with which it is "constantly and successfully turning the tables," a form of domination allied in a pact with "the bourgeois self-assertion of the subject."[2]

Any possible alternative to the world of the exchange society and of the universal "social web of delusion"[3] would not emerge in a pure state *in* this world. In it, the negative dialectic represents the adequate organon of knowledge—perhaps the only adequate organon of knowledge at all if it is considered as a "second reflection," as a reaction to a constitutive break within the subject. It would be one with a radical crack in history, with the "event," as Adorno calls it using Heidegger's word, that "leads out."

As with Heidegger, Adorno's philosophical attitude seems to have been "informed" by this event; it seems connected to it without his ever wanting to call it by name. This philosophical attitude is described in the last passage of *Minima Moralia:* a philosophy of the "as if," which would undertake the attempt "to contemplate all things as they would present themselves from the standpoint of redemption." This attempt, however, as Adorno points out in a kind of reprise of the previous section on the dialectic, is so marked by "impossibility," that "the question of the reality or unreality of redemption itself hardly matters" in light of the demand placed on the thinker to think "without velleity [Willkür] or violence, entirely from felt contact with [the world's] objects," while the gaze upon these objects is determined and at the same time distorted from the outset by the "scope of existence."[4]

If the subject, as Adorno contends in *Negative Dialectics,* is the latest incarnation of myth and at the same time something equal to

2. Adorno, *Minima Moralia*, 245–46.

3. Theodor W. Adorno: *Aesthetic Theory,* trans. Robert Huppot-Kentor (Minneapolis: University of Minnesota Press, 1997), 231.

4. Adorno, *Minima Moralia*, 247.

its oldest incarnation,[5] but the other can only be appropriated to us through the exertion of the subjective thought, then the meaning of "counterthinking" ["Denken gegen sich selbst"] becomes apparent. The self, hypostatized by certain psychological schools as the "core" of our being, subjective identity, is always already distorted by self-preservation which in its institutionalized form, according to Horkheimer and Adorno, as hardening and petrifaction of conditions and thus of subjects, does away with the very self it was supposed to preserve.

The exertion Adorno demands of the subject if it is to think authentically, to experience authentically, is identical with what Hegel refers to in the introduction to the *Phenomenology of Mind* as the "path of despair" and what he describes in the preface as the "life of the mind," which endures death and dwells upon the negative. But the "magical power" that for Hegel in the process of the self-experience and self-apprehension of mind on the path to absolute knowledge "inverts" the negative into "being," this "magical power" is for Adorno a potential deception, a rationalization of that which thought has already obscured in its effort to be binding.

Adorno holds that within the world dominated by totally utilitarian rationality, the difference between thinking and that which is thought cannot be invalidated, but one must ask oneself whether Adorno does not borrow from the realm of the philosophy of history arguments for the self-criticism of the subject—that the subject does not even exist yet (incidentally, a typical figure of thought for Adorno)—and confound them with arguments of an ontological quality, ones that concern subjectivity's mode of being between self-consciousness, language, sexuality, and death and that constitute themselves anew in any given historical context; arguments, however, that do not conceal the fundamental crack necessitated by finitude and mortality.

Suffering, and history as the "quintessence of suffering," become the starting points for the thought of Critical Theory; they do so as much on the basis of the faithfulness to the truth about the course of history and about the condition of people in a world that for Adorno is to be interpreted as a "figure of injustice" as they do on the basis of a fundamental experience that conceives of suffering as an essential motor of knowledge: "The need to lend a voice to suffering is a condition of all truth."[6]

---

5. Theodor W. Adorno, *Negative Dialectics*, trans. E. B. Ashton, (New York: Continuum, 1973).

6. Adorno, *Negative Dialectics*, 17–18.

This sentence refers back to Schopenhauer, in whose philosophy, Adorno maintains, "suffering appears as a 'mere phenomenon,' its very shabbiness and meanness make its seriousness evident."[7]

Schopenhauer is the philosopher who continues to counter the merely subsistent, the empirical world with the world of ideas and of the In-Itself. Thus does he carry on the traditional dualism, and yet, as Horkheimer formulated, he "did not deify" the In-Itself, the "actual essence." Nowhere does Schopenhauer identify himself with that which is; he breaks through the nineteenth century's belief in progress, the idea that there is meaning in history. All optimism, which he famously referred to as "wicked," founders for him on the nameless, perennial suffering of the majority. Hegel spoke of history as the "slaughterhouse in which the happiness of peoples, the wisdom of states, and the virtue of individuals are brought to be sacrificed," but Schopenhauer is the one who denies to this process any and all meaning.

For Schopenhauer, subjectivity is in itself already appearance and life that transpires, condemned in advance by age, sickness, and death, shadowy and unredeemed in constant inevitability, blinded and left to pick its way through a bed of glowing coals, accorded but a few moments of respite and peace, which only serve to help keep in motion the machinery of self-preservation.

If mere existence is not bad enough, it is all the more uncanny and horrible when it reveals itself to be mere appearance:

> Just as the boatman sits in his small boat, trusting his frail craft in a stormy sea that is boundless in every direction, rising and falling with the howling, mountainous waves, so in the midst of a world full of suffering and misery the individual calmly sits, supported by and trusting the *principium individuationis* [. . .] His vanishing person, his extentionless present, his momentary gratification, these alone have reality for him [. . .] Till then, there lives only in the innermost depths of his consciousness the wholly obscure presentiment that all this [. . .] indeed [. . .] has a connexion with him from which the *principium individuationis* cannot protect him. From this presentiment arises that ineradicable *dread*, common to all human beings [. . .], which suddenly seizes them, when they become puzzled over the *principium individuationis* [. . .].[8]

---

7. Theodor W. Adorno: *In Search of Wagner*, Rodney Livingstone, (n.p.: NLB, 1981) 146.

8. Arthur Schopenhauer, *The World as Will and Representation*, volume 1, trans. E.F.J. Payne (New York: Dover, 1969) 352–53.

Schopenhauer's philosophy is that stormy sea into which the individual is plunged only to awaken in horror to the awareness of his interconnection with everything else, his entanglement in a story of mutual destruction, prolonged suffering, inescapable descent and ultimate demise. Although such a condition is inherent in the concept of the will, this very will is utterly bereft of any meaning, of any claim to truth. Schopenhauer's thought, which in his critique of Hegel attacks the optimism of Hegel's system, as Adorno does later, lacks an ultimate foothold; indeed, it fundamentally lacks any safeguard at all.

In his essay "Schopenhauer Today," Horkheimer points out that the bursting asunder of world process and mind affects the concept of truth itself, which without a residual trace of theology is an untenable one:

> Accordingly, truth is preserved nowhere but in perishable men themselves and is as perishable as they are. The striving toward truth, an exertion that for Schopenhauer is freed from the servitude to all externally posited ends, moves through the course of his work in stringently logical fashion toward the self-negation of the concept of truth. From the blind will as the being [Wesen] follows the antinomy that the affirmation of eternal, true being [Sein] cannot endure in the face of truth.[9]

This antinomy, which forces the subject to think something that shatters its identity and delivers this subject over to a being that is an un-being, a monstrosity, anticipates the exertion that for Adorno is demanded of the subject. Schopenhauer's metaphysics becomes a hermeneutics of the world of experience, whereby immediacy is construed, ultimately by means of an intuitive somatic experience, as the path to the solution of the "riddle of the world." It is the will-nature of the body that precedes and always predetermines all knowledge, and the will-nature arrived at through analogy for all other beings. The thing-in-itself, the essence of the world, "this substrate of all appearances, and subsequently of nature in its entirety," is nothing other "than that with which we are immediately acquainted and intimately familiar; that which we find in the innermost reaches of our own selves as will"; self and essence of the world become identical, but in such a way that destroys what we perceive in the world of representation, of individuation, of self-

9. Max Horkheimer, "Die Aktualität Schopenhauers," *Schopenhauer-Jahrbuch* 42 (1961) 12–25.

preservation, as self: counterthinking. This mystical thought of the unity of world and self repeats itself where Schopenhauer explains that the world is "self-knowledge of the will."[10]

The thought that the will "turns," that it, "having achieved complete self-knowledge, [. . .] freely denied itself," leads to the Epicurean motif in Schopenhauer's pessimism, in his philosophy of pain and suffering: the negation of the will, its turning against itself, "shows" a dimension of experience that for us remains generally inaccessible and that, conversely, seems to motivate Schopenhauer's affect, his insistence upon the gloominess of existence: "that peace, [. . .] that oceanlike calmness of the spirit, that deep tranquillity, that unshakable confidence and serenity."[11]

As Adorno noticed without keeping this conclusion in mind that "[g]rayness could not fill us with despair if our minds did not harbor the concept of different colors, scattered traces of which are not absent from the negative whole,"[12] and reproached Schopenhauer for being the "spokesman of the spell." If Schopenhauer supplies with his image of happiness as that serenity the "concept of different colors" as well, then Adorno's reservation against the total subsumption in which existence for Schopenhauer always persists in its course, in its inevitability, remains; so that happiness, as Nietzsche suspiciously maintained, appears only as quietism.

The self that has awakened to its own phenomenality and to the realization that the world it faces is "nothing" fortifies itself anew with the image of that serenity which remains essentially inaccessible to us:

> We then look with deep and painful yearning at that state, beside which the miserable and desperate nature of our own appears in the clearest light by the contrast. Yet this consideration is the only one that can permanently console us, when, on the one hand, we have recognized incurable suffering and endless misery as essential to the phenomenon of the will, to the world, and on the other see the world melt away with the abolished will, and retain before us only empty nothingness.[13]

In Adorno's complex dialectic, the subject is raised out of itself by pain, nature, or aesthetic experience and attempts to transcend

---

10. Schopenhauer, *The World as Will and Representation 1*, 410.
11. Ibid., 411.
12. Adorno, *Negative Dialectics*, 377–78.
13. Schopenhauer, *The World as Will and Representation 1*, 411.

itself and the existent. In doing so it is addressed by an objective tendency that shows such pain, nature, or aesthetic experience and at the same time preserves itself in this process, through which it undertakes the attempt to see the world in the light of redemption, in which violence no longer distorts the intentions and the relations of things and beings. What Schopenhauer's subject does is to undertake the attempt to see the world as will in the light of that serenity "whose mere reflection" on faces in paintings by Raffael and Corregio overwhelms us and helps us to transcend the torment of existence between misery and nothing: in the light of redemption and the light of serenity, which protect the subject from sinking completely in the thought of that which it abolishes.

For Schopenhauer, aesthetic experience and pity lead into a dimension of experience in which self-preservation and thus the subject sublate themselves and the will is extinguished; in which with the extinguishing of the will everything becomes "nothing," the famous last word of *The World as Will and Representation*,[14] but that Epicurean motif and the gaze at the bliss of the saints reveal an intention which can only preserve itself in a negative manner: the subject's knowledge, driven on by the wish to be *permanently* free of pain, to cancel itself out, to anticipate death, drifts in the radical dichotomy between the world of purposes and the second world of contemplation and the will that turns. Because it is nothing that awaits us anyway, this nothing becomes the sole positive content.

For Adorno, who like Schopenhauer conceives of suffering as the starting point of thought and who sees in pain, in shock, as well as in aesthetic experience outstanding moments that respectively remind the subject of that which it in fact intends, individually and socially, this experience does not become nothing par excellence, but becomes rather the measure for a totally different kind of socialization.

This alternative to traditional socialization, however, cannot do away with that fundamental crack in the subject that is necessitated by our "mortal nature" itself and that becomes the "failure principle" par excellence that Adorno would like to sublate. Second reflection, which breaks the subject's attempt to grasp its other—nature in the subject, and the objects—and allows the other to be the other, potentially becomes a step forward in knowledge that sublates a historical philosophy of redemption. The dichotomy

---

14. Ibid., 412.

between misery and nothing, the latter of which amounts at the same time to happiness, becomes for Adorno a movement in which truth is thought of as amounting to *promesse du bonheur* and yet every tangible form thereof remains untrue.

Adorno moves his concept of a "transformed sensuality" to the place that for Schopenhauer is occupied by nothing; a place that nevertheless might mean something similar.

In his essay on Eichendorff, Adorno speaks of Schumann's "Piano Fantasy" and sees in its third movement an affinity with Eichendorff's refined and yielding gesture of scorning even his own right to existence. As the motto of his understanding of Eichendorff's oeuvre, Adorno cites the line *Und ich mag mich nicht bewahren* [Nay, I will not spare myself] from the poem "Frische Fahrt" [Brisk ride]. This gesture is for him in the end transformed into a love in which the ego "no longer becomes callous and entrenched within itself," but rather "wants to make amends for the primordial injustice of being ego at all."[15]

Throughout Adorno's works there are numerous passages which not only accentuate the dominance the so-called reality-proficient subject exerts over itself—which as dominance over internal and external nature leads then to the reification of the world and to the emptying of the subject—but which go on to stress the guilt inherent in subjectivity itself, in differentiation in this emphatic sense. For the very reason that this thought is less applicable to Eichendorff than Adorno would have it, as one would have to admit after critical scrutiny, the question of its origin becomes all the more intriguing. This remarkable thesis has its own tradition, indeed one which Adorno expressly pointed out on a number of occasions. It can be traced back in this form, at any rate in its systematic formulation, to the philosophy of Schopenhauer, and thence it is incorporated into the thought of critical theory, where Adorno gives it a different, updated accent.

The central concepts Schopenhauer employs to designate the contradiction of all individuation, "principium individuationis" and "Veil of Maya," recur in Adorno's philosophy, sometimes changed, sometimes not: what Adorno refers to as the "social web of delusion"[16] (even more clearly in the earlier formulation "tech-

---

15. Theodor W. Adorno: "In Memory of Eichendorff," from *Notes to Literature*, volume 1, ed. Rolf Tiedemann, trans. Shierry Weber Nicholsen (New York/Oxford: Columbia Univ. Pr. 1991), 64.

16. Adorno: *Aesthetic Theory*, 231 and passim.

nological veil''[17]), which obscures people's consciousness of themselves and of their real social situation, is nothing other than a
sociologically and psychoanalytically modified version of Schopenhauer's "Veil of Maya." As we know, Schopenhauer makes the
bold leap of translating the Kantian concepts of *Ding an sich*
[thing-in-itself] and *Erscheinung* [phenomenon] as *Wille* [will] and
Vorstellung [representation], whereby "will" takes on the connota-
tion of "real, essential, substantial" and "representation" that of
"unreal, apparent, accidental."

The phenomena of the world are conceived as necessary ideas of
objects for a subject which according to the principle of sufficient
reason constitutes the objects as such in the forms of space and
time, which are a priori forms of intuition. In other words, object
and subject can be spoken of, respectively, only as matter which
requires constitution for us and as beings which carry out this act
of constitution a priori and which can experience themselves only
in this act. Experience can come about only under the condition of
the validity of the principle of sufficient reason, i.e., in the four
forms of causality. At the same time, however, this "only" is subject
to a further limitation, to the extent that the world, which Schopenhauer is seeking to *understand* and not to *explain,* consists not only
of representation, but also of will, whose metaphysical essence we
can, remarkably enough, experience in an immediate fashion—by
means of the body, which is given to us in experience in a twofold
manner.

Metaphysics, i.e., the answer to the inquiry into being-in-the-
whole with the requisite derivation of being from a supreme principle, is tied to a somatic experience, so to speak, to a vague inkling
we receive. This recurs with Adorno, for example in the "Meditations on Metaphysics,"[18] when he allows metaphysics—which traditionally postulated a supreme *intellectual* principle and insofar
stood in strict opposition to materialism—to be inscribed within
the blindest layer of the somatic.

> The somatic, unmeaningful stratum of life is the stage of suffering,
> of the suffering which in the camps, without any consolation, burned
> every soothing feature out of the mind, and out of culture, the mind's
> objectification. The point of no return has been reached in the pro-

---

17. Theodor W. Adorno and Max Horkheimer: *Dialectic of Enlightenment,*
trans. John Cumming (New York: Herder and Herder, 1972).
18. Adorno: *Negative Dialectics,* 361ff.

cess which irresistibly forced metaphysics to join what it was once conceived against. [. . .] Children sense some of this in the fascination that issues from the flayer's zone, from carcasses, from the repulsively sweet odor of putrefaction, and from the opprobrious terms used for that zone.[19]

As concerns the world as representation and the principle of sufficient reason one can say: "Space, time, and causality are ordering structures with which cognizant subjectivity arranges everything that becomes for it the object of experience."[20] Time, space, and causality are themselves different formulations of the one principle of sufficient reason, which forms for us a necessary precondition for experience, but with the particular accent that Schopenhauer, in exploiting the ambiguity of *Vorstellung* [representation, idea]—and this radically contradicts Kant's use of the word *Erscheinung* [phenomenon, appearance]—at the same time intimates that the experience of the "world as representation" is not the entire experience of the world. If Kant aimed his epistemological critique at the postulation of metaphysical axioms, which as such can in no way be derived from our experience, then Schopenhauer sees the world itself as an enigma—a thought completely alien to Kant and Hegel, most likely—an enigma that awaits its disentanglement. This, however, is most certainly not accomplished by my making use of the forms of intuition necessary to me nor the forms of knowledge familiar to me. The real world is always at the same time the veiling of that which in this world is solely real. The enigma "world," however, can never be completely disentangled.

Space and time are for Schopenhauer the "principium individuationis," i.e., the principle by means of which an individual is recognized as an individual. Outside of space and time no individuals exist. At this juncture, the ambiguity of "Vorstellung" [representation, idea] recurs, this time with regard to the individuation principle. The latter refers on the one hand to the way in which the will manifests or presents itself through all imagining [vorstellenden] beings and on the other hand to the way in which these beings experience themselves and suffer as individuals, without for the most part ever knowing that what they are in substance is nothing individual whatsoever; neither is it anything general that they can

---

19. Adorno: *Negative Dialectics*, 365–66.
20. Ulrich Pothast: *Die eigentlich metaphysische Tätigkeit*, (Frankfurt/Main: Suhrkamp, 1982) 34.

grasp the same way in which they believe to experience themselves as individuals.

The notion of the phenomenality [Scheinhaftigkeit] of a subjectivity that conceives of itself as something ultimate, something absolutely immune to all delusion [unhintergehbar] and incapable of being mistaken for something else is very close to Adorno's thought, just as Schopenhauer's decisive consciousness-critical shift within German idealism vis-a-vis Hegel becomes important for Adorno; i.e., to discover the substance of individuality not in something intellectual, but in something instinctually somatic and for the most part unconscious, which establishes the unity of the world in a completely different way than through the positing of a habitual subjectivity of beings.

To prove his point, Adorno cites on a number of occasions a passage from the fourth book of *The World as Will and Representation:*

> But this double character of our inner being does not rest on a self-existent unity, otherwise it would be possible for us to be conscious of ourselves *in ourselves and independently of the objects of knowing and willing.* Now we simply cannot do this, but as soon as we enter into ourselves in order to attempt it, and wish for once to know ourselves fully by directing our knowledge inwards, we lose ourselves in a bottomless void; we find ourselves like a hollow glass globe, from the emptiness of which a voice speaks. But the cause of this voice is not to be found in the globe, and since we want to comprehend ourselves, we grasp with a shudder nothing but a wavering and unstable phantom.[21]

That the duplicity of our being does not rest in an independently existing unity, that no knowledge can come close enough to inspect a crack that shows itself only after the fact, that any attempt to find, in ourselves alone, unity with what we are in substance is doomed to failure, all of this constituted for Adorno at the same time a critique of bourgeois society, which deludes the individual caught within the struggle for self-preservation with the notion that he is a unique individual, while the organization of society prevents any true individuation.

The notion that consciousness of ourselves cannot be brought about independently of our consciousness of the objects of knowledge and will leads in Adorno's thought to the notion of the pre-

---

21. Schopenhauer, *The World as Will and Representation* 1, 278.

dominance of the object in the subject-object dialectic. Here is his commentary on the Schopenhauer passage cited:

> Thus he [Schopenhauer] called the mythical deception of the pure self by its name, null and void. It is an abstraction. What presents itself as an original entity, a monad, is only the result of a social division of the social process. Precisely as an absolute, the individual is a mere reflection of property relations. In him the fictitious claim is made that what is biologically one must logically precede the social whole, from which it is only isolated by force, and its contingency is held up as a standard of truth. Not only is the self entwined in society; it owes society its existence in the most literal sense. All its content comes from society, or at any rate from its relation to the object. It grows richer the more freely it develops and reflects this relation, while it is limited, impoverished and reduced by the separation and hardening that it lays claim to as an origin.[22]

Here, as many stages in the theory have been worked through to conceive of abstract metaphysical determinations and their dialectic as an expression of antagonistic social conditions as—and Adorno would surely see it thus—the abstractly and unhistorically formulated truth has received its actual binding historical-concrete substance.

Schopenhauer says: "All this as a whole does not really belong to *what* appears, to *what* has entered the form of the representation, but only to this form itself."[23] His fundamental doubt of our ability to understand the essence of things by means of a cognitive faculty defined as "clear and definite," recurs, mediated by various other stages (above all Nietzsche's philosophy), in Adorno's thought, in his critique of cognition under the dominion of the identity principle, whose universality and validity assumes for us and for our purposes *the* very position and function that Schopenhauer ascribes to the validity of the principle of sufficient reason. For both philosophers it is consequently the aesthetic experience that is accorded the preeminent stature, for this is the only experience that leads out of the cognition of the world after our previously occurring "preconditioning," a process carried out in the interest of our self-preservation. For this reason, Adorno (in his *Aesthetic Theory*) credited Schopenhauer with being the *first* adequately to have construed—just as Adorno construes, in accordance with Marx and Lukacs,

---

22. Adorno, *Minima Moralia*, 153–54.
23. Schopenhauer, *The World as Will and Representation 1*, 120.

the world of the social web of delusion—the essence of aesthetic experience as the renunciation of the world of utilitarian ends and the principle of exchange, indeed as experience, which radically forces the subject out of that subjectivity constrained by the ends of self-preservation.

The subject that orders and comes to know the world on the basis of the principle of sufficient reason is not the same as the one that contemplates the essence of a thing as an idea and loses itself in the face of the object of experience.

In the province of the will and of the knowledge of the will, however, it is not actually the mode of knowledge peculiar to art that applies, but rather the more intuitively felt awareness of the interrelatedness of things.

So what does the world as will look like, considering that Schopenhauer negates it in the end, whereby aesthetic experience and its great ethic of pity serve as the passageway to "nothing," the last word of his magnum opus?

If in the end a state of strife prevails, in an almost paradoxical manner, between will and knowledge, which as understanding and reason is initially nothing other than the organon of self-preservation, then the state that prevails in the world as will is essentially one of battle and annihilation, insofar as will, in the compulsion to objectify itself, interprets itself within the world, so to speak, moving through a succession of objectifications, each one of which is corresponded to by an idea in the Platonic sense, whereby one idea potentially consumes the other.

Schopenhauer understands ideas as "every definite and fixed *grade of the will's objectification,* in so far as it is thing-in-itself and is therefore foreign to plurality. These grades are, to be sure, related to individual things as their eternal forms, or as their prototypes."[24] The emergence of ideas as phenomena, in the sense of a succession of steps moving from a lower-level to a higher-level objectification of will, transpires in a merciless struggle.

The unity of will throughout all of its stages of objectification, in which will at the same time consumes itself—for it has nothing better to do, one could say—makes itself known by way of an inner relatedness that shows itself in all of its manifestations from one to the next.

Schopenhauer argues further: "Now if the objects appearing in these forms are not to be empty phantoms, but are to have a

---

24. Schopenhauer, *The World as Will and Representation 1,* 130.

meaning, they must point to something, must be the expression of something, which is not, like themselves, object, representation, something existing merely relatively, namely for a subject."[25]

For us, then, the emphasis shall lie on the one hand upon the latent negation of the sharp distinction between the world as representation and the world as will, on the other hand upon the recurrence in Adorno's aesthetics (with particular emphasis in his investigations on the beauty of nature) of the concept of *expression* and the idea of the relatedness of beings to one another, a relatedness that is somehow always sensed by these beings and that forms the prerequisite for the possibility of Schopenhauer's analogical inference.

For Adorno, the truth inherent in works of art is a function of the extent to which they realize with human means the speech of the non-human. To experience this nonhuman is to experience the beauty of nature, the perceivable order expressed by nature. At the same time, it is to experience something that has not yet even come to be.

The notion of a historicity of nature implies that nature requires human assistance to achieve its true being and at the same time that the human being can only become human by taking part in this possible nonviolent process of coming-to-terms with nature. It is a prerequisite to this process that man recognizes his own naturalness but at the same time does not subsume himself to it.

To forget the beauty of nature is to forget why we are on "this poor earth" in the first place.

With this, the possibility of reconciliation is inscribed into—if one may beg its existence—nature as will, whereby "nature" here is taken to include human nature. It is this possibility alone that underlies the pathos of salvation and the claim to happiness with which Adorno counters Schopenhauer, even if the former shares for the most part the latter's description of the subjugation of the world to the nonsensuality of the will, the perpetuation of suffering and transitoriness.

The very notion of experience (a notion that has become in a completely new sense central to modern philosophy—one need only think in a more narrow sense of Benjamin, Heidegger, or indeed of Adorno) means of course the state of being touched by an other that is at the same time not completely other, that itself has to take steps toward appropriation, toward inclination—an "ob-

---

25. Schopenhauer, *The World as Will and Representation 1*, 119.

ject'' that the "subject" can appropriate without destroying it and in experiencing it becomes something else. To experience means not to return the same as one was before and no longer to know what had previously rendered the world plausible. Experience takes one beyond appropriation and brings one to an other.

The expression of the experienced virtually exceeds the appropriation through which alone experience is possible.

> Nature's eloquence is damaged by the objectivation that is a result of studied observation [. . .]. If nature can in a sense only be seen blindly, the aesthetic imperatives of unconscious apperception and remembrance are at the same time archaic vestiges incompatible with the increasing maturation of reason. [. . .] Genetically, aesthetic comportment may require familiarity with natural beauty in childhood [. . .] Its [natural beauty's] essential indeterminateness is manifest in the fact that every part of nature, as well as everything made by man that has congealed into nature, is able to become beautiful, luminous from within. [. . .] Each can step in for the other, and it is in this constant fluctuation, not in any unequivocal order of relationships, that natural beauty lives [. . .]. A qualitative distinction in natural beauty can be sought, if at all, in the degree to which something not made by human beings is eloquent: in its expression. What is beautiful in nature is what appears to be more than what is literally there. Without receptivity there would be no such objective expression, but it is not reducible to the subject; natural beauty points to the primacy of the object in subjective experience. Natural beauty is perceived as both: as authoritatively binding and as something incomprehensible that questioningly awaits its solution.[26]

So much for Adorno's aesthetics. Let us return then to the world of will and the role of reason:

> The will, which hitherto followed its tendency in the dark with extreme certainty and infallibility, has at this stage kindled a light for itself. This was a means that became necessary for getting rid of the disadvantage which would result from the throng and the complicated nature of its phenomena, and would accrue precisely to the most perfect of them. [. . .] That complicated, many-sided, flexible being, man, who is extremely needy and exposed to innumerable shocks and injuries, had to be illuminated by a twofold knowledge in order to be able to exist.[27]

---

26. Adorno, *Aesthetic Theory*, 69ff.
27. Schopenhauer, *The World as Will and Representation 1*, 150–51.

This context serves as a basis for the explication of the consideration, passed along by Nietzsche, that is to become central for Adorno: that even in that stage of rational reflection which has gone the furthest to render itself independent, an impulse of self-preservation manifests itself; that reason is essentially the means to an end, the end being the creation of better living conditions, and that reason's degeneration into instrumental reason is at the same time the forgetting of its actual origin and task: "The concept of progress is dialectical in a strictly unmetaphorical sense, in that its organon, reason, is one; a nature-dominating level and a reconciling level do not exist separate and disjunct within reason, rather both share all its determinations. The one moment inverts into its other only in that it literally reflects itself, in that reason applies reason to itself and in its self-restriction emancipates itself from the demon of identity,"[28] i.e., remembers that it is something which has become, by means of the memory of its origin in necessity. Reason is a praxis and as such is goal-oriented; the bodily will-impulse of Schopenhauer, however, as an expression of Will's infinitude and self-consumption, which can be countered only by deconstruction through cognition and the resulting asceticism, is the perennial deferment of goals, in so far as each one proves illusory. If for Adorno the reminder of the bodily neediness of man and the rootedness of reason—for all its apparent independence from the body—in bodily impulses gives rise to the categorical imperative to make the fulfillment or the reflection of these needs the supreme goal of the efforts of reason, then for Schopenhauer it is the impossibility of such fulfillment and the intimation of the transience of all individuals that form the basis for his argumentation which leads, in the fourth book of *The World as Will and Representation*, by way of a principle of the negation of will, to life, and ultimately perhaps to the utter extinction of the human race:

> The basis of all willing, however, is need, lack, and hence pain, and by its very nature and origin it is therefore destined to pain. If, on the other hand, it lacks objects of willing, because it is at once deprived of them again by too easy a satisfaction, a fearful emptiness and boredom come over it; in other words, its being and its existence itself become an intolerable burden for it. Hence its life swings like a pendulum to and fro between pain and boredom, and these two

---

28. Theodor W. Adorno: "Progress", in *Critical Models. Interventions and Catchwords*, trans. Henry W. Pickford (New York: Columbia University Press, 1998) 152.

are in fact its ultimate constituents. This has been expressed very quaintly by saying that, after man had placed all pains and torments in hell, there was nothing left for heaven but boredom.[29]

Schopenhauer's well-known consequences are quite gloomy indeed, and some of the tragedy and futility that human existence takes on when regarded from this point of view is communicated by Adorno's philosophy as well, which even if it ultimately takes exception to Schopenhauer's conclusions may well be regarded as the true successor to his pessimism in this century, and in which the nearly cataleptic despondency expressed in Schopenhauer's description of the world of will has become open despair.

Schopenhauer invokes a line from Calderon's *Life Is a Dream:* "For the greatest guilt of man/ Is that he was born at all."

This guilt is for him the cause of the death of the individual phenomenon. This guilt stems from the fact of our very existence, which shares in the suffering of the whole world, to the extent that it remains for the most part caught up in the principium individuationis; behind this is the notion that the very world itself is burdened with guilt and as a moral phenomenon stands in need of negation. The pathos of compassion, to the extent that the compassionate one sees wherever he looks human and animal suffering and a world dwindling away, places the accent of guiltiness on the practice of that person who—owing to the necessarily individuating nature of his perceptions—is incapable of such compassion, i.e., the anamnesis of his original similarity with everything. This incapability stems solely from his status as an individual who as such assumes in the interest of self-preservation that the drama of the perpetually self-similar will, played out upon the stage of history, is being performed for him alone, for his own particular ends and in the interest of his ephemeral well-being.

To the extent that existence always entails individuality [Ichheit], existence, like individuality, is always burdened with guilt. This very thought is inherited by Adorno, mediated by psychoanalysis and social theory. Such mediation, however, endows the guilt in its metaphysical quality, the quality denoted by the notion of original sin, with an apparent expiability, insofar as the guilt is reflected in its necessity. The moral pathos and the tone of despair with which Adorno refers to the incessancy of suffering and violence in the world (even if this reference is made on the basis of historical expe-

---

29. Schopenhauer, *The World As Will and Representation* 1, 312.

riences) nevertheless allow the notion of guilt to take on once again the dimensions of original sin. And subsequent reflection, the reminder of the necessity of having arrived at this state of affairs by the process of becoming, offer no recompense for this having-become on the basis of the subsequence of the reflection. This is one reason why for Adorno all praxis ultimately seemed closed off and paradoxically, why Schopenhauer's negation of the will to life—a negation, to be sure, which with Schopenhauer carries an Epicurean accent—returns in Adorno.

Guilt, or the nonexistence of the right to be a self at all, means for Adorno to be mindful of the violence people had to inflict upon each other in order to form an identical self, a formation process he deems on the other hand necessary to the self-preservation of the individual otherwise helplessly subject to the predominance of nature or society.

> The dread of losing the self and of abrogating altogether with the self the barrier between oneself and other life, the fear of death and destruction, is intimately associated with a promise of happiness which threatened civilization in every moment.[30]

In sympathy with this threat, Adorno, who would also like to sympathize with asceticism, counters Schopenhauer's characterization of the satisfied will, of happiness, which in its ephemerality is followed immediately by boredom, with the proposition that the boredom that according to Schopenhauer befalls people when they waver in their unremitting efforts at self-preservation is a thoroughly bourgeois phenomenon, i.e., a reflex of false living within the social web of delusion, which misleads individuals into regarding their permanent self-destruction through self-preservation as a necessity of nature. In this context, he turns his attention to the ''ennui'' of the ruling class:

> None who profit by the profit system may exist within it without shame, and this deforms even the undeformed joys, although the excesses envied by the philosophers may at times have been by no means as boring as they [i.e. those who profit from the profit system] assure us. [. . .] The dictum *omne animal post coitum triste est* was concocted by bourgeois contempt for man; nowhere more than here does humanity differ from creaturely gloom. It is not ecstasy but socially approved love that is followed by disgust [. . .]. The tran-

---

30. Max Horkheimer and Theodor W. Adorno, *Dialectic of Enlightenment*, 33.

sience of pleasure, the mainstay of asceticism, attests that except in the *minutes heureuses,* when the lover's forgotten life shines back in the loved one's limbs, there is, as yet, no pleasure at all.[31]

If Adorno embraces the pleasure principle as the telos of self-preservation, so does he recognize in the failure and destruction present in the course of human lives the false social organization which prolongs even further the guilt of being a self at all, because it does not allow people the prerogative of forgetting themselves in the face of the devotion to some other, a devotion that forms the prerequisite to their becoming true individuals, individuated in experience, at all. He understands this experience as the successful experience of the nature that we ourselves are, and of the similarity with the external nature that comes at us from without, finally as the appropriate experience of art with its dialectic of nonconceptual knowledge and utopia. If the *Aesthetic Theory* ends with the notion of a wedding in trepidation of Eros and knowledge, then a very early mimetic behavior returns at the highest plane, a behavior that has as its prerequisite the notion of a nature united with man in self-preservation, transience, and expression, the reconciled version of the identity principle.

The real possibility of this reconciliation seemed to Adorno so lacking, this claim to identity was perhaps also so absolute, that the ambivalence he exhibits between ecstasy and asceticism returns in the tone of his philosophy, which did not want to limit itself to music as the only means to endure the foreknowledge of paradise.

He characterized the love with which he associated the above-mentioned third movement of Schumann's *Piano Fantasy* as death-obsessed and self-forgetting, and something of the ambivalence expressed in this range has communicated itself to his entire thinking.

The obsession with death is the tender sympathy with transience, a sympathy that empathizes with the wish to be *after all* and that might well receive consolation in knowing that transience brings an end to suffering as well. It is at the same time the moment that reminds us most emphatically of our similarity with all of nature, the one that should help to bring about that state of self-forgetting in which happiness, as the momentary, qualitative experience of reconciliation, might compensate us for the short time we are granted to dwell upon this earth.

Translated by Daniel Theisen

---

31. Adorno: *Minima Moralia,* 176.

Max Horkheimer and
Theodor W. Adorno

ON THE CONCEPT OF ENLIGHTENMENT

In the most general sense of progressive thought, the Enlightenment has always aimed at liberating men from fear and establishing their sovereignty. Yet the fully enlightened earth radiates disaster triumphant. The program of the Enlightenment was the disenchantment of the world; the dissolution of myths and the substitution of knowledge for fancy. Bacon, the "father of experimental philosophy,"[1] had defined its motives. He looked down on the masters of tradition, the "great reputed authors" who first "believe that others know that which they know not; and after themselves know that which they know not. But indeed facility to believe, impatience to doubt, temerity to answer, glory to know, doubt to contradict, end to gain, sloth to search, seeking things in words, resting in part of nature; these and the like have been the things which have forbidden the happy match between the mind of man and the nature of things; and in place thereof have married it to vain notions and blind experiments: and what the posterity and issue of so honorable a match may be, it is not hard to consider. Printing, a gross invention; artillery, a thing that lay not far out of the way; the needle, a thing partly known before: what a change have these three things made in the world in these times; the one in state of learning, the other in the state of war, the third in the state of treasure, commodities, and navigation! And those, I say, were but stumbled upon and lighted upon by chance. Therefore, no doubt, the sovereignty of man lieth hid in knowledge; wherein many things are reserved, which kings with their treasure cannot buy, nor with their force command; their spials and intelligencers can give no news of them,

---

1. Voltaire, *Lettres Philosophiques*, XII, *Oeuvres Complètes* (Garnier: Paris, 1879), vol. 22, p. 118.

their seamen and discoverers cannot sail where they grow; now we govern nature in opinions, but we are thrall unto her in necessity: but if we would be led by her in invention, we should command her by action."[2]

Despite his lack of mathematics, Bacon's view was appropriate to the scientific attitude that prevailed after him. The concordance between the mind of man and the nature of things that he had in mind is patriarchal: the human mind, which overcomes superstition, is to hold sway over a disenchanted nature. Knowledge, which is power, knows no obstacles: neither in the enslavement of men nor in compliance with the world's rulers. As with all the ends of bourgeois economy in the factory and on the battlefield, origin is no bar to the dictates of the entrepreneurs: kings, no less directly than businessmen, control technology; it is as democratic as the economic system with which it is bound up. Technology is the essence of this knowledge. It does not work by concepts and images, by the fortunate insight, but refers to method, the exploitation of others' work, and capital. The "many things" which, according to Bacon, "are reserved," are themselves no more than instrumental: the radio as a sublimated printing press, the dive bomber as a more effective form of artillery, radio control as a more reliable compass. What men want to learn from nature is how to use it in order wholly to dominate it and other men. That is the only aim. Ruthlessly, in despite of itself, the Enlightenment has extinguished any trace of its own self-consciousness. The only kind of thinking that is sufficiently hard to shatter myths is ultimately self-destructive. In face of the present triumph of the factual mentality, even Bacon's nominalist credo would be suspected of a metaphysical bias and come under the same verdict of vanity that he pronounced on scholastic philosophy. Power and knowledge are synonymous.[3] For Bacon as for Luther, "knowledge that tendeth but to satisfaction, is but as a courtesan, which is for pleasure, and not for fruit or generation." Not "satisfaction, which men call truth," but "operation," "to do the business," is the "right mark": for ". . . what is the true end, scope, or office of knowledge, which I have set down to consist not in any plausible, delectable, reverend or admired discourse, or any satisfactory arguments, but in effecting and working,

---

2. Bacon, "In Praise of Human Knowledge" *(Miscellaneous Tracts upon Human Knowledge), The Works of Francis Bacon,* ed. Basil Montagu (London, 1825), vol. 1, pp. 254ff.

3. Cf. Bacon, *Novum Organum, Works,* vol. 14, p. 31.

and in discovery of particulars not revealed before, for the better endowment and help of man's life."[4] There is to be no mystery—which means, too, no wish to reveal mystery.

The disenchantment of the world is the extirpating of animism. Xenophanes derides the multitude of deities because they are but replicas of the men who produced them, together with all that is contingent and evil in mankind; and the most recent school of logic denounces—for the impressions they bear—the words of language, holding them to be false coins better replaced by neutral counters. The world becomes chaos, and synthesis salvation. There is said to be no difference between the totemic animal, the dreams of the ghost-seer, and the absolute Idea. On the road to modern science, men renounce any claim to meaning. They substitute formula for concept, rule and probability for cause and motive. Cause was only the last philosophic concept which served as a yardstick for scientific criticism: so to speak because it alone among the old ideas still seemed to offer itself to scientific criticism, the latest secularization of the creative principle. Substance and quality, activity and suffering, being and existence: to define these concepts in a way appropriate to the times was a concern of philosophy after Bacon—but science managed without such categories. They were abandoned as *idola theatri* of the old metaphysics, and assessed as being even then memorials of the elements and powers of the prehistory for which life and death disclosed their nature in myths and became interwoven in them. The categories by which Western philosophy defined its everlasting natural order marked the spots once occupied by Oncus and Persephone, Ariadne and Nereus. The pre-socratic cosmologies preserve the moment of transition. The moist, the indivisible, air, and fire, which they hold to be the primal matter of nature, are already rationalizations of the mythic mode of apprehension. Just as the images of generation from water and earth, which came from the Nile to the Greeks, became here hylozoistic principles, or elements, so all the equivocal multitude of mythical demons were intellectualized in the pure form of ontological essences. Finally, by means of the Platonic ideas, even the patriarchal gods of Olympus were absorbed in the philosophical *logos*. The Enlightenment, however, recognized the old powers in the Platonic and Aristotelian aspects of metaphysics, and opposed as superstition the claim that truth is predictable of universals. It asserted that

---

4. Bacon, "Valerius Terminus: Of the Interpretation of Nature" *(Miscellaneous Tracts upon Human Knowledge)*, *Works*, vol. 1, p. 281.

in the authority of universal concepts, there was still discernible fear of the demonic spirits which men sought to portray in magic rituals, hoping thus to influence nature. From now on, matter would at last be mastered without any illusion of ruling or inherent powers, of hidden qualities. For the Enlightenment, whatever does not conform to the rule of computation and utility is suspect. So long as it can develop undisturbed by any outward repression, there is no holding it. In the process, it treats its own ideas of human rights exactly as it does the older universals. Every spiritual resistance it encounters serves merely to increase its strength. Which means that enlightenment still recognizes itself even in myths. Whatever myths the resistance may appeal to, by virtue of the very fact that they become arguments in the process of opposition, they acknowledge the principle of dissolvent rationality for which they reproach the Enlightenment. Enlightenment is totalitarian.

Enlightenment has always taken the basic principle of myth to be anthropomorphism, the projection onto nature of the subjective. In this view, the supernatural, spirits and demons, are mirror images of men who allow themselves to be frightened by natural phenomena. Consequently the many mythic figures can all be brought to a common denominator, and reduced to the human subject. Oedipus' answer to the Sphinx's riddle: "It is man!" is the Enlightenment stereotype repeatedly offered as information, irrespective of whether it is faced with a piece of objective intelligence, a bare schematization, fear of evil powers, or hope of redemption. In advance, the Enlightenment recognizes as being and occurrence only what can be apprehended in unity: its ideal is the system from which all and everything follows. Its rationalist and empiricist versions do not part company on that point. Even though the individual schools may interpret the axioms differently, the structure of scientific unity has always been the same. Bacon's postulate of *una scientia universalis*,[5] whatever the number of fields of research, is as inimical to the unassignable as Leibniz's *mathesis universalis* is to discontinuity. The multiplicity of forms is reduced to position and arrangement, history to fact, things to matter. According to Bacon, too, degrees of universality provide an unequivocal logical connection between first principles and observational judgments. De Maistre mocks him for harboring `une idole d'échelle.`"[6] Formal logic was

---

5. Bacon, *De Augmentis Scientiarum, Works*, vol. 8, p. 152.

6. *Les Soirées de Saint-Pétersbourg, Oeuvres Complètes* (Lyon, 1891), vol. 4, p. 256.

the major school of unified science. It provided the Enlightenment thinkers with the schema of the calculability of the world. The mythologizing equation of Ideas with numbers in Plato's last writings expressed the longing of all demythologization: number became the canon of the Enlightenment. The same equations dominate bourgeois justice and commodity exchange. "Is not the rule, `Si inaequalibus aequalia addas, omnia erunt inaequalia,`' an axiom of justice as well as of the mathematics? And is there not a true coincidence between commutative and distributive justice, and arithmetical and geometrical proportion?"[7] Bourgeois society is ruled by equivalence. It makes the dissimilar comparable by reducing it to abstract quantities. To the Enlightenment, that which does not reduce to numbers, and ultimately to the one, becomes illusion; modern positivism writes it off as literature. Unity is the slogan from Parmenides to Russell. The destruction of gods and qualities alike is insisted upon.

Yet the myths which fell victim to the Enlightenment were its own products. In the scientific calculation of occurrence, the computation is annulled which thought had once transferred from occurrence into myths. Myth intended report, naming, the narration of the Beginning; but also presentation, confirmation, explanation: a tendency that grew stronger with the recording and collection of myths. Narrative became didactic at an early stage. Every ritual includes the idea of activity as a determined process which magic can nevertheless influence. This theoretical element in ritual won independence in the earliest national epics. The myths, as the tragedians came upon them, are already characterized by the discipline and power that Bacon celebrated as the "right mark." In place of the local spirits and demons there appeared heaven and its hierarchy; in place of the invocations of the magician and the tribe the distinct gradation of sacrifice and the labor of the unfree mediated through the word of command. The Olympic deities are no longer directly identical with elements, but signify them. In Homer, Zeus represents the sky and the weather, Apollo controls the sun, and Helios and Eos are already shifting to an allegorical function. The gods are distinguished from material elements as their quintessential concepts. From now on, being divides into the *logos* (which with the progress of philosophy contracts to the monad, to a mere point of reference), and into the mass of all things and creatures without. This single distinction between existence proper and real-

---

7. Bacon, *Advancement of Learning, Works*, vol. 2, p. 126.

ity engulfs all others. Without regard to distinctions, the world becomes subject to man. In this the Jewish creation narrative and the
religion of Olympia are at one: ". . . and let them have dominion
over the fish of the sea, and over the fowl of the air, and over the
cattle, and over all the earth, and over every creeping thing that
creepeth upon the earth."[8] "O Zeus, Father Zeus, yours is the dominion of the heavens, and you oversee the works of man, both
wicked and just, and even the wantonness of the beasts; and righteousness is your concern."[9] "For so it is that one atones straight-
away, and another later; but should one escape and the threatening
decree of the gods not reach him, yet it will certainly be visited at
last, if not upon him then upon his children or another generation."[10] Only he who always submits survives in the face of the
gods. The awakening of the self is paid for by the acknowledgement
of power as the principle of all relations. In view of the unity of this
ratio, the divorcement between God and man dwindles to the degree of irrelevancy to which unswervable reason has drawn attention since even the earliest critique of Homer. The creative god and
the systematic spirit are alike as rulers of nature. Man's likeness to
God consists in sovereignty over existence, in the countenance of
the lord and master, and in command.

Myth turns into enlightenment, and nature into mere objectivity.
Men pay for the increase of their power with alienation from that
over which they exercise their power. Enlightenment behaves
toward things as a dictator toward men. He knows them insofar as
he can manipulate them. The man of science knows things insofar
as he can make them. In this way their potentiality is turned to his
own ends. In the metamorphosis the nature of things, as a substratum of domination, is revealed as always the same. This identity
constitutes the unit of nature. It is a presupposition of the magical
invocation as little as the unity of the subject. The shaman's rites
were directed to the wind, the rain, the serpent without, or the
demon in the sick man, but not to materials or specimens. Magic
was not ordered by one, identical spirit: it changed like the cultic
masks which were supposed to accord with the various spirits.
Magic is utterly untrue, yet in it domination is not yet negated by
transforming itself into the pure truth and acting as the very ground
of the world that has become subject to it. The magician imitates

---

8. Genesis I. 26.
9. Archilochos, fr. 87.
10. Solon, fr. 13.25.

demons; in order to frighten them or to appease them, he behaves frighteningly or makes gestures of appeasement. Even though his task is impersonation, he never conceives of himself as does the civilized man for whom the unpretentious preserves of the happy hunting ground become the unified cosmos, the inclusive concept for all possibilities of plunder. The magician never interprets himself as the image of the invisible power; yet this is the very image in which man attains to the identity of self that cannot disappear through identification with another, but takes possession of itself once and for all as an impenetrable mask. It is the identity of the spirit and its correlate, the unity of nature, to which the multiplicity of qualities falls victim. Disqualified nature becomes the chaotic matter of mere classification, and the all-powerful self becomes mere possession—abstract identity. In magic there is specific representation. What happens to the enemy's spear, hair or name, also happens to the individual; the sacrificial animal is massacred instead of the god. Substitution in the course of sacrifice marks a step toward discursive logic. Even though the hind offered up for the daughter, and the lamb for the first-born, still had to have specific qualities, they already represented the species. They already exhibited the nonspecificity of the example. But the holiness of the *hic et nunc*, the uniqueness of the chosen one into which the representative enters, radically marks it off, and makes it unfit for exchange. Science prepares the end of this state of affairs. In science there is no specific representation: and if there are no sacrificial animals there is no god. Representation is exchanged for the fungible—universal interchangeability. An atom is smashed not in representation but as a specimen of matter, and the rabbit does not represent but, as a mere example, is virtually ignored by the zeal of the laboratory. Because the distinctions in functional science are so fluid that everything is subsumed in the same manner, the scientific object is petrified, and the fixed ritual of former times appears flexible because it attributed the other to the one. The world of magic retained distinctions whose traces have disappeared even in linguistic form. The multitudinous affinities between existents are suppressed by the single relation between the subject who bestows meaning and the meaningless object, between rational significance and the chance vehicle of significance. On the magical plane, dream and image were not mere signs for the thing in question, but were bound up with it by similarity or names. The relation is one not of intention but of relatedness. Like science, magic pursues aims, but seeks to achieve them by mimesis—not by progressively distancing itself from the object. It is not grounded in the "sovereignty of ideas," which the primitive, like the neurotic, is said to ascribe to himself;[11] there can be no "overevaluation of mental processes as against reality" where there is no radical distinction between thoughts and reality. The "unshakable confidence in the possibility of world domination,"[12] which Freud anachronistically ascribes to magic, corresponds to realistic world domination only in terms of a more skilled science. The replacement of the milieu-bound practices of the medicine man by all-inclusive industrial technology required first of all the autonomy of ideas in regard to objects that was achieved in the reality-adjusted ego.

As a linguistically expressed totality, whose claim to truth suppresses the older mythic belief, the national religion or patriarchal solar myth is itself an Enlightenment with which the philosophic form can compare itself on the same level. And now it has its requital. Mythology itself set off the unending process of enlightenment in which ever and again, with the inevitability of necessity, every specific theoretic view succumbs to the destructive criticism that it is only a belief—until even the very notions of spirit, of truth and, indeed, enlightenment itself, have become animistic magic. The principle of fatal necessity, which brings low the heroes of myth and derives as a logical consequence from the pronouncement of the oracle, does not merely, when refined to the stringency of formal logic, rule in every rationalistic system of Western philosophy, but itself dominates the series of systems which begins with the hierarchy of the gods and, in a permanent twilight of the idols, hands down an identical content: anger against insufficient righteousness. Just as the myths already realize enlightenment, so enlightenment with every step becomes more deeply engulfed in mythology. It receives all its matter from the myths, in order to destroy them; and even as a judge it comes under the mythic curse. It wishes to extricate itself from the process of fate and retribution, while exercising retribution on that process. In the myths everything that happens must atone for having happened. And so it is in enlightenment: the fact becomes null and void, and might as well not have happened. The doctrine of the equivalence of action and reaction asserted the power of repetition over reality, long after men had renounced the illusion that by repetition they could iden-

---

11. Cf. Freud, *Totem und Tabu (Totem and Taboo)*, *Gesammelte Werke*, vol. 9, pp. 106ff.

12. *Totem und Tabu*, p. 110.

tify themselves with the repeated reality and thus escape its power. But as the magical illusion fades away, the more relentlessly in the name of law repetition imprisons man in the cycle—that cycle whose objectification in the form of natural law he imagines will ensure his action as a free subject. The principle of immanence, the explanation of every event as repetition, that the Enlightenment upholds against mythic imagination, is the principle of myth itself. That arid wisdom that holds there is nothing new under the sun, because all the pieces in the meaningless game have been played, and all the great thoughts have already been thought, and because all possible discoveries can be construed in advance and all men are decided on adaptation as the means to self-preservation—that dry sagacity merely reproduces the fantastic wisdom that it supposedly rejects: the sanction of fate that in retribution relentlessly remakes what has already been. What was different is equalized. That is the verdict which critically determines the limits of possible experience. The identity of everything with everything else is paid for in that nothing may at the same time be identical with itself. Enlighten-ment dissolves the injustice of the old inequality—unmediated lord-ship and mastery—but at the same time perpetuates it in universal mediation, in the relation of any one existent to any other. It does what Kierkegaard praises his Protestant ethic for, and what in the Heraclean epic cycle is one of the primal images of mythic power; it excises the incommensurable. Not only are qualities dissolved in thought, but men are brought to actual conformity. The blessing that the market does not enquire after one's birth is paid for by the barterer, in that he models the potentialities that are his by birth on the production of the commodities that can be bought in the mar-ket. Men were given their individuality as unique in each case, dif-ferent to all others, so that it might all the more surely be made the same as any other. But because the unique self never wholly disappeared, even after the liberalistic epoch, the Enlightenment has always sympathized with the social impulse. The unity of the manipulated collective consists in the negation of each individual: for individuality makes a mockery of the kind of society which would turn all individuals to the one collectivity. The horde which so assuredly appears in the organization of the Hitler Youth is not a return to barbarism but the triumph of repressive equality, the disclosure through peers of the parity of the right to injustice. The phony Fascist mythology is shown to be the genuine myth of antiq-uity, insofar as the genuine one saw retribution, whereas the false one blindly doles it out to the sacrifices. Every attempt to break the natural thralldom, because nature is broken, enters all the more deeply into that natural enslavement. Hence the course of European civilization. Abstraction, the tool of enlightenment, treats its objects as did fate, the notion of which it rejects: it liquidates them. Under the leveling domination of abstraction (which makes everything in nature repeatable), and of industry (for which abstraction ordains repetition), the freedom themselves finally came to form that "herd" which Hegel has declared to be the result of the Enlightenment.

The distance between subject and object, a presupposition of abstraction, is grounded in the distance from the thing itself which the master achieved through the mastered. The lyrics of Homer and the hymns of the Rig-Veda date from the time of territorial dominion and the secure locations in which a dominant warlike race established themselves over the mass of vanquished natives. The first god among the gods arose with this civil society in which the king, as chieftain of the arms-bearing nobility, holds down the conquered to the earth, whereas physicians, soothsayers, craftsmen and merchants see to social intercourse. With the end of a nomadic existence, the social order is created on a basis of fixed property. Mastery and labor are divided. A proprietor like Odysseus "manages from a distance a numerous, carefully gradated staff of cowherds, shepherds, swineherds and servants. In the evening, when he has seen from his castle that the countryside is illumined by a thousand fires, he can compose himself for sleep with a quiet mind: he knows that his upright servants are keeping watch lest wild animals approach, and to chase thieves from the preserves which they are there to protect."[13] The universality of ideas as developed by discursive logic, domination in the conceptual sphere, is raised up on the basis of actual domination. The dissolution of the magical heritage, of the old diffuse ideas, by conceptual unity, expresses the hierarchical constitution of life determined by those who are free. The individuality that learned order and subordination in the subjection of the world, soon wholly equated truth with the regulative thought without whose fixed distinctions universal truth cannot exist. Together with mimetic magic, it tabooed the knowledge which really concerned the object. Its hatred was extended to the image of the vanquished former age and its imaginary happiness. The chthonic gods of the original inhabitants are banished to the hell to which,

---

13. G. Glotz, *Histoire Grècque,* vol. 1 in *Histoire Ancienne* (Paris, 1938), pp. 137ff.

according to the sun and light religion of Indra and Zeus, the earth is transformed.

Heaven and hell, however, hang together. Just as the name of Zeus, in nonexclusive cults, was given to a god of the underworld as well as to a god of light; just as the Olympian gods had every kind of commerce with the chthonic deities: so the good and evil powers, salvation and disaster, were not unequivocally distinct. They were linked together like coming up and passing away, life and death, summer and winter. The gloomy and indistinct religious principle that was honored as mana in the earliest known stages of humanity, lives on in the radiant world of Greek religion. Everything unknown and alien is primary and undifferentiated: that which transcends the confines of experience; whatever in things is more than their previously known reality. What the primitive experiences in this regard is not a spiritual as opposed to a material substance, but the intricacy of the Natural in contrast to the individual. The gasp of surprise which accompanies the experience of the unusual becomes its name. It fixes the transcendence of the unknown in relation to the known, and therefore terror as sacredness. The dualization of nature as appearance and sequence, effort and power, which first makes possible both myth and science, originates in human fear, the expression of which becomes explanation. It is not the soul which is transposed to nature, as psychologism would have it; mana, the moving spirit, is no projection, but the echo of the real supremacy of nature in the weak souls of primitive men. The separation of the animate and the inanimate, the occupation of certain places by demons and deities, first arises from this preanimism, which contains the first lines of the separation of subject and object. When the tree is no longer approached merely as tree, but as evidence for an Other, as the location of mana, language expressed the contradiction that something is itself and at one and the same time something other than itself, identical and not identical.[14] Through the deity, language is transformed from tautology to language. The concept, which some would see as the sign-unit for whatever is comprised under it, has from the beginning been instead the product of dialectical thinking in which everything is always that which it is, only because it becomes that which it is not. That was the original form of objectifying definition, in which con-

---

14. This is how Hubert and Mauss interpret "sympathy," or *mimesis:* "*L'un est le tout, tout est dans l'un, la nature triomphe de la nature.*" H. Hubert and M. Mauss, "*Théorie générale de la Magie,*" in: *L'Année Sociologique,* 1902–3, p. 100.

cept and thing are separated. The same form which is already far advanced in the Homeric epic and confounds itself in modern positivist science. But this dialectic remains impotent to the extent that it develops from the cry of terror which is the duplication, the tautology, of terror itself. The gods cannot take fear away from man, for they bear its petrified sound with them as they bear their names. Man imagines himself free from fear when there is no longer anything unknown. That determines the course of demythologication, of enlightenment, which compounds the animate with the inanimate just as myth compounds the inanimate with the animate. Enlightenment is mythic fear turned radical. The pure immanence of positivism, its ultimate product, is no more than a so to speak universal taboo. Nothing at all may remain outside, because the mere idea of outsideness is the very source of fear. The revenge of the primitive for death, when visited upon one of his kin, was sometimes appeased by reception of the murderer into his own family; this, too, signified the infusion of alien blood into one's own, the generation of immanence. The mythic dualism does not extend beyond the environs of existence. The world permeated by mana and even the world of Indian and Greek myth know no exits, and are eternally the same. Every birth is paid for with death, every fortune with misfortune. Men and gods may try in their short space to assess fate in other terms than the blind course of destiny, but in the end existence triumphs over them. Even their justice, which is wrested from fatality, bears the marks of fatality: it corresponds to the look which men—primitives, Greeks and barbarians alike—cast from a society of pressure and misery on the circumambient world. Hence, for mythic and enlightened justice, guilt and atonement, happiness and unhappiness were sides of an equation. Justice is subsumed in law. The shaman wards off danger by means of its image. Equivalence is his instrument; and equivalence regulates punishment and reward in civilization. The mythic representations can also be traced back in their entirety to natural conditions. Just as the Gemini—the constellation of Castor and Pollux—and all other symbols of duality refer to the inevitable cycle of nature, which itself has its ancient sign in the symbol of the egg from which they came, so the balance held by Zeus, which symbolizes the justice of the entire patriarchal world, refers back to mere nature. The step from chaos to civilization, in which natural conditions exert their power no longer directly but through the medium of the human consciousness, has not changed the principle of equivalence. Indeed, men paid for this very step by worshipping what they were once in thrall to only in the same way as all other creatures. Before, the fetishes were subject to the law of equivalence. Now equivalence itself has become a fetish. The blindfold over Justitia's eyes does not only mean that there should be no assault upon justice, but that justice does not originate in freedom.

The doctrine of the priests was symbolic in the sense that in it sign and image were one. Just as hieroglyphs bear witness, so the word too originally had a pictorial function, which was transferred to myths. Like magical rites, myths signify self-repetitive nature, which is the core of the symbolic: a state of being or a process that is presented as eternal, because it incessantly becomes actual once more by being realized in symbolic form. Inexhaustibility, unending renewal and the permanence of the signified are not mere attributes of all symbols, but their essential content. The representations of creation in which the world comes forth from the primal mother, the cow, or the egg, are symbolic—unlike the Jewish Genesis. The elders' mockery of the all-too-human gods left the core untouched. The gods were not wholly individual. They still had something of mana in them, for they embodied nature as universal power. With their pre-animistic characteristics they are prominent in the Enlightenment. Beneath the coy veil of the Olympian *chronique scandaleuse*, there was already apparent the doctrine of the mixture, pressure, and impact of the elements, which presently established itself as science and turned the myths into fantastic images. With the clean separation of science and poetry, the division of labor it had already helped to effect was extended to language. For science the word is a sign: as sound, image, and word proper it is distributed among the different arts, and is not permitted to reconstitute itself by their addition, by synesthesia, or in the composition of the *Gesamtkunstwerk.* As a system of signs, language is required to resign itself to calculation in order to know nature, and must discard the claim to be like her. As image, it is required to resign itself to mirror-imagery in order to be nature entire, and must discard the claim to know her. With the progress of enlightenment, only authentic works of art were able to avoid the mere imitation of that which already is. The practicable antithesis of art and science, which tears them apart as separate areas of culture in order to make them both manageable as areas of culture ultimately allows them, by dint of their own tendencies, to blend with one another even as exact contraries. In its neopositivist version, science becomes aestheticism, a system of detached signs devoid of any intention that would transcend the system: it becomes the game which mathematicians have for long proudly asserted is their concern. But the art of integral representability, even in its techniques, subscribed to positive science, and in fact adapts to the world yet again, becoming ideological duplication, partisan reproduction. The separation of sign and image is irremediable. Should unconscious self-satisfaction cause it once again to become hypostatized, then each of the two isolated principles tends toward the destruction of truth.

In the relationship of intuition (i.e., direct perception) and concept, philosophy already discerned the gulf which opened with that separation, and again tries in vain to close it: philosophy, indeed, is defined by this very attempt. For the most part it has stood on the side from which it derives its name. Plato banned poetry with the same gesture that positivism used against the theory of ideas *(Ideenlehre)*. With his much-renowned art, Homer carried out no public or private reforms, and neither won a war nor made any discovery. We know of no multitude of followers who might have honored or adored him. Art must first prove its utility.[15] For art, as for the Jews, imitation is proscribed. Reason and religion deprecate and condemn the principle of magic enchantment. Even in resigned self-distancing from real existence, as art, it remains dishonest; its practitioners become travelers, latter-day nomads who find no abiding home under the established what-has-come-to-be. Nature must no longer be influenced by approximation, but mastered by labor. The work of art still has something in common with enchantment: it posits its own, self-enclosed area, which is withdrawn from the context of profane existence, and in which special laws apply. Just as in the ceremony the magician first of all marked out the limits of the area where the sacred powers were to come into play, so every work of art describes its own circumference which closes it off from actuality. This very renunciation of influence, which distinguishes art from magical sympathy, retains the magic heritage all the more surely. It places the pure image in contrast to animate existence, the elements of which it absorbs. It is in the nature of the work of art, or aesthetic semblance, to be what the new, terrifying occurrence became in the primitive's magic: the appearance of the whole in the particular. In the work of art that duplication still occurs by which the thing appeared as spiritual, as the expression of mana. This constitutes its aura. As an expression of totality art lays claim to the dignity of the absolute. This sometimes causes philosophy to

---

15. Cf. Plato, *Republic*, Book 10.

allow it precedence to conceptual knowledge. According to Schelling, art comes into play where knowledge forsakes mankind. For him it is "the prototype of science, and only where there is art may science enter in."[16] In his theory, the separation of image and sign is "wholly canceled by every single artistic representation."[17] The bourgeois world was but rarely open to such confidence in art. Where it restricted knowledge, it usually did so not for the sake of art, but in order to make room for faith. Through faith the militant religiousness of the new age hoped to reconcile Torquemada, Luther, Mohammed, spirit, and real life. But faith is a privative concept: it is destroyed as faith if it does not continually display its contradistinction to, or conformity with, knowledge. Since it is always set upon the restriction of knowledge, it is itself restricted. The attempt of Protestant faith to find, as in prehistory, the transcendental principle of truth (without which belief cannot exist) directly in the word itself, and to reinvest this with symbolic power, has been paid for with obedience to the word, and not to the sacred. As long as faith remains unhesitatingly tied—as friend or foe—to knowledge, it perpetuates the separation in the very course of the struggle to overcome it: its fanaticism is the occasion of its untruth, the objective admission that he who only has faith, for that very reason no longer has it. Bad conscience is its second nature. In the secret consciousness of the deficiency—necessarily inherent in faith—of its immanent contradiction in making reconciliation a vocation, lies the reason why the integrity of all believers has always been a sensitive and dangerous thing. The atrocities of fire and sword, Counter-Reformation and Reformation, have occurred not as exaggerations but as realizations of the principle of faith itself. Faith constantly reveals itself to be of the same cut as the world-history which it would dictate to—in modern times, indeed, it becomes its favorite instrument, its particular stratagem. It is not merely the Enlightenment of the eighteenth century that, as Hegel confirmed, is relentless but—as no one knew better than he—the advance of thought itself. The lowest and the highest insight alike manifest that distance from truth which makes apologists liars. The paradoxical nature of faith ultimately degenerates into a swindle, and becomes the myth of the twentieth century; and its irrationality turns it into an instrument of rational administration by the wholly enlightened as they steer society toward barbarism.

---

16. *Erster Entwurf eines Systems der Naturphilosophie*, S. 5, *Werke*, Abt. 1, vol. 2, p. 623.

17. *Ibid.*, p. 626.

When language enters history its masters are priests and sorcerers. Whoever harms the symbols is, in the name of the supernatural powers, subject to their earthly counterparts, whose representatives are those chosen organs of society. What happened previously is hid in darkness. The dread which gives to mana, wherever it is met within ethnology, is always sanctioned—at least by the tribal elders. Unidentified, volatile mana was rendered consistent by men and forcibly materialized. Soon the magicians peopled every spot with emanations and made a multiplicity of sacred rites concordant with the variety of sacred places. They expanded their professional knowledge and their influence with the expansion of the spirit world and its characteristics. The nature of the sacred being transferred itself to the magicians, who were privy to it. In the first stages of nomadic life the members of the tribe still took an individual part in the process of influencing the course of nature. Men hunted game, while women did the work which could be produced without strict command. It is impossible to determine to what extent habit contributed to so simple an arrangement. In it, the world is already divided into the territory of power and the profane area; as the emanation of mana, the course of nature is elevated to become the norm, and submission to it is required. But even though, despite all submission, the savage nomad still participated in the magic which determined the lines of that submission, and clothed himself as his quarry in order to stalk it, in later times intercourse with spirits and submission were assigned to different classes: the power is on the one side, and obedience on the other. For the vanquished (whether by alien tribes or by their own cliques), the recurrent, eternally similar natural processes become the rhythm of labor according to the beat of cudgel and whip which resounds in every barbaric drum and every monotonous ritual. The symbols undertake a fetishistic function. In the process, the recurrence of nature which they signify is always the permanence of the social pressure which they represent. The dread objectified as a fixed image becomes the sign of the established domination of the privileged. Such is the fate of universal concepts, even when they have discarded everything pictorial. Even the deductive form of science reflects hierarchy and coercion. Just as the first categories represented the organized tribe and its power over the individual, so the whole logical order, dependency, connection, progression, and union of concepts is grounded in the corresponding conditions of social reality—that is, of the division of labor.[18] But of course this social character of categories of thought is not, as Durkheim asserts, an expression of social solidarity, but evidence of the inscrutable unity of society and domination. Domination lends increased consistency and force to the social whole in which it establishes itself. The division of labor to which domination tends serves the dominated whole for the end of self-preservation. But then the whole as whole, the manifestation of its immanent reason, necessarily leads to the execution of the particular. To the individual, domination appears to be the universal: reason in actuality. Through the division of labor imposed on them, the power of all the members of society—for whom as such there is no other course—amounts over and over again to the realization of the whole, whose rationality is reproduced in this way. What is done to all by the few, always occurs as the subjection of individuals by the many: social repression always exhibits the masks of repression by a collective. It is this unity of the collectivity and domination, and not direct social universality, solidarity, which is expressed in thought forms. By virtue of the claim to universal validity, the philosophic concepts with which Plato and Aristotle represented the world, elevated the conditions they were used to substantiate to the level of true reality. These concepts originated, as Vico puts it,[19] in the marketplace of Athens; they reflected with equal clarity the laws of physics, the equality of full citizens and the inferiority of women, children and slaves. Language itself gave what was asserted, the conditions of domination, the universality that they had assumed as the means of intercourse of a bourgeois society. The metaphysical emphasis, and sanction by means of ideas and norms, were no more than a hypostatization of the rigidity and exclusiveness which concepts were generally compelled to assume wherever language united the community of rulers with the giving of orders. As a mere means of reinforcing the social power of language, ideas became all the more superfluous as this power grew, and the language of science prepared the way for their ultimate desuetude. The suggestion of something still akin to the terror of the fetish did not inhere in conscious justification; instead the unity of collectivity and domination is revealed in the universality neces-

---

18. See Emile Durkheim, ``*De Quelques Formes Primitives de Classification,*'' in: *L'Année Sociologique*, vol. 4, 1903, pp. 66ff.

19. Giambattista Vico, *Scienza Nuova (Principles of a New Science of the Common Nature of Nations)*.

sarily assumed by the bad content of language, both metaphysical and scientific. Metaphysical apology betrayed the injustice of the status quo least of all in the incongruence of concept and actuality. In the impartiality of scientific language, that which is powerless has wholly lost any means of expression, and only the given finds its neutral sign. This kind of neutrality is more metaphysical than metaphysics. Ultimately, the Enlightenment consumed not just the symbols but their successors, universal concepts, and spared no remnant of metaphysics apart from the abstract fear of the collective from which it arose. The situation of concepts in the face of the Enlightenment is like that of men of private means in regard to industrial trusts: none can feel safe. Even if logical positivism still allowed leeway to probability, ethnological positivism puts it in its place: "Our vague ideas of chance and quintessence are pale shadows of this much richer notion"[20]—that is, of magical substance.

As a nominalist movement, the Enlightenment calls a halt before the *nomen,* the exclusive, precise concept, the proper name. Whether proper names were originally species names as well, can no longer be ascertained, yet the former have not shared the fate of the latter. The substantial ego refuted by Hume and Mach is not synonymous with the name. In Jewish religion, in which the idea of the patriarchate culminates in the destruction of myth, the bond between name and being is still recognized in the ban on pronouncing the name of God. The disenchanted world of Judaism conciliates magic by negating it in the idea of God. Jewish religion allows no word that would alleviate the despair of all that is mortal. It associates hope only with the prohibition against calling on what is false as God, against invoking the finite as the infinite, lies as truth. The guarantee of salvation lies in the rejection of any belief that would replace it: it is knowledge obtained in the denunciation of illusion. Admittedly, the negation is not abstract. The contesting of every positive without distinction, the stereotype formula of vanity, as used by Buddhism, sets itself above the prohibition against naming the Absolute with names: just as far above as its contrary, pantheism; or its caricature, bourgeois skepticism. Explanations of the world as all or nothing are mythologies, and guaranteed roads to redemption are sublimated magic practices. The self-satisfaction of knowing in advance and the transfiguration of negativity into redemption are untrue forms of resistance against deception. The justness of the image is preserved in the faithful pursuit of its prohi-

---

20. Hubert and Mauss, p. 118.

bition. This pursuit, "determinate negativity"(Hegel) does not receive from the sovereignty of the abstract concept any immunity against corrupting intuition, as does skepticism, to which both true and false are equally vain. Determinate negation rejects the defective ideas of the absolute, the idols, differently than does rigorism, which confronts them with the Idea that they cannot match up to. Dialectic, on the contrary, interprets every image as writing. It shows how the admission of its falsity is to be read in the lines of its features—a confession that deprives it of its power and appropriates it for truth. With the notion of determinate negativity, Hegel revealed an element that distinguishes the Enlightenment from the positivist degeneracy to which he attributes it. By ultimately making the conscious result of the whole process of negation—totality in system and in history—into an absolute, he of course contravened the prohibition and himself lapsed into mythology.

This did not happen merely to his philosophy as the apotheosis of progressive thought, but to the Enlightenment itself, as the sobriety which it thought distinguished it from Hegel and from metaphysics. For enlightenment is as totalitarian as any system. Its untruth does not consist in what its romantic enemies have always reproached it for: analytical method, return to elements, dissolution through reflective thought; but instead in the fact that for enlightenment the process is always decided from the start. When in mathematical procedure the unknown becomes the unknown quantity of an equation, this marks it as the well-known even before any value is inserted. Nature, before and after the quantum theory, is that which is to be comprehended mathematically; even what cannot be made to agree, indissolubility and irrationality, is converted by means of mathematical theorems. In the anticipatory indentification of the wholly conceived and mathematized world with truth, enlightenment intends to secure itself against the return of the mythic. It confounds thought and mathematics. In this way the latter is, so to speak, released and made into an absolute instance. "An infinite world, in this case a world of idealities, is conceived as one whose objects do not accede singly, imperfectly, and as if by chance to our cognition, but are attained by a rational, systematically unified method—in a process of infinite progression—so that each object is ultimately apparent according to its full inherent being. . . . In the Galilean mathematization of the world, however, *this selfness* is idealized under the guidance of the new mathematics: in modern terms, it becomes itself a mathematical multiplicity."[21] Thinking objectifies itself to become an automatic, self-activating process; an impersonation of the machine that it produces itself so that ultimately the machine can replace it. Enlightenment[22] has put aside the classic requirement of thinking about thought—Fichte is its extreme manifestation—because it wants to avoid the precept of dictating practice that Fichte himself wished to obey. Mathematical procedure became, so to speak, the ritual of thinking. In spite of the axiomatic self-restriction, it establishes itself as necessary and objective: it turns thought into a thing, an instrument—which is its own term for it. But this kind of mimesis, in which universal thought is equalized, so turns the actual into the unique, that even atheism itself is subjected to the ban on metaphysics. For positivism, which represents the court of judgment of enlightened reason, to digress into intelligible worlds is no longer merely forbidden, but meaningless prattle. It does not need—fortunately—to be atheistic, because objectified thinking cannot even raise the problem. The positivist censor lets the established cult escape as willingly as art—as a cognition-free special area of social activity; but he will never permit that denial of it which itself claims to be knowledge. For the scientific mind, the separation of thought from business for the purpose of adjusting actuality, departure from the privileged area of real existence, is as insane and self-destructive as the primitive magician would consider stepping out of the magic circle he has prepared for his invocation; in both cases the offense against the taboo will actually result in the malefactor's ruin. The mastery of nature draws the circle into which the criticism of pure reason banished thought. Kant joined the theory of its unceasingly laborious advance into infinity with an insistence on its deficiency and everlasting limitation. His judgment is an oracle. There is no form of being in the world that science could not penetrate, but what can be penetrated by science is not being. According to Kant, philosophic judgment aims at the new; and yet it recognizes nothing new, since it always merely recalls what reason has always deposited in the object. But there is a reckoning for this form of thinking that considers itself secure in the various departments of science—secure from the dreams of a ghost-seer: world domination over nature turns against the thinking subject himself;

21. Edmund Husserl, "*Die Krisis der europäischen Wissenschaften und die transzendentale Phänomenologie,*" in: *Philosophia* (Belgrade, 1936), pp. 95ff.

22. Cf. Schopenhauer, *Parerga und Paralipomena,* vol. 2, §, 356; *Werke,* ed. Deussen, vol. 5, p. 671.

nothing is left of him but that eternally same *I think* that must accompany all my ideas. Subject and object are both rendered ineffectual. The abstract self, which justifies record-making and systematization, has nothing set over against it but the abstract material which possesses no other quality than to be a substrate of such possession. The equation of spirit and world arises eventually, but only with a mutual restriction of both sides. The reduction of thought to a mathematical apparatus conceals the sanction of the world as its own yardstick. What appears to be the triumph of subjective rationality, the subjection of all reality to logical formalism, is paid for by the obedient subjection of reason to what is directly given. What is abandoned is the whole claim and approach of knowledge: to comprehend the given as such; not merely to determine the abstract spatio-temporal relations of the facts which allow them just to be grasped, but on the contrary to conceive them as the superficies, as mediated conceptual moments which come to fulfillment only in the development of their social, historical, and human significance. The task of cognition does not consist in mere apprehension, classification, and calculation, but in the determinate negation of each immediacy. Mathematical formalism, however, whose medium is number, the most abstract form of the immediate, instead holds thinking firmly to mere immediacy. Factuality wins the day; cognition is restricted to its repetition; and thought becomes mere tautology. The more the machinery of thought subjects existence to itself, the more blind its resignation in reproducing existence. Hence enlightenment returns to mythology, which it never really knew how to elude. For in its figures mythology had the essence of the status quo: cycle, fate, and domination of the world reflected as the truth and deprived of hope. In both the pregnancy of the mythical image and the clarity of the scientific formula, the everlastingness of the factual is confirmed and mere existence pure and simple expressed as the meaning which it forbids. The world as a gigantic analytic judgment, the only one left over from all the dreams of science, is of the same mold as the cosmic myth which associated the cycle of spring and autumn with the kidnapping of Persephone. The uniqueness of the mythic process, which tends to legitimize factuality, is deception. Originally the carrying off of the goddess was directly synonymous with the dying of nature. It repeated itself every autumn, and even the repetition was not the result of the buried one but the same every time. With the rigidification of the consciousness of time, the process was fixed in the past as a unique one, and in each new cycle of the seasons an attempt was made ritually to appease fear of death by recourse to what was long past. But the separation is ineffective. Through the establishment of a unique past, the cycle takes on the character of inevitability, and dread radiates from the age-old occurrence to make every event its mere repetition. The absorption of factuality, whether into legendary prehistory or into mathematical formalism, the symbolical relation of the contemporary to the mythic process in the rite or to the abstract category in science, makes the new appear as the predetermined, which is accordingly the old. Not existence but knowledge is without hope, for in the pictorical or mathematical symbol it appropriates and perpetuates existence as a schema.

In the enlightened world, mythology has entered into the profane. In its blank purity, the reality which has been cleansed of demons and their conceptual descendants assumes the numinous character which the ancient world attributed to demons. Under the title of brute facts, the social injustice from which they proceed is now as assuredly sacred a preserve as the medicine man was sacrosanct by reason of the protection of his gods. It is not merely that domination is paid for by the alienation of men from the objects dominated: with the objectification of spirit, the very relations of men—even those of the individual to himself—were bewitched. The individual is reduced to the nodal point of the conventional responses and modes of operation expected of him. Animism spiritualized the object, whereas industrialism objectifies the spirits of men. Automatically, the economic apparatus, even before total planning, equips commodities with the values which decide human behavior. Since, with the end of free exchange, commodities lost all their economic qualities except for fetishism, the latter has extended its arthritic influence over all aspects of social life. Through the countless agencies of mass production and its culture the conventionalized modes of behavior are impressed on the individual as the only natural, respectable, and rational ones. He defines himself only as a thing, as a static element, as success or failure. His yardstick is self-preservation, successful or unsuccessful approximation to the objectivity of his function and the models established for it. Everything else, idea and crime, suffers the force of the collective, which monitors it from the classroom to the trade union. But even the threatening collective belongs only to the deceptive surface, beneath which are concealed the powers which manipulate it as the instrument of power. Its brutality, which keeps the individual up to scratch, represents the true quality of men as little as value represents the things which he consumes. The demonically distorted form which things and men have assumed in the light of unprejudiced cognition, indicates domination, the principle which effected the specification of mana in spirits and gods and occurred in the jugglery of magicians and medicine men. The fatality by means of which prehistory sanctioned the incomprehensibility of death is transferred to wholly comprehensible real existence. The noontide panic fear in which men suddenly became aware of nature as totality has found its like in the panic which nowadays is ready to break out at every moment: men expect that the world, which is without any issue, will be set on fire by a totality which they themselves are and over which they have no control.

The mythic terror feared by the Enlightenment accords with myth. Enlightenment discerns it not merely in unclarified concepts and words, as demonstrated by semantic language-criticism, but in any human assertion that has no place in the ultimate context of self-preservation. Spinoza's "*Conatus sese conservandi primum et unicum virtutis est fundamentum*"[23] contains the true maxim of all Western civilization, in which the religious and philosophical differences of the middle class are reconciled. The self (which, according to the methodical extirpation of all natural residues because they are mythological, must no longer be either body or blood, or soul, or even the natural I), once sublimated into the transcendental or logical subject, would form the reference point of reason, of the determinative instance of action. Whoever resigns himself to life without any rational reference to self-preservation would, according to the Enlightenment—and Protestantism—regress to prehistory. Impulse as such is as mythic as superstition; to serve the god not postulated by the self is as idiotic as drunkenness. Progress has prepared the same fate for both adoration and descent into a state of directly natural being, and has anathematized both the self-abandonment of thought and that of pleasure. The social work of every individual in bourgeois society is mediated through the principle of self; for one, labor will bring an increased return on capital; for others, the energy for extra labor. But the more the process of self-preservation is effected by the bourgeois division of labor, the more it requires the self-alienation of the individuals who must model their body and soul according to the technical apparatus. This again is taken into account by enlightened thought: in the end the transcendental subject of cognition is apparently abandoned as

---

23. *Ethica,* Pars. IV. Propos, XXII. Coroll.

the last reminiscence of subjectivity and replaced by the much smoother work of automatic control mechanisms. Subjectivity has given way to the logic of the allegedly indifferent rules of the game, in order to dictate all the more unrestrainedly. Positivism, which finally did not spare thought itself, the chimera in a cerebral form, has removed the very last insulating instance between individual behavior and the social norm. The technical process, into which the subject has objectified itself after being removed from the consciousness, is free of the ambiguity of mythic thought as of all meaning altogether, because reason itself has become the mere instrument of the all-inclusive economic apparatus. It serves as a general tool, useful for the manufacture of all other tools, firmly directed toward its end, as fateful as the precisely calculated movement of material production, whose result for mankind is beyond all calculation. At last its old ambition, to be a pure organ of ends, has been realized. The exclusiveness of logical laws originates in this unique functional significance, and ultimately in the compulsive nature of self-preservation. And self-preservation repeatedly culminates in the choice between survival and destruction, apparent again in the principle that of two contradictory propositions only one can be true and only one false. The formalism of this principle, and of the entire logic in which form it is established, derives from the opacity and complexity of interests in a society in which the maintenance of forms and the preservation of individuals coincide only by change. The derivation of thought from logic ratifies in the lecture room the reification of man in the factory and the office. In this way the taboo encroaches upon the anathematizing power, and enlightenment upon the spirit which it itself comprises. Then, however, nature as true self-preservation is released by the very process which promised to extirpate it, in the individual as in the collective destiny of crisis and armed conflict. If the only norm that remains for theory is the ideal of unified science, practice must be subjected to the irrepressible process of world history. The self that is wholly comprehended by civilization resolves itself in an element of the inhumanity which from the beginning has aspired to evade civilization. The primordial fear of losing one's own name is realized. For civilization, pure natural existence, animal and vegetative, was the absolute danger. One after the other, mimetic, mythic and metaphysical modes of behavior were taken as superseded eras, any reversion to which was to be feared as implying a reversion of the self to that mere state of nature from which it had estranged itself with so huge an effort, and which therefore struck such terror into the self. In every century, any living reminiscence of olden times, not only of nomadic antiquity but all the more of the pre-patriarchal stages, was most rigorously punished and extirpated from human consciousness. The spirit of enlightenment replaced the fire and the rack by the stigma it attached to all irrationality, because it led to corruption. Hedonism was moderate, finding the extreme no less odious than did Aristotle. The bourgeois ideal of naturalness intends not amorphous nature, but the virtuous mean. Promiscuity and asceticism, excess and hunger, are directly identical, despite the antagonism, as power of disintegration. By subjecting the whole of life to the demands of its maintenance, the dictatorial minority guarantees, together with its own security, the persistence of the whole. From Homer to modern times, the dominant spirit wishes to steer between the Scylla of a return to mere reproduction and the Charybdis of unfettered fulfillment; it has always mistrusted any star other than that of the lesser evil. The new German pagans and warmongers want to set pleasure free once more. But under the pressure of labor, through the centuries, pleasure has learned self-hatred, and therefore in the state of totalitarian emancipation remains mean and disabled by self-contempt. It remains in the grip of the self-preservation to which it once trained reason—deposed in the meantime. At the turning points of Western civilization, from the transition to Olympian religion up to the Renaissance, Reformation, and bourgeois atheism, whenever new nations and classes more firmly repressed myth, the fear of uncomprehended, threatening nature, the consequence of its very materialization and objectification, was reduced to animistic superstition, and the subjugation of nature was made the absolute purpose of life within and without. If in the end self-preservation has been automated, so reason has been abandoned by those who, as administrators of production, entered upon its inheritance and now fear it in the persons of the disinherited. The essence of enlightenment is the alternative whose ineradicability is that of domination. Men have always had to choose between their subjection to nature or the subjection of nature to the Self. With the extension of the bourgeois commodity economy, the dark horizon of myth is illumined by the sun of calculating reason, beneath whose cold rays the seed of the new barbarism grows to fruition. Under the pressure of domination human labor has always led away from myth—but under domination always returns to the jurisdiction of myth.

The entanglement of myth, domination, and labor is preserved in one of the Homeric narratives. Book 12 of *The Odyssey* tells of the encounter with the Sirens. Their allurement is that of losing oneself in the past. But the hero to whom the temptation is offered has reached maturity through suffering. Throughout the many mortal perils he has had to endure, the unity of his own life, the identity of the individual, has been confirmed for him. The regions of time part for him as do water, earth, and air. For him, the flood of that-which-was has retreated from the rock of the present, and the future lies cloudy on the horizon. What Odysseus left behind him entered into the nether world; for the self is still so close to prehistoric myth, from whose womb it tore itself, that its very own experienced past becomes mythic prehistory. And it seeks to encounter that myth through the fixed order of time. The three-fold schema is intended to free the present moment from the power of the past by referring that power behind the absolute barrier of the unrepeatable and placing it at the disposal of the present as practicable knowledge. The compulsion to rescue what is gone as what is living instead of using it as the material of progress was appeased only in art, to which history itself appertains as a presentation of past life. So long as art declines to pass as cognition and is thus separated from practice, social practice tolerates it as it tolerates pleasure. But the Sirens' song has not yet been rendered powerless by reduction to the condition of art. They know "everything that ever happened on this so fruitful earth,"[24] including the events in which Odysseus himself took part, "all those things that Argos's sons and the Trojans suffered by the will of the gods on the plains of Troy."[25] While they directly evoke the recent past, with the irresistible promise of pleasure as which their song is heard, they threaten the patriarchal order which renders to each man his life only in return for his full measure of time. Whoever falls for their trickery must perish, whereas only perpetual presence of mind forces an existence from nature. Even though the Sirens know all that has happened, they demand the future as the price of that knowledge, and the promise of the happy return is the deception with which the past ensnares the one who longs for it. Odysseus is warned by Circe, that divinity of reversion to the animal, whom he resisted and who therefore gives him strength to resist other powers of disintegration. But the allurement of the Sirens remains superior;

---

24. *The Odyssey* 12, 191. (Since the authors' translation differs at certain concise points from the best-known English versions, this and other passages quoted here are near-literal prose renderings of the German.—Trans.)

25. *The Odyssey* 12, 189–90.

no one who hears their song can escape. Men had to do fearful things to themselves before the self, the identical, purposive, and virile nature of man, was formed, and something of that recurs in every childhood. The strain of holding the I together adheres to the I in all stages; and the temptation to lose it has always been there with the blind determination to maintain it. The narcotic intoxication which permits the atonement of deathlike sleep for the euphoria in which the self is suspended, is one of the oldest social arrangements which mediate between self-preservation and self-destruction—an attempt of the self to survive itself. The dread of losing the self and of abrogating together with the self the barrier between oneself and other life, the fear of death and destruction, is intimately associated with a promise of happiness which threatened civilization in every moment. Its road was that of obedience and labor, over which fulfillment shines forth perpetually—but only as illusive appearance, as devitalized beauty. The mind of Odysseus, inimical both to his own death and to his own happiness, is aware of this. He knows only two possible ways to escape. One of them he prescribes for his men. He plugs their ears with wax, and they must row with all their strength. Whoever would survive must not hear the temptation of that which is unrepeatable, and he is able to survive only by being unable to hear it. Society has always made provision for that. The laborers must be fresh and concentrate as they look ahead, and must ignore whatever lies to one side. They must doggedly sublimate in additional effort the drive that impels to diversion. And so they become practical.—The other possibility Odysseus, the seigneur who allows the others to labor for themselves, reserves to himself. He listens, but while bound impotently to the mast; the greater the temptation the more he has his bonds tightened—just as later the burghers would deny themselves happiness all the more doggedly as it drew closer to them with the growth of their own power. What Odysseus hears is without consequence for him; he is able only to nod his head as a sign to be set free from his bonds; but it is too late; his men, who do not listen, know only the song's danger but nothing of its beauty, and leave him at the mast in order to save him and themselves. They reproduce the oppressor's life together with their own, and the oppressor is no longer able to escape his social role. The bonds with which he has irremediably tied himself to practice, also keep the Sirens away from practice: their temptation is neutralized and becomes a mere object of contemplation—becomes art. The prisoner is present at a concert, an inactive eavesdropper like later concertgoers, and his spirited call for liberation fades like applause. Thus the enjoyment of art and manual labor break apart as the world of prehistory is left behind. The epic already contains the appropriate theory. The cultural material is in exact correlation to work done according to command; and both are grounded in the inescapable compulsion to social domination of nature.

Measures such as those taken on Odysseus's ship in regard to the Sirens form presentient allegory of the dialectic of enlightenment. Just as the capacity of representation is the measure of domination, and domination is the most powerful thing that can be represented in most performances, so the capacity of representation is the vehicle of progress and regression at one and the same time. Under the given conditions, exemption from work—not only among the unemployed but even at the other end of the social scale—also means disablement. The rulers experience existence, with which they need no longer concern themselves, only as a substratum, and hence wholly ossify into the condition of the commanding self. Primitive man experienced the natural thing merely as the evasive object of desire. "But the master, who has interposed the servant between it and himself, in this way relates himself only the dependence of the thing and enjoys it pure; however, he leaves the aspect of [its] independence to the servant, who works upon it."[26] Odysseus is represented in labor. Just as he cannot yield to the temptation to self-abandonment, so, as proprietor, he finally renounces even participation in labor, and ultimately even its management, whereas his men—despite their closeness to things—cannot enjoy their labor because it is performed under pressure, in desperation, with senses stopped by force. The servant remains enslaved in body and soul; the master regresses. No authority has yet been able to escape paying this price, and the apparent cyclical nature of the advance of history is partly explained by this debilitation, the equivalent of power. Mankind, whose versatility and knowledge become differentiated with the division of labor, is at the same time forced back to anthropologically more primitive stages, for with the technical easing of life the persistence of domination brings about a fixation of the instincts by means of heavier repression. Imagination atrophies. The disaster is not merely that individuals might remain behind society or its material production. Where the evolution of the machine has already turned into that of

---

26. Hegel, *Phenomenology of Spirit*. Trans. A. V. Miller. Oxford University Press, 1977, p. 116.

the machinery of domination (so that technical and social tendencies, always interwoven, converge in the total schematization of
men), untruth is not represented merely by the outdistanced. As
against that, adaptation to the power of progress involves the progress of power, and each time anew brings about those degenerations
which show not unsuccessful but successful progress to be its contrary. The curse of irresistible progress is irresistible regression.

This regression is not restricted to the experience of the sensuous
world bound up with the circumambient animate, but at the same
time affects the self-dominant intellect, which separates from sensuous experience in order to subjugate it. The unification of intellectual functions by means of which domination over the senses is
achieved, the resignation of thought to the rise of unanimity, means
the impoverishment of thought and of experience: the separation
of both areas leaves both impaired. The restriction of thought to
organization and administration, practiced by rulers from the cunning Odysseus to the naive managing directors of today, necessarily
implies the restriction which comes upon the great as soon as it is
no longer merely a question of manipulating the small. Hence the
spirit becomes the very apparatus of domination and self-domina-
tion which bourgeois thought has always mistakenly supposed it to
be. The stopped ears which the pliable proletarians have retained
ever since the time of the myth have no advantage over the immo-
bility of the master. The over-maturity of society lives by the immaturity of the dominated. The more complicated and precise the
social, economic, and scientific apparatus with whose service the
production system has long harmonized the body, the more impoverished the experiences which it can offer. The elimination of qualities, their conversion into functions, is translated from science by
means of rationalized modes of labor to the experiential world of
nations, and tends to approximate it once more to that of the am-
phibians. The regression of the masses today is their inability to
hear the unheard-of with their own ears, to touch the unappre-
hended with their own hands—the new form of delusion which de-
poses every conquered mythic form. Through the mediation of the
total society which embraces all relations and emotions, men are
once again made to be that against which the evolutionary law of
society, the principle of self, had turned: mere species beings, exactly like one another through isolation in the forcibly united collectivity. The oarsmen, who cannot speak to one another, are each
of them yoked in the same rhythm as the modern worker in the
factory, movie theater, and collective. The actual working condi-

tions in society compel conformism—not the conscious influences which also made the suppressed men dumb and separated them from truth. The impotence of the worker is not merely a stratagem of the rulers, but the logical consequence of the industrial society into which the ancient Fate—in the very course of the effort to escape it—has finally changed.

But this logical necessity is not conclusive. It remains tied to domination, as both its reflection and its tool. Therefore its truth is no less questionable than its evidence is irrefutable. Of course thought has always sufficed concretely to characterize its own equivocation. It is the servant that the master cannot check as he wishes. Domination, ever since men settled down, and later in the commodity society, has become objectified as law and organization and must therefore restrict itself. The instrument achieves independence: the mediating instance of the spirit, independently of the will of the master, modifies the directness of economic injustice. The instruments of domination, which would encompass all—language, weapons, and finally machines—must allow themselves to be encompassed by all. Hence in domination the aspect of rationality prevails as one that is also different from it. The ''objectivity'' of the means, which makes it universally available, already implies the criticism of that domination as whose means thought arose. On the way from mythology to logistics, thought has lost the element of self-reflection, and today machinery disables men even as it nurtures them. But in the form of machines the alienated *ratio* moves toward a society which reconciles thought in its fixed form as a material and intellectual apparatus with all the freed living, and refers to society itself as the real subject of thought. The specific origin of thought and its universal perspective have always been inseparable. Today, with the transformation of the world into industry, the perspective of universality, the social realization of thought, extends so far that in its behalf the rulers themselves disavow thought as mere ideology. The bad conscience of cliques which ultimately embody economic necessity is betrayed in that its revelations, from the intuitions of the Leader to the dynamic Weltanschauung, no longer recognize (in marked contrast to earlier bourgeois apologetics) their own misdeeds as necessary consequences of statutory contexts. The mythological lies of mission and destiny which they use as substitutes never declare the whole truth: gone are the objective laws of the market which ruled in the actions of the entrepreneurs and tended toward catastrophe. Instead the conscious decision of the managing directors executes as results (which are more obligatory than the blindest price-mechanisms) the old law of value and hence the destiny of capitalism. The rulers themselves do not believe in any objective necessity, even though they sometimes describe their concoctions thus. They declare themselves to be the engineers of world history. Only the ruled accept as unquestionable necessity the course of development that with every decreed rise in the standard of living makes them so much more powerless. When the standard of living of those who are still employed to service the machines can be assured with a minimal part of the working time available to the rulers of society, the superfluous remainder, the vast mass of the population, is drilled as yet another battalion—additional material to serve the present and future great plans of the system. The masses are fed and quartered as the army of the unemployed. In their eyes, .their reduction to mere objects of the administered life, which preforms every sector of modern existence including language and perception, represents objective necessity, against which they believe there is nothing they can do. Misery as the antithesis of power and powerlessness grows immeasurably, together with the capacity to remove all misery permanently. Each individual is unable to penetrate the forest of cliques and institutions which, from the highest levels of command to the last professional rackets, ensure the boundless persistence of status. For the union boss, let alone the director, the proletarian (should he ever come face to face with him) is nothing but a supernumerary example of the mass, while the boss in his turn has to tremble at the thought of his own liquidation.

The absurdity of a state of affairs in which the enforced power of the system over men grows with every step that takes it out of the power of nature, denounces the rationality of the rational society as obsolete. Its necessity is illusive, no less than the freedom of the entrepreneurs who ultimately reveal their compulsive nature in their inevitable wars and contracts. This illusion, in which a wholly enlightened mankind has lost itself, cannot be dissolved by a philosophy which, as the organ of domination, has to choose between command and obedience. Without being able to escape the confusion which still ensnares it in prehistory, it is nevertheless able to recognize the logic of either-or, of consequence and antinomy, with which it radically emancipated itself from nature, as this very nature, unredeemed and self-alienated. Thinking, in whose mechanism of compulsion nature is reflected and persists, inescapably reflects its very own self as its own forgotten nature—as a mechanism of compulsion. Ideation is only an instrument. In thought, men distance themselves from nature in order thus imaginatively to present it to themselves—but only in order to determine how it is to be dominated. Like the thing, the material tool, which is held on to in different situations as the same thing, and hence divides the world as the chaotic, manysided, and disparate from the known, one, and identical, the concept is the ideal tool, fit to do service for everything, wherever it can be applied. And so thought becomes illusionary whenever it seeks to deny the divisive function, distancing and objectification. All mystic unification remains deception, the impotently inward trace of the absolved revolution. But while enlightenment maintains its justness against any hypostatization of utopia and unfailingly proclaims domination to be disunion, the dichotomy between subject and object that it will not allow to be obscured becomes the index of the untruth of that dichotomy and of truth. The proscription of superstition has always signified not only the progress of domination but its compromise. Enlightenment is more than enlightenment—the distinct representation of nature in its alienation. In the self-cognition of the spirit as nature in disunion with itself, as in prehistory, nature calls itself to account; no longer directly, as mana—that is, with the alias that signifies omnipotence—but as blind and lame. The decline, the forfeiture, of nature consists in the subjugation of nature without which spirit does not exist. Through the decision in which spirit acknowledges itself to be domination and retreats into nature, it abandons the claim to domination which makes it a vassal of nature. Even though in the flight from necessity, in progress and civilization, mankind cannot hold the course without abandoning knowledge itself, at least it no longer mistakes the ramparts that it erects against necessity (the institutions and practices of subjection that have always redounded on society from the subjugation of nature) for guarantees of the freedom to come. Every progress made by civilization has renewed together with domination that prospect of its removal. Whereas, however, real history is woven out of a real suffering that is not lessened in proportion to the growth of means for its abrogation, the realization of the prospect is referred to the notion, the concept. For it does not merely, as science, distance men from nature, but, as the self-consideration of thought that in the form of science remains tied to blind economic tendency, allows the distance perpetuating injustice to be measured. By virtue of this remembrance of nature in the subject, in whose fulfillment the unacknowledged truth of all culture lies hidden, enlightenment is universally opposed to domination; and the call to check enlightenment resounded even in the time of Vanini[27] less out of fear of exact science than out of that hatred of undisciplined ideas which emerges from the jurisdiction of nature even as it acknowledges itself to be nature's very dread of its own self. The priests always avenged mana on the prophet of enlightenment, who propitiated mana by a terror-stricken attitude to what went by the name of terror, and the augurs of the Enlightenment were one with the priests in their hybris. In its bourgeois form, the Enlightenment had lost itself in its positivistic aspect long before Turgot and d'Alembert. It was never immune to the exchange of freedom for the pursuit of self-preservation. The suspension of the concept, whether in the name of progress or of culture—which had already long before tacitly leagued themselves against the truth—opened the way for falsehood. And this in a world that verified only evidential propositions, and preserved thought—degraded to the achievement of great thinkers—as a kind of stock of superannuated cliches, no longer to be distinguished from truth neutralized as a cultural commodity.

But to recognize domination, even in thought itself, as unreconciled nature, would mean a slackening of the necessity whose perpetuity socialism itself prematurely confirmed as a concession to reactionary common sense. By elevating necessity to the status of the basis for all time to come, and by idealistically degrading the spirit for ever to the very apex, socialism held on all too surely to the legacy of bourgeois philosophy. Hence the relation of necessity to the realm of freedom would remain merely quantitative and mechanical, and nature, posited as wholly alien—just as in the earliest mythology—would become totalitarian and absorb freedom together with socialism. With the abandonment of thought, which in its reified form of mathematics, machine, and organization avenges itself on the men who have forgotten it, enlightenment has relinquished its own realization. By taking everything unique and individual under its tutelage, it left the uncomprehended whole the freedom, as domination, to strike back at human existence and consciousness by way of things. But true revolutionary practice depends on the intransigence of theory in the face of the insensibility with which society allows thought to ossify. It is not the material prerequisites of fulfillment—liberated technology as such—which jeopardize fulfillment. That is asserted by those sociologists who are again searching for an antidote, and—should it be a collectivist

---

27. Lucilio Vanini, a quasipantheistic Italian philosopher (1584–1619) sentenced and burned for blasphemy by the Inquisition.—Tr.

measure—to master the antidote.[28] Guilt is a context of social delusion. The mythic scientific respect of the peoples of the earth for the status quo that they themselves unceasingly produce, itself finally becomes positive fact: the oppressor's fortress in regard to which even revolutionary imagination despises itself as utopism and decays to the condition of pliable trust in the objective tendency of history. As the organ of this kind of adaptation, as a mere construction of means, the Enlightenment is as destructive as its romantic enemies accuse it of being. It comes into its own only when it surrenders the last remaining concordance with the latter and dares to transcend the false absolute, the principle of blind domination. The spirit of this kind of unrelenting theory would turn even the mind of relentless progress to its end. Its herald Bacon dreamed of the many things "which kings with their treasure cannot buy, nor with their force command," of which "their spials and intelligencers can give no news." As he wished, they fell to the burghers, the enlightened heirs of those kings. While bourgeois economy multiplied power through the mediation of the market, it also multiplied its objects and powers to such an extent that for their administration not just the kings, not even the middle classes are no longer necessary, but all men. They learn from the power of things to dispense at last with power. Enlightenment is realized and reaches its term when the nearest practical ends reveal themselves as the most distant goal now attained, and the lands of which "their spials and intelligencers can give no news," that is, those of the nature despised by dominant science, are recognized as the lands of origin. Today, when Bacon's utopian vision that we should "command nature by action"—that is, in practice—has been realized on a tellurian scale, the nature of the thralldom that he ascribed to unsubjected nature is clear. It was domination itself. And knowledge, in which Bacon was certain the "sovereignty of man lieth hid," can now become the dissolution of domination. But in the face of such a possibility, and in the service of the present age, enlightenment becomes wholesale deception of the masses.

Translated by John Cumming

---

28. "The supreme question that confronts our generations today—the question to which all other problems are merely corollaries—is whether technology can be brought under control. . . . Nobody can be sure of the formula by which this end can be achieved. . . . We must draw on all the resources to which access can be had. . . ." (*The Rockefeller Foundation: A Review for 1943* [New York, 1944], pp. 33ff.).

Walter Benjamin

THESES ON THE PHILOSOPHY OF HISTORY

1

The story is told of an automaton constructed in such a way that it
could play a winning game of chess, answering each move of an
opponent with a countermove. A puppet in Turkish attire and with
a hookah in its mouth sat before a chessboard placed on a large
table. A system of mirrors created the illusion that this table was
transparent from all sides. Actually, a little hunchback who was an
expert chess player sat inside and guided the puppet's hand by
means of strings. One can imagine a philosophical counterpart to
this device. The puppet called "historical materialism" is to win all
the time. It can easily be a match for anyone if it enlists the services
of theology, which today, as we know, is wizened and has to keep
out of sight.

2

"One of the most remarkable characteristics of human nature,"
writes Lotze, "is, alongside so much selfishness in specific instances,
the freedom from envy which the present displays toward the future." Reflection shows us that our image of happiness is thoroughly colored by the time to which the course of our own
existence has assigned us. The kind of happiness that could arouse
envy in us exists only in the air we have breathed, among people
we could have talked to, women who could have given themselves
to us. In other words, our image of happiness is indissolubly bound
up with the image of redemption. The same applies to our view of
the past, which is the concern of history. The past carries with it a
temporal index by which it is referred to redemption. There is a
secret agreement between past generations and the present one.
Our coming was expected on earth. Like every generation that preceded us, we have been endowed with a *weak* Messianic power, a

power to which the past has a claim. That claim cannot be settled cheaply. Historical materialists are aware of that.

3

A chronicler who recites events without distinguishing between major and minor ones acts in accordance with the following truth: nothing that has ever happened should be regarded as lost for history. To be sure, only a redeemed mankind receives the fullness of its past—which is to say, only for a redeemed mankind has its past become citable in all its moments. Each moment it has lived becomes a *citation à l'ordre du jour*—and that day is Judgment Day.

4

> *Seek for food and clothing first, then*
> *the Kingdom of God shall be added unto you.*
> —G. W. F. Hegel, 1807

The class struggle, which is always present to a historian influenced by Marx, is a fight for the crude and material things without which no refined and spiritual things could exist. Nevertheless, it is not in the form of the spoils which fall to the victor that the latter make their presence felt in the class struggle. They manifest themselves in this struggle as courage, humor, cunning, and fortitude. They have retroactive force and will constantly call in question every victory, past and present, of the rulers. As flowers turn toward the sun, by dint of a secret heliotropism the past strives to turn toward that sun which is rising in the sky of history. A historical materialist must be aware of this most inconspicuous of all transformations.

5

The true picture of the past flits by. The past can be seized only as an image which flashes up at the instant when it can be recognized and is never seen again. "The truth will not run away from us": in the historical outlook of historicism these words of Gottfried Keller mark the exact point where historical materialism cuts through historicism. For every image of the past that is not recognized by the present as one of its own concerns threatens to disappear irretrievably. (The good tidings which the historian of the past brings with throbbing heart may be lost in a void the very moment he opens his mouth.)

6

To articulate the past historically does not mean to recognize it "the way it really was" (Ranke). It means to seize hold of a memory as it flashes up at a moment of danger. Historical materialism wishes to retain that image of the past which unexpectedly appears to man singled out by history at a moment of danger. The danger affects both the content of the tradition and its receivers. The same threat hangs over both: that of becoming a tool of the ruling classes. In every era the attempt must be made anew to wrest tradition away from a conformism that is about to overpower it. The Messiah comes not only as the redeemer, he comes as the subduer of Antichrist. Only that historian will have the gift of fanning the spark of hope in the past who is firmly convinced that *even the dead* will not be safe from the enemy if he wins. And this enemy has not ceased to be victorious.

7

*Consider the darkness and the great cold
In this vale which resounds with mysery.*
—Bertolt Brecht, *The Threepenny Opera*

To historians who wish to relive an era, Fustel de Coulanges recommends that they blot out everything they know about the later course of history. There is no better way of characterizing the method with which historical materialism has broken. It is a process of empathy whose origin is the indolence of the heart, *acedia*, which despairs of grasping and holding the genuine historical image as it flares up briefly. Among medieval theologians it was regarded as the root cause of sadness. Flaubert, who was familiar with it, wrote: *"Peu de gens devineront combien il a fallu etre triste pour ressusciter Carthage."*[1] The nature of this sadness stands out more clearly if one asks with whom the adherents of historicism actually empathize. The answer is inevitable: with the victor. And all rulers are the heirs of those who conquered before them. Hence, empathy with the victor invariably benefits the rulers. Historical materialists know what that means. Whoever has emerged victorious participates to this day in the triumphal procession in which the present rulers step over those who are lying prostrate. According to traditional practice, the spoils are carried along in the procession. They are called cultural treasures, and a historical materialist views them with cautious detachment. For without exception the cultural treasures he surveys have an origin which he cannot contemplate with-

---

1. "Few will be able to guess how sad one had to be in order to resuscitate Carthage."

out horror. They owe their existence not only to the efforts of the great minds and talents who have created them, but also to the anonymous toil of their contemporaries. There is no document of civilization which is not at the same time a document of barbarism. And just as such a document is not free of barbarism, barbarism taints also the manner in which it was transmitted from one owner to another. A historical materialist therefore dissociates himself from it as far as possible. He regards it as his task to brush history against the grain.

8

The tradition of the oppressed teaches us that the "state of emergency" in which we live is not the exception but the rule. We must attain to a conception of history that is in keeping with this insight. Then we shall clearly realize that it is our task to bring about a real state of emergency, and this will improve our position in the struggle against Fascism. One reason why Fascism has a chance is that in the name of progress its opponents treat it as a historical norm. The current amazement that the things we are experiencing are "still" possible in the twentieth century is *not* philosophical. This amazement is not the beginning of knowledge—unless it is the knowledge that the view of history which gives rise to it is untenable.

9

My wing is ready for fight,
I would like to turn back.
If I stayed timeless time,
I would have little luck.
—Gerhard Scholem

A Klee painting named *Angelus Novus* shows an angel looking as though he is about to move away from something he is fixedly contemplating. His eyes are staring, his mouth is open, his wings are spread. This is how one pictures the angel of history. His face is turned toward the past. Where we perceive a chain of events, he sees one single catastrophe which keeps piling wreckage upon wreckage and hurls it in front of his feet. The angel would like to stay, awaken the dead, and make whole what has been smashed. But a storm is blowing from Paradise; it has got caught in his wings with such violence that the angel can no longer close them. This storm irresistibly propels him into the future to which his back is turned, while the pile of debris before him grows skyward. This storm is what we call progress.

10

The themes which monastic discipline assigned to friars for meditation were designed to turn them away from the world and its affairs. The thoughts which we are developing here originate from similar considerations. At a moment when the politicians in whom the opponents of Fascism had placed their hopes are prostrate and confirm their defeat by betraying their own cause, these observations are intended to disentangle the political worldlings from the snares in which the traitors have entrapped them. Our consideration proceeds from the insight that the politicians' stubborn faith in progress, their confidence in their "mass basis," and, finally, their servile integration in an uncontrollable apparatus have been three aspects of the same thing. It seeks to convey an idea of the high price our accustomed thinking will have to pay for a conception of history that avoids any complicity with the thinking to which these politicians continue to adhere.

11

The conformism which has been part and parcel of Social Democracy from the beginning attaches not only to its political tactics but to its economic views as well. It is one reason for its later breakdown. Nothing has corrupted the German working class so much as the notion that it was moving with the current. It regarded technological developments as the fall of the stream with which it thought it was moving. From there it was but a step to the illusion that the factory work which was supposed to tend toward technological progress constituted a political achievement. The old Protestant ethics of work was resurrected among German workers in secularized form. The Gotha Program[2] already bears traces of this confusion, defining labor as "the source of all wealth and all culture." Smelling a rat, Marx countered that ". . . the man who possesses no other property than his labor power" must of necessity become "the slave of other men who have made themselves the owners. . . ." However, the confusion spread, and soon thereafter Josef Dietzgen proclaimed: "The savior of modern times is called work. The . . . improvement . . . of labor constitutes the wealth

---

2. The Gotha Congress of 1875 united the two German Socialist parties, one led by Ferdinand Lassalle, the other by Karl Marx and Wilhelm Liebknecht.

which is now able to accomplish what no redeemer has ever been able to do." This vulgar-Marxist conception of the nature of labor bypasses the question of how its products might benefit the workers while still not being at their disposal. It recognizes only the progress in the mastery of nature, not the retrogression of society; it already displays the technocratic features later encountered in Fascism. Among these is a conception of nature which differs ominously from the one in the Socialist utopias before the 1848 revolution. The new conception of labor amounts to the exploitation of nature, which with naïve complacency is contrasted with the exploitation of the proletariat. Compared with this positivistic conception, Fourier's fantasies, which have so often been ridiculed, prove to be surprisingly sound. According to Fourier, as a result of efficient cooperative labor, four moons would illuminate the earthly night, the ice would recede from the poles, sea water would no longer taste salty, and beasts of prey would do man's bidding. All this illustrates a kind of labor which, far from exploiting nature, is capable of delivering her of the creations which lie dormant in her womb as potentials. Nature, which, as Dietzgen puts it, "exists gratis," is a complement to the corrupted conception of labor.

12
We need history, but not the way a spoiled loafer
in the garden of knowledge needs it.
—Friedrich Nietzsche, *On the Use*
and Abuse of History

Not man or men but the struggling, oppressed class itself is the depository of historical knowledge. In Marx it appears as the last enslaved class, as the avenger that completes the task of liberation in the name of generations of the downtrodden. This conviction, which had a brief resurgence in the Spartacist group,[3] has always been objectionable to Social Democrats. Within three decades they managed virtually to erase the name of Blanqui, though it had been the rallying sound that had reverberated through the preceding century. Social Democracy thought fit to assign to the working class the role of the redeemer of future generations, in this way cutting the sinews of its greatest strength. This training made the working class forget both its hatred and its spirit of sacrifice, for both are

---

3. Leftist group, founded by Karl Liebknecht and Rosa Luxemburg at the beginning of World War I in opposition to the pro-war policies of the German Socialist party, later absorbed by the Communist party.

nourished by the image of enslaved ancestors rather than that of liberated grandchildren.

13
Every day our cause becomes clearer and people get smarter.
—Wilhelm Dietzgen, *Die Religion der Sozialdemokratie*

Social Democratic theory, and even more its practice, have been formed by a conception of progress which did not adhere to reality but made dogmatic claims. Progress as pictured in the minds of Social Democrats was, first of all, the progress of mankind itself (and not just advances in men's ability and knowledge). Secondly, it was something boundless, in keeping with the infinite perfectibility of mankind. Thirdly, progress was regarded as irresistible, something that automatically pursued a straight or spiral course. Each of these predicates is controversial and open to criticism. However, when the chips are down, criticism must penetrate beyond these predicates and focus on something that they have in common. The concept of the historical progress of mankind cannot be sundered from the concept of its progression through a homogeneous, empty time. A critique of the concept of such a progression must be the basis of any criticism of the concept of progress itself.

14
Origin is the goal.
—Karl Kraus, *Worte in Versen*, vol. 1

History is the subject of a structure whose site is not homogeneous, empty time, but time filled by the presence of the now [*Jetztzeit*].[4] Thus, to Robespierre ancient Rome was a past charged with the time of the now which he blasted out of the continuum of history. The French Revolution viewed itself as Rome reincarnate. It evoked ancient Rome the way fashion evokes costumes of the past. Fashion has a flair for the topical, no matter where it stirs in the thickets of long ago; it is a tiger's leap into the past. This jump, however, takes place in an arena where the ruling class gives the commands. The same leap in the open air of history is the dialectical one, which is how Marx understood the revolution.

---

4. Benjamin says "*Jetztzeit*" and indicates by the quotation marks that he does not simply mean an equivalent to *Gegenwart*, that is, present. He clearly is thinking of the mystical *nunc stans*.

15

The awareness that they are about to make the continuum of history explode is characteristic of the revolutionary classes at the moment of their action. The great revolution introduced a new calendar. The initial day of a calendar serves as a historical time-lapse camera. And, basically, it is the same day that keeps recurring in the guise of holidays, which are days of remembrance. Thus the calendars do not measure time as clocks do; they are monuments of a historical consciousness of which not the slightest trace has been apparent in Europe in the past hundred years. In the July revolution an incident occurred which showed this consciousness still alive. On the first evening of fighting it turned out that the clocks in towers were being fired on simultaneously and independently from several places in Paris. An eye-witness, who may have owed his insight to the rhyme, wrote as follows:

> Who would have believed it! we are told that new Joshuas
> at the foot of every tower, as though irritated with
> time itself, fired at the dials in order to stop the day.

16

A historical materialist cannot do without the notion of a present which is not a transition, but in which time stands still and has come to a stop. For this notion defines the present in which he himself is writing history. Historicism gives the "eternal" image of the past; historical materialism supplies a unique experience with the past. The historical materialist leaves it to others to be drained by the whore called "Once upon a time" in historicism's bordello. He remains in control of his powers, man enough to blast open the continuum of history.

17

Historicism rightly culminates in universal history. Materialistic historiography differs from it as to method more clearly than from any other kind. Universal history has no theoretical armature. Its method is additive; it musters a mass of data to fill the homogeneous, empty time. Materialistic historiography, on the other hand, is based on a constructive principle. Thinking involves not only the flow of thoughts, but their arrest as well. Where thinking suddenly stops in a configuration pregnant with tensions, it gives that configuration a shock, by which it crystallizes into a monad. A historical materialist approaches a historical subject only where he encounters it as a monad. In this structure he recognizes the sign of a Messianic cessation of happening, or, put differently, a revolutionary chance in the fight for the oppressed past. He takes cognizance of it in order to blast a specific era out of the homogeneous course of history—blasting a specific life out of the era or a specific work out of the lifework. As a result of this method, the lifework is preserved in this work and at the same time canceled;[5] in the lifework, the era; and in the era, the entire course of history. The nourishing fruit of the historically understood contains time as a precious but tasteless seed.

18

"In relation to the history of organic life on earth," writes a modern biologist, "the paltry fifty millennia of Homo sapiens constitute something like two seconds at the close of a twenty-four-hour day. On this scale, the history of civilized mankind would fill one-fifth of the last second of the last hour." The present, which, as a model of Messianic time, comprises the entire history of mankind in an enormous abridgment, coincides exactly with the stature which the history of mankind has in the universe.

A

Historicism contents itself with establishing a causal connection between various moments in history. But no fact that is a cause is for that very reason historical. It became historical posthumously, as it were, through events that may be separated from it by thousands of years. A historian who takes this as his point of departure stops telling the sequence of events like the beads of a rosary. Instead, he grasps the constellation which his own era has formed with a definite earlier one. Thus he establishes a conception of the present as the "time of the now" which is shot through with chips of Messianic time.

B

The soothsayers who found out from time what it had in store certainly did not experience time as either homogeneous or empty. Anyone who keeps this in mind will perhaps get an idea of how

---

5. The Hegelian term *aufheben* in its threefold meaning: to preserve, to elevate, to cancel.

past times were experienced in remembrance—namely, in just the same way. We know that the Jews were prohibited from investigating the future. The Torah and the prayers instruct them in remembrance, however. This stripped the future of its magic, to which all those succumb who turn to the soothsayers for enlightenment. This does not imply, however, that for the Jews the future turned into homogeneous, empty time. For every second of time was the strait gate through which the Messiah might enter.

Translated by Harry Zohn

Leo Löwenthal

TERROR'S ATOMIZATION OF MAN

There is a widely held option that the fascist terror was just an ephemeral episode in modern history, now happily behind us. That opinion I cannot share. I believe that it is deeply rooted in the trends of modern civilization, and especially in the pattern of modern economy.

Indeed the reluctance to face squarely and explore fully the phenomena of terror and their implications is itself a lingering phenomenon of the terror.

Those who live with terror are under powerful compulsion not to speculate about it or to increase their knowledge of it. But this does not explain the remarkable reserve and resignation displayed in the face of totalitarian terror by the fact-loving Western world. The West shrank from the facts of the fascist terror, though they were available from reliable sources, until they were forced upon it in the unmasked horrors of Buchenwald, Oswiecim, Belsen, and Dachau. It shrinks today from the facts of the terror that is succeeding the end of the military war. The self-preserving numbness of the terror-ridden countries seems to be matched by a psychological mass repression, an unconscious flight from truth, in the countries where civilization survives.

Essentially, the modern system of terror amounts to the atomization of the individual. We shudder at the tortures inflicted on the physical bodies of men; we should not be less appalled by its menace to the spirit of man. Terror accomplishes its work of dehumanization through the total integration of the population into collectivities, and then depriving them of the psychological means of direct communication in spite of—rather because of—the tremendous communications apparatus to which they are exposed. The individual under terrorist conditions is never alone and always alone. He becomes numb and rigid not only in relation to his neighbor but also in relation to himself; fear robs him of the power of spontaneous emotional or mental reaction. Thinking becomes a stupid crime; it endangers his life. The inevitable consequence is that stupidity spreads as a contagious disease among the terrorized population. Human beings live in a state of stupor, in a moral coma.

Let us examine more closely the main phenomena of terror in action.

Directness and Omnipotence

One of the basic functions of terror is to wipe out the rational connection between government decisions and individual fate. The wholesale arrest of people during the first stages of totalitarian terror, the mixing in the concentration camps of the most diverse elements of the population for the most diverse reasons, fulfills precisely this function of elimination of individual differences and claims before the apparatus of power. The qualitative difference between the imprisoned lawbreaker and the rest of the population does not exist between the victims of terror within the concentration camps and those outside. The principle of selection of the forced workers of the camps is direct terroristic calculation. They are in the majority trapped in mass arrests, with no question of individual guilt involved and no hope of limited punishment.

That the concentration camps are far more representative of the population at large than is the traditional penal institution is made ominously clear by the fact that they are supervised not by a specialized body of civil servants but by units of that same secret police that oppresses the population at large.

This interruption of the causal relation between what a person does and what happens to him fulfills one of the chief aims of modern terror, namely:

The Breakdown of the Continuum of Experience

With the breakdown of legal rationality and its clear relation to the individual fate, this fate itself becomes so enigmatic as to lose all meaning. The individual does not know what he may experience; and what he has already experienced is no longer important for his person or his future. The normal rhythm of youth, manhood, old age, of education, career, success or failure, is completely disrupted. The creative faculties of fantasy, imaginations, memory become meaningless and tend to atrophy where they can no longer bring about any desired change in the individual's fate.

Of course this transformation of a human being from an individual whose essence is continuity of experience and memory into a unit of atomized reactions is carried further among the trapped victims than among the population at large. But the difference is only in degree, and if we cite only examples from reports from the detention camps, it must always be remembered that the population at large was aware of both mass arrests and the terror within the concentration camps. Thus the terror actually visited upon the bodies of Jews, "radicals," Poles, and others terrorized the minds of all, which was indeed its primary function.

The breakdown of memory and experience has been described by a German psychologist, Kurt Bondy, who was himself in a concentration camp for a time:

"This uncertainty about the duration of the imprisonment is probably what unnerves the men most. . . . They try to forget. The past becomes uncertain and nebulous, the picture of their family and friends indistinct. . . . Here are the roots of hopelessness, apathy, indifference, despair, distrust, and egocentricity."

Thus life becomes a chain of expected, avoided, or materialized shocks, and thus the atomized experiences heighten the atomization of the individual. Paradoxically, in a terrorist society, in which everything is most carefully planned, the plan for the individual is to have no plan; to become and to remain a mere object, a bundle of conditioned reflexes that amply respond to a series of manipulated and calculated shocks.

The Breakdown of Personality

In a system that reduces life to a chain of disconnected reactions to shock, personal communication tends to lose all meaning. The superego—the agency of conscience—in which people have stored the mechanism of moral decency, is repressed by what I may call a Hitler-ego, meaning that the inhibitions produced by conscience yield to inhibitions or drives produced by mechanical reactions and imitations. Neither the terrorized nor the terrorist is any longer a personality in the traditional sense. They are mere material conforming to situations created by a power utterly independent of themselves. An underground report by a prisoner escaped from Oswiecim tells how the camp system "destroyed every social tie in a victim and reduced his spiritual life to a fear-driven desire to prolong existence, be it only for a day or an hour." And a keen observer with personal experience in two camps, Dr. Bruno Bettelheim, now

[1945] with the University of Chicago, has studied this deterioration to its end in loss of the vital passions:

"This outside world which continued to live as if nothing had happened was in the minds of the new prisoners represented by those whom they used to know, namely: by their relatives and friends. But even this hatred was very subdued in the old prisoners. It seemed that, as much as they had forgotten to love their kin, they had lost the ability to hate them . . . they were unable to feel strongly about anybody."

A similar shrinking of the personality to a cluster of conditioned reflexes has been observed among the guards. In his report, *A Year in Treblinka*, Yankel Wiernik describes the practitioners of terror as automata devoid of passion or remorse, who performed their given tasks as soon as some higher-up pressed a button. Bettelheim describes their dehumanization in these words:

"Having been educated in a world which rejected brutality, they felt uneasy about what they were doing. It seemed that they, too, had an emotional attitude toward their acts of brutality which might be described as a feeling of unreality. After having been guards in the camp for some time, they got accustomed to inhuman behavior, they became 'conditioned' to it; it then became part of their 'real' life."

And there is, above all, the corroborating evidence provided by these automata themselves in the trials currently being held in Germany. They admit the most atrocious crimes but show not the slightest sense of guilt. Their inhuman conduct was justified, they maintain, because it was ordered by their superiors.

The Struggle for Survival

The old system of culture, from abstract philosophical metaphysics to the institutions of religion and education, had the result of permeating mankind with the idea that only rational behavior that included respect for the rights, claims, and needs of others could guarantee one's own survival. Under terror such behavior may be equivalent to self-annihilation. Terrorism wipes out the causal relation between social conduct and survival, and confronts the individual with the naked force of nature—that is, of denatured nature—in the form of the all-powerful terrorist machine. What the terror aims to bring about, and enforces through its tortures, is that people shall come to act in harmony with the law of terror, namely, that their whole calculation shall have but one aim: self-perpetuation. The more people become ruthless seekers after their own survival, the more they become psychological pawns and puppets of a system that knows no other purpose than to keep itself in power.

Former inmates of Nazi detention camps confirm this regression to sheer Darwinism—or perhaps one should say infantilism:

> The urge of self-preservation, bestial fear, hunger and thirst led to a complete transformation of the majority of the prisoners. . . . In many cases the sense of responsibility towards others disappeared entirely, as well as the least feeling of consideration of their common lot. Many a prisoner carried on a wild, ruthless, and thoroughly senseless struggle for his individual survival.

Reduction to Natural Material

What the terrorist masters fear most is that their victims may recover their awareness of belonging to a whole, to human history. The complete victory of totalitarianism would be identical with the complete forgetting of history, that is, with a mankind become void of reflection, or in other words with a mankind solely become natural material. To quote Hitler:

> A violently active, dominating, intrepid, brutal youth—that is what I am after. Youth must be all those things. It must be indifferent to pain. There must be no weakness or tenderness in it. I want to see once more in its eyes the gleam of pride and independence of the beast of prey. . . . I intend to have an athletic youth—that is the first and chief thing. In this way I shall eradicate the thousands of years of human domestication. Then I shall have in front of me the pure and noble natural material. With that I can create the new order.

Here, if we discard the flowery adjectives, is a classic admission of fascist aims and ends. Mankind, having become domesticated again, becomes part of the overabundance of nature. It thus becomes material indeed, for exploitation where needed and for annihilation where not—in any case, mere material to be *processed*. Modern terror always looks at people with the eyes either of the big monopolist surveying raw materials or of the undertaker anticipating the disposal of the useless human corpse.

This attitude is perfectly illustrated in reports describing the initiation of inmates in the Nazi concentration camps of Eastern Europe:

> At the one side we surrendered our baggage; at the other side we had to undress and to surrender our clothing and pieces of value. Naked

then, we went into another barrack, where our heads and beards were shaved and disinfected with lysol. When we walked out of this barrack each of us was given a number. . . . With these numbers in our hands we were chased into a third barrack where the reception took place. This "reception" consisted in that our numbers were tattooed on the left breast. Then they proceeded to take the data of each person and brought us, divided in groups of hundreds, into a cellar, later into another barrack, where we were given striped prisoners' clothes and wooden shoes.

There is a striking analogy between this treatment of human beings and that of merchandise shipped into the inventory rooms of a large department store or factory. It is a planful handling of materials for certain purposes. According to the witnesses, the system became so streamlined that only the really useful human merchandise was tagged. He who got no number was a reject; he was disposed of. And as in any oversized administrative unit, no one cared to take the blame for mistakes. Even if the merchandise had been rejected by mistake, it was destroyed:

Since the prisoners were checked according to numbers and not according to their names, an error could easily be made which would be disastrous. If the "block-writer" had marked "dead" a number which in reality was still alive—a thing which can happen in these extreme cases of great mortality—the mistake was corrected by putting to death the holder of the number.

Wiernik describes the reduction of the human being into nothing more significant or valuable than a potential cadaver:

It was a continuous coming and going, and death without end. I learned to look at every live person as a prospective corpse in the nearest future. I appraised him with my eyes and thought of his weight; who was going to carry him to his grave; how severe a beating would he get while doing it? It was terrible, but nonetheless true. Would you believe that a human being, living under such conditions, could at times smile and jest?

These are hard facts, and they justify one's saying that within the logic of terror, man has himself become a fact of raw nature. And death gains the rationality of putting surplus human material to use: "The Germans carried out mass round-ups of Jews in the city. They spared neither men, women, nor children. The adults they simply murdered, while the children were given away to the Hitler Jugend squads as shooting targets.''

Assimilation to the Terrorists

Terror reaches its peak of success when the victim loses his awareness of the gulf between himself and his tormentors. With the complete breakdown of the personality the most primitive historical force, imitation, becomes openly prevalent in the dehumanized atmosphere of totalitarianism. This ultimate state in regression is described by Bettelheim:

> A prisoner had reached the final stage of adjustment to the camp situation when he had changed his personality so as to accept as his own the values of the Gestapo. . . .
>
> Old prisoners who seemed to have a tendency to identify themselves with the Gestapo did so not only in respect to aggressive behavior. They would try to arrogate to themselves old pieces of Gestapo uniforms. . . . This identification with their torturers went so far as copying their leisure-time activities. One of the games played by the guards was to find out who could stand to be hit longest without uttering a complaint. This game was copied by the old prisoners, as though they had not been hit often enough without needing to repeat this experience as a game.
>
> Other problems in which most old prisoners made their peace with the values of the Gestapo included the race problem, although race discrimination had been alien to their scheme of values before they were brought into the camp.

Can one imagine a greater triumph for any system than this adoption of its values and behavior by its powerless victims? When we again recall that the difference between the effect of terror upon the population within and without the concentration camp is one of degree rather than kind, we have here an appalling index to the magnitude of the so-called problem of reeducation in Central Europe.

So much for the atomization of the individual. What are some of the social consequences of a regime of terror?

It is characteristic of a terrorist regime that its tools and practices increase in efficiency, quantity, and cruelty. Terror grows by what it feeds on—its excesses beget the need for ever greater terror. Under this increasing oppression the victims cease to anticipate an end of terror; they hope only for its alleviation.

Thus terror, by its own inner dynamics, perpetuates its sovereignty. Its victims lose the power to envisage a different order of life. They become absolutely dependent, materially and spiritually. They are receivers of doles, from such rewards as the "Strength through Joy" benefits all the way down to the spoiled food and contaminated water of the concentration camp.

This, I think, explains the behavior of a good many Germans toward the Allied armies. It is a continuity of frozen reactions. The aloofness of some and the abject toadying of others to the military powers are alike the result of their long alienation from genuinely experienced values and convictions.

Another result is the emergence of an infantile collectivity. Terrorist atomization has resulted in almost complete destruction of the old institutions of society. Most important, because the family was the basic unit of society, is the weakening of family ties. The complete dependence of parents on the whims of the terrorist hierarchy; the state policy of training children to inform on their parents; the regimentation of youth; the "social engineering" that shifts masses of people about with as little respect for family ties as in the worst phases of chattel slavery; the creation of millions of orphans through mass extermination of adults; all these are practices that the totalitarian governments have made horribly familiar. And all these practices inevitably and designedly disrupt family relationships and deprive the young of reliance upon the warmth and security of family life.

The result is an upsurge of a feeling of adolescent collectivity, rootless and ruthless, in which the concept of the family is supplanted by the image of a cynical, tough, destructive, joyfully cruel, and extremely resentful community, frighteningly reminiscent of Hitler's vision of brutally domesticated and therefore brutal natural material.

Finally, the pattern of terrorist oppression has had its influence on the behavior of liberated groups and individuals. Without moralizing about the legitimacy or appropriateness of revenge, it must be said that reprisals that betray a resort to the means of the totalitarian enemy have a deep significance for the tasks of peace. It has been truly said that the system of terror that Mussolini introduced into Western Europe enjoyed a sinister triumph in the orgy of vengeance over the dead bodies of the fascist dictator and his mistress. It triumphed when French girls were paraded with shaved heads before a vituperative populace in punishment for intimate relations with German soldiers. The "humane and orderly" transfer of Germans from liberated Poland was foreshadowed in the remark made to Jan Karski by a girl member of the Polish underground: "The moment the Germans are defeated a ruthless mass terror must be organized. The imported Germans must be expelled from the vicinity by the same methods by which they were settled here—by force and ruthless extermination."

What is there in modern civilization that has set this terror loose among us? I should like to venture this thesis: Mankind today has so tremendously improved its technology as to render itself largely superfluous. Modern machinery and methods of organization have made it possible for a relatively small minority of managers, technicians, and skilled workers to keep the whole industrial apparatus going. Society has reached the stage of potential mass unemployment; and mass employment is increasingly a manipulated product of the state and state-like powers that channelize surplus mankind into public works, including armies and official or semiofficial political organizations, in order to keep it at once alive and under control.

This is to say that large masses of workers have lost all creative relation to the productive process. They live in a social and economic vacuum. Their dilemma is the precondition of terror. It provides the totalitarian forces with a road to power and an object for its exercise. For them, terror is the institutionalized administration of large strata of mankind as surplus.

Certain cultural tendencies emerging from the crisis of the liberal era may be cited as contributing to the rise of terror.

Under the impact of mass production, people have learned to live in patterns, not only material but also spiritual. They tend to accept uncritically entire systems or opinions and attitudes, as if ideological tie-in sales were forced upon them. To be a progressive is ipso facto to be for democracy, for the New Deal, for the Negroes, for the Jews, for Soviet Russia, and many other things. To be an isolationist is, or was, to be ipso facto against Great Britain, against Soviet Russia, against the intellectuals, against the Jews, and many other things.

It is not so much that people believe in these configurations of stereotypes as that they themselves become stereotyped appendages of this or that big cultural or political monopoly. Reason, consistency, personal experience no longer matter. One might say, for example, that there are no true anti-Semites any more, because anti-Semitism is not so much a reaction to anything experienced as specifically Jewish as it is a behavior pattern tied in with adherence to a certain cultural ticket. And this shrinking of genuine experience makes it all the more difficult to counteract distorted and fallacious stereotypes. The cultural monopoly, integrating a whole chain of attitudes, itself exercises a psychologically terroristic impact on which the individual yields.

The fearful discrepancy between the moral traditions of individualism and the mass crimes of modern collectivism has left modern man in a moral no-man's land. He still holds to the moral concepts of middle-class society—conscience, decency, self-respect, the dignity of man—but the social foundations of these concepts are crumbling. The overwhelming scale of power, size, destruction, extermination in the modern world make individual moral scruples, problems, and conflict seem puny and irrelevant.

To cite a drastic example, the ethical issue involved in *Hamlet*, which may be considered a classical document of morality after the dissolution of medieval culture, is the question whether or not a time "out of joint" can be righted if Hamlet becomes the judge and executioner of his father's murderer. In the face of present-day physical and moral catastrophe this issue is almost ridiculous.

The individual today realizes, more or less consciously, that his moral values do not greatly matter, because not much depends any more, either materially or spiritually, upon his decisions. He feels alone, deprived of the material and moral heritage that was the basis of his existence in liberal society. He is exposed to tremendous fury and aggression. He had become a potential paranoiac. In this condition he is ready to accept the most insane ideologies and patterns of domination and persecution.

The facists were the first to spot the connection between potential material poverty and real spiritual poverty, and to exploit it rationally and systematically on a mass scale. They realize that in order to subjugate and control the surplus population it was necessary to burn into people's minds the awareness of physical and spiritual menace, and to extirpate the whole frame of moral and emotional reference within which people had traditionally attempted to survive personal calamity. Hitler himself, in a conversation with Rauschning, once expressed the fascist need of terror and brutality. According to Rauschning:

> He had not the slightest liking for concentration camps and secret police and the like but these things were simply necessities from which there was no getting away. "Unless you are prepared to be pitiless, you will get nowhere. . . . Domination is never founded on

humanity, but, regarded from the narrow civilian angle, on crime. Terrorism is absolutely indispensable in every case of the founding of a new power. . . . Even more important than terrorism is the systematic modification of the ideas and feelings of the masses. We have to control those."

Hegel once said, "How fortunate the institution which has no history." Our age of terror is history, and one of its blackest chapters. But the dreams of freedom and happiness that terror would destroy are also part of history.

It is only by applying the efforts of reason—in its theory and practice—to the phenomena of terror, their roots and their consequences, that mankind can hope to wrest itself from the most sinister threat and ultimately pathetic fate in which it has ever become involved.

The dreams of Western civilization may still become reality if mankind can free itself from its use of human beings as surplus or commodities or means. Otherwise we too may face the terror.

Herbert Marcuse

ON HEDONISM

The idealist philosophy of the bourgeois era attempted to comprehend the universal, which was supposed to realize itself in and through isolated individuals, under the notion of reason. The individual appears as an ego isolated from and against others in its drives, thoughts, and interests. This isolating individuation is overcome and a common world constructed through the reduction of concrete individuality to the subject of mere thought, the rational ego. Operating among men who at first follow only their particular interests, the laws of reason eventually succeed in bringing about community. The universal validity of at least some forms of intuition and of thought can be securely established, and certain general maxims of conduct can be derived from the rationality of the person. Insofar as the individual partakes of universality only as a rational being and not with the empirical manifold of his needs, wants, and capacities, this idea of reason implicitly contains the sacrifice of the individual. His full development could not be admitted into the realm of reason. The gratification of his wants and capacities, his happiness, appears as an arbitrary and subjective element that cannot be brought into consonance with the universal validity of the highest principle of human action.

> For it is every man's own special feeling of pleasure and pain that decides in what he is to place his happiness, and even in the same subject this will vary with the difference of his wants according as this feeling changes, and thus a law which is *subjectively necessary* (as a law of nature) is *objectively* a very *contingent* practical principle, which can and must be very different in different subjects, and therefore can never furnish a law. . . .[1]

---

1. Kant, *Critique of Practical Reason.* T. H. Abbott, trans. London: Longmans, 1909, pp. 112–13.

Happiness is of no matter, for happiness does not lead beyond the individual in all his contingency and imperfection. Hegel saw the history of humanity as burdened with this irredeemable misfortune. Individuals must be sacrificed for the sake of the universal, for there is no preestablished harmony between the general and the particular interest, or between reason and happiness. The progress of reason realizes itself against the happiness of individuals.

> Happy is he who has adapted his existence to his particular character, will, and choice and thus enjoys himself in his existence. History is not the stage of happiness. In it, the periods of happiness are empty pages. . . .[2]

The universal follows its course in disregard of individuals, and history, when comprehended, appears as the monstrous Calvary of the spirit.

Hegel fought against eudaemonism in the interest of historical progress. As such, the eudaemonistic principle of "making happiness and pleasure the highest good" is not false, according to Hegel. Rather, the baseness of eudaemonism is that it transposes the fulfillment of desire and the happiness of individuals into a "vulgar world and reality." In accordance with this eudaemonism, the individual is supposed to be reconciled to this common and base world. The individual should "trust in this world and yield himself to it and be able to devote himself to it without sin." Eudaemonism sins against historical reason, according to Hegel, in that it lets the culmination of human existence be prescribed and tainted by bad empirical reality.

Hegel's critique of eudaemonism expresses insight into the required objectivity of happiness. If happiness is no more than the immediate gratification of particular interests, then eudaemonism contains an irrational principle that keeps men within whatever forms of life are given. Human happiness should be something other than personal contentment. Its own title points beyond mere subjectivity.

Both ancient and bourgeois eudaemonism viewed happiness essentially as such a subjective condition. Insofar as men can and should attain happiness within the status prescribed them by the established social order, this doctrine contains a moment of resignation and approbation. Eudaemonism comes into contradiction with the principle of the critical autonomy of reason.

---

2. Hegel, *Vorlesungen über die Geschichte.* Werke IX. Ed. Gans. Berlin 1840–47, p. 34.

The contraposition of happiness and reason goes all the way back to ancient philosophy. The relegation of happiness to chance, to that which cannot be controlled and is not dominated, to the irrational power of conditions that are essentially external to the individual, so that happiness at most "supervenes" on its aims and goals—this resigned relationship to happiness is contained in the Greek concept of arche. One is happy in the realm of "external goods," which do not fall within the freedom of the individual, but rather are subject to the opaque contingency of the social order of life. True felicity, the fulfillment of individuals' highest potentialities, thus cannot consist in what is commonly called happiness, but must be sought in the world of the soul and the mind.

It is against this internalization of happiness, which accepts as inevitable the anarchy and unfreedom of the external conditions of existence, that the hedonistic trends of philosophy have protested. By identifying happiness with pleasure, they were demanding that man's sensual and sensuous potentialities and needs, too, should find satisfaction—that in them, too, man should enjoy his existence without sinning against his essence, without guilt and shame. In the principle of hedonism, in an abstract and undeveloped form, the demand for the freedom of the individual is extended into the realm of the material conditions of life. Insofar as the materialistic protest of hedonism preserves an otherwise proscribed element of human liberation, it is linked with the interest of critical theory.

Two types of hedonism are commonly distinguished: the Cyrenaic and the Epicurean trends. The Cyrenaics' point of departure is the thesis that the fulfillment of specific instincts and wants of the individual is associated with the feeling of pleasure. Happiness consists in having these individual pleasures as often as possible.

> Our end is particular pleasure, whereas happiness is the sum total of all individual pleasures, in which are included both past and future pleasures. Particular pleasure is desirable for its own sake, whereas happiness is desirable not for its own sake, but for the sake of particular pleasures.[3]

What the individual instincts and wants may be makes no difference; their moral evaluation is not based upon their "nature." They are a matter of custom, of social convention. Pleasure is all that matters. It is the only happiness that the individual is allotted.

---

3. Diogenes Laertius, *Lives of Eminent Philosophers I*. R. D. Hicks, trans. New York: Putnam, p. 217.

". . . pleasure does not differ from pleasure nor is one pleasure more pleasant than another."

And now the materialist protest against internalization:

> . . . bodily pleasures are far better than mental pleasures, and bodily pains far worse than mental pains . . .[4]

Even rebellion against sacrificing the individual to the hypostatized community is preserved: "It was reasonable . . . for the good man not to risk his life in the defence of his country, for he would never throw wisdom away to benefit the unwise."[5]

This hedonism fails to differentiate not only between individual pleasures but also between the individuals who enjoy them. They are to gratify themselves just as they are, and the world is to become an object of possible enjoyment just as it is. In its relegation of happiness to immediate abandon and immediate enjoyment, hedonism accords with circumstances located in the structure of antagonistic society itself; they become clear only in their developed form.

In this form of society, the world as it is can become an object of enjoyment only when everything in it, men and things, is accepted as it appears. Its essence, that is, those potentialities which emerge as the highest on the basis of the attained level of the productive forces and of knowledge, is not present to the subject of enjoyment. For since the life process is not determined by the true interests of individuals creating, in solidarity, their existence through contending with nature, these potentialities are not realized in the decisive social relations. They can only appear to consciousness as lost, atrophied, and repressed. Any relationship to men and things going beyond their immediacy, any deeper understanding, would immediately come upon their essence, upon that which they could be and are not, and would then suffer from their appearance. Appearance becomes visible in the light of unrealized potentialities. Then it is no longer one beautiful moment among others so much as something evanescent which is lost and cannot be restored. Faults and blemishes of the objects of enjoyment are then burdened with the general ugliness and general unhappiness, whereas in immediacy they can even become a source of pleasure. Contingency in relations to men and things and the accompanying obstacles, losses, and renunciations become an expression of the anarchy and injustice of the whole, of a society in which even the most personal relations are determined by the economic law of value.

---

4. Ibid., p. 219.
5. Ibid., p. 227.

In this society, all human relationships transcending immediate encounter are not relations of happiness: especially not relationships in the labor process, which is regulated with regard not to the needs and capacities of individuals but rather to profit on capital and the production of commodities. Human relations are class relations, and their typical form is the free labor contract. This contractual character of human relationships has spread from the sphere of production to all of social life. Relationships function only in their reified form, mediated through the class distribution of the material output of the contractual partners. If this functional depersonalization were ever breached, not merely by that back-slapping familiarity which only underscores the reciprocal functional distance separating men but rather by mutual concern and solidarity, it would be impossible for men to return to their normal social functions and positions. The contractual structure upon which this society is based would be broken.

Contract, however, does not encompass all interpersonal relations. Society has released a whole dimension of relationships whose value is supposed to consist precisely in their not being determined by contractual achievements and contractual services. These are relationships in which individuals are in the relation of "persons" to one another and in which they are supposed to realize their personality. Love, friendship, and companionship are such personal relations, to which Western culture has relegated man's highest earthly happiness. But they cannot sustain happiness, precisely when they are what they are intended to be. If they are really to guarantee an essential and permanent community among individuals, they must be based on comprehending understanding of the other. They must contain uncompromising knowledge. To this knowledge the other reveals himself not merely in the uninterrupted immediacy of sensual appearance that can be desired and enjoyed as beautiful, through satisfaction with appearance, but rather in his essence, as he really is. His image will thus include ugliness, injustice, inconstancy, decay, and ephemerality not as subjective properties that could be overcome by understanding concern but rather as the effects of the intervention of social necessities into the personal sphere. These necessities actually constitute the instincts, wants, and interests of the person in this society. Accordingly the very essence of the person expresses itself in modes of behavior to which the other (or the person himself) reacts with disappointment, concern, sympathy, anxiety, infidelity, jealousy, and sorrow. Culture has transfigured these feelings and given them tragic consecration.

In fact, they subvert reification. In the behavior to which they are a response, the individual wants to release himself from a situation whose social law he has hitherto obeyed, whether marriage, occupation, or any other obligation in which he has accepted morality. He wants to follow his passions. In an order of unfreedom, however, passion is deeply disorderly and hence immoral. When not diverted toward generally desired goals, it leads to unhappiness.

This is not the only way in which personal relations are linked to pain and unhappiness. The development of personality also means the development of knowledge: insight into the structures of the reality in which one lives. These structures being what they are, every step of cognition removes the individual from immediate abandonment to appearance and from ready acceptance of the ideology that conceals its essence. Thus knowledge destroys proffered happiness. If the individual really acts on his knowledge, he is led either to struggle against the status quo or to renunciation. Knowledge does not help him attain happiness, yet without if he reverts to reified relationships. This is an inescapable dilemma. Enjoyment and truth, happiness and the essential relations of individuals are disjunctions.

By not concealing this dichotomy, consistent hedonism fulfilled a progressive function. It did not pretend that, in an anarchic society, happiness could be found in a developed, harmonic "personality" based on the highest achievements of culture. Hedonism is useless as ideology and in no way admits of being employed to justify an order associated with the suppression of freedom and the sacrifice of the individual. For such a purpose it must first be morally internalized or revised in a utilitarian sense. Hedonism advocates happiness equally for all individuals. It does not hypostatize a community in which happiness is negated without regard to the individuals. It is meaningful to speak of the progress of universal reason realizing itself in the face of the unhappiness of individuals, but general happiness apart from the happiness of individuals is a meaningless phrase.

Hedonism is the opposite pole to the philosophy of reason. In abstract fashion, both movements of thought have preserved potentialities of existing society that point to a real human society. The philosophy of reason has emphasized the development of the productive forces, the free rational shaping of the conditions of life, the domination of nature, and the critical autonomy of the associated individuals. Hedonism has stressed the comprehensive unfolding and fulfillment of individual wants and needs, emancipation from an inhuman labor process, and liberation of the world for the purposes of enjoyment. In society up to the present, the two doctrines have been incompatible, as are the principles that they represent. The idea of reason aims at universality, at a society in which the antagonistic interests of "empirical" individuals are canceled. To this community, however, the real fulfillment of individuals and their happiness remains alien and external; they must be sacrificed. There is no harmony between the general and the particular interest, between reason and happiness. If the individual believes that both interests are in accord, he becomes the victim of a necessary and salutary illusion; reason outwits the individuals. The true interest (of universality) reifies itself in opposition to the individuals and becomes a power that overwhelms them.

Hedonism wants to preserve the development and gratification of the individual as a goal within an anarchic and impoverished reality. But the protest against the reified community and against the meaningless sacrifices which are made to it leads only deeper into isolation and opposition between individuals as long as the historical forces that could transform the established society into a true community have not matured and are not comprehended. For hedonism, happiness remains something exclusively subjective. The particular interest of the individual, just as it is, is affirmed as the true interest and is justified against every and all community. This is the limit of hedonism: its attachment to the individualism of competition. Its concept of happiness can be derived only by abstracting from all universality and community. Abstract happiness corresponds to the abstract freedom of the monadic individual. The concrete objectivity of happiness is a concept for which hedonism finds no evidence.

This inevitable entanglement of even the most radical eudaemonism is a proper target of Hegel's critique. For it reconciles particular happiness with general unhappiness. Hedonism is not untrue because the individual is supposed to seek and find his happiness in a world of injustice and of misery. To the contrary, the hedonistic principle as such rebels often enough against this order. If it were ever to take hold of the masses, they would scarcely tolerate unfreedom and would be made completely unsuited for heroic domestication. The apologetic aspect of hedonism is located at a deeper level. It is to be found in hedonism's abstract conception of the subjective side of happiness, in its inability to distinguish between true and false wants and interests and between true and false enjoyment. It accepts the wants and interests of individuals as simply given and as valuable in themselves. Yet these wants and interests themselves, and not merely their gratification, already contain the stunted growth, the repression, and the untruth with which men grow up in class society. The affirmation of the one already contains the affirmation of the other.

The inability of hedonism to apply the category of truth to happiness, its fundamental relativism, is not a logical or epistemological fault of a philosophical system. It can be neither corrected within the system nor eliminated by a more comprehensive and better philosophical system. It originates in the form of social relations to which hedonism is linked, and all attempts to avoid it through immanent differentiation lead to new contradictions.

The second type of hedonism, the Epicurean, represents such an attempt at immanent differentiation. The identification of the highest good with pleasure is retained, but a specific kind of pleasure is, as "true" pleasure, opposed to all others. The undifferentiated gratification of whatever wants are given is all too often obviously followed by pain, whose magnitude is the basis for a differentiation of individual pleasures. There are wants and desires whose satisfaction is succeeded by pain that only serves to stimulate new desires, destroying man's peace of mind and health. Therefore,

> . . . we do not choose every pleasure whatsoever, but ofttimes pass over many pleasures when a greater annoyance ensues from them. And ofttimes we consider pains superior to pleasures when submission to the pains for a long time brings us as a consequence a greater pleasure.[6]

Reason, whose foresight makes possible a comparison of the values of momentary pleasure and later pain, becomes the adjudicator of pleasure. It may itself even become the highest pleasure.

> It is not an unbroken succession of drinking-bouts and of revelry, not sexual love, not the enjoyment of the fish and other delicacies . . . which produce a pleasant life; it is sober reasoning, searching out the grounds of every choice and avoidance, and banishing those beliefs through which the greatest tumults take possession of the soul.[7]

Reason grants man that moderate enjoyment which reduces risk and offers the prospect of permanently balanced health. The differentiating evaluation of pleasure ensues therefore with regard to the greatest possible security and permanence of pleasure. This method

---

6. Ibid., vol. 2, p. 655.
7. Ibid., p. 657.

expresses fear of the insecurity and badness of the conditions of life, the invincible limitation of enjoyment. It is a negative hedonism. Its principle is less the pleasure to be striven for than the pain to be avoided. The truth against which pleasure is to be measured is only evasion of conflict with the established order: the socially permitted if not desired form of pleasure. The "sage's" tranquility is the goal: an idea in which the concept of pleasure as well as the concept of the sage are deprived of their meaning. Pleasure perishes, inasmuch as the cautious, measured, and withdrawn relationship of the individual to men and things resists their dominion over him precisely where this dominion brings real happiness: as enjoyable abandon. In the antagonistic ordering of existence, happiness is encountered as something withdrawn from the autonomy of the individual, something that can be neither achieved nor controlled by reason. The element of extraneousness, contingency, and gratuitousness is here an essential component of happiness. It is just in this external-ity, in this innocent, unburdened, harmonious conjunction of the individual with something in the world, that pleasure consists. In the historical situation of individuals up to the present, it is not what reason has achieved nor what the soul experiences that can be called happiness (for these are necessarily tainted with unhappi-ness). To the contrary, only "externalized" pleasure, i.e., sensuality, can be called happiness. In reified social relationships, sensuality, and not reason, is the "organ" of happiness.

In the antithesis of reason and sensuality (or sensuousness), as it has been worked out in the development of philosophy, sensuality has increasingly acquired the character of a lower, baser human faculty, a realm lying on this side of true and false and of correct and incorrect, a region of dull, undiscriminating instincts. Only in epistemology has the connection between sensuousness and truth been preserved. Here the decisive aspect of sensuality has been re-tained: receptivity that is open and that opens itself (to experience). This quality contradicts sensuality's allegedly dull instinctual char-acter. Precisely through this receptivity, this open abandon to ob-jects (men and things), sensuality can become a source of happiness. For in it, in complete immediacy, the individual's isolation is over-come. Objects can occur to him here without their essential media-tion through the social life process and, consequently, without their unhappy side becoming constitutive of pleasure. In the process of knowledge, in reason, quite the reverse holds. Here the individual's spontaneity necessarily comes up against the object as against something foreign. Reason must overcome the latter quality and comprehend the object in its essence, not only as it is presented and appears but as it has become. The method of reason has always been held to be the way of attaining clarity about the origin and principle of beings. This method implicitly referred to history. To be sure, history was understood not as real history but only transcendentally. Nevertheless, that process of comprehension worthy of the title of reason absorbed enough of the mutability, the insecurity, the conflicts, and suffering of reality to make the application of the term *pleasure* appear false in this realm. When Plato and Aristotle connected reason with pleasure, they did not establish reason as one of (or the best of) the individual pleasures in the sense of the hedonists. Rather, reason appears as the highest human potentiality and therefore, necessarily, as the highest human pleasure. Here, in the fight against hedonism, the concept of pleasure is taken out of the sphere to which the hedonists had relegated it and held up in opposition to this entire sphere.

The situation is different when, as in the case of Epicurus, reason is made a pleasure or pleasure is made reasonable within hedonism itself. This gives rise to that ideal of the satisfied sage in which both pleasure as well as reason have lost their meaning. The sage, then, would be the person whose reason and whose pleasure never go too far. They never are followed through to the end because, if they were, they would come upon knowledge that negates enjoyment. The sage's reason would be so limited from the start that it would only be occupied with the calculation of risks and with the psychic technique of extracting the best from everything. Such reason has abdicated its claim to truth. It appears only as subjective cunning and private expertise, calmly acquiescing in the persistence of general unreason and enjoying not so much what is allotted or occurs to it as itself.

Hedonism embodies a correct judgment about society. That the receptivity of sensuality and not the spontaneity of reason is the source of happiness results from antagonistic work relations. They are the real form of the attained level of human reason. It is in them that the extent of possible freedom and possible happiness is decided. If this form is one in which the productive forces are disposed of in the interest of the smallest social groups, in which the majority of men are separated from the means of production, and in which labor is performed not in accordance with the capacities and needs of individuals but according to the requirements of the process of profitable production, then happiness cannot be general within it. Happiness is restricted to the sphere of consumption.

Radical hedonism was formulated in the ancient world and draws a moral conclusion from the slave economy. Labor and happiness are essentially separated. They belong to different modes of existence. Some men are slaves in their essence, others are free men. In the modern epoch the principle of labor has become general. Everyone is supposed to work and everyone is supposed to be rewarded in accordance with his work. But since the distribution of social labor proceeds according to the opaque necessity of the capitalist law of value, no rational relation is established between production and consumption, between labor and enjoyment. Gratification occurs as a contingency that is to be accepted. Reason rules only behind the backs of individuals in the reproduction of the whole that takes place despite anarchy. For the individual in pursuit of his own interests, reason's role is at most a personal calculation in choosing among given possibilities. And it is in this atrophied form that reason depreciated to the idea of the sage. If reason cannot be effective in the process of production as free communal decision about the state of human existence (within specific historical and natural conditions), then it can certainly not be effective in the process of consumption.

The restriction of happiness to the sphere of consumption, which appears separated from the process of production, stabilizes the particularity and the subjectivity of happiness in a society in which rational unity of the process of production and consumption, of labor and enjoyment, has not been brought about. The rejection by idealistic ethics of hedonism just because of the latter's essential particularity and subjectivity is founded upon a justified criticism: Does not happiness, with its immanent demand for increase and permanence, require that, within happiness itself, the isolation of individuals, the reification of human relations, and the contingency of gratification be done away with? Must not happiness become compatible with truth? On the other hand, none other than isolation, reification, and contingency have been the dimensions of happiness in previous society. Hedonism, therefore, has been right precisely in its falsehood insofar as it has preserved the demand for happiness against every idealization of unhappiness. The truth of hedonism would be its abolition by and preservation in a new principle of social organization, not in a different philosophical principle.

Philosophy has attempted in various ways to save the objectivity of happiness and to comprehend it under the category of truth and universality. Such attempts are to be found in ancient eudaemonism, in the Catholic philosophy of the Middle Ages, in humanism, and in the French Enlightenment. If inquiry into the possible objectivity of happiness is not extended to the structure of the social organization of humanity, its result is bound to run aground on social contradictions. Inasmuch, however, as the philosophical critique at least refers decisively to the historical problem at hand as a task of historical practice, we shall discuss in what follows the first and most important controversy with hedonism.

Plato's critique of hedonism (on two different levels in the *Gorgias* and *Philebus*) worked out for the first time the concept of true and false wants and true and false pleasure. Here truth and falsehood are categories that are supposed to be applicable to every individual pleasure. The critique takes its departure from the essential conjunction of pleasure and pain. Every pleasure is connected with pain, since pleasure is the removal and fulfillment of a want (lack, privation) that as such is felt as painful. Pleasure, therefore, cannot be "the good" or happiness, because it contains its own opposite: unless it were possible to find an "unmixed" pleasure, one essentially separated from pain. In the *Philebus* (51 b ff.) what remains as unmixed, true pleasure is in the last analysis only pleasure in lines, sounds, and colors that are "beautiful in themselves," in other words, enjoyment released from all painful desire and restricted to inorganic objects. This enjoyment is obviously too empty to be happiness. Designating inorganic entities as the object of pure pleasure shows decisively that in the given form of existential relations true pleasure is not only separated from the soul, which, as the seat of desire and longing, is necessarily also the source of pain, but is also separated from all essential personal relationships. Unmixed pleasure is to be had only in those things which are most removed from the social life process. The receptivity of open abandonment to the object of enjoyment, which Plato recognizes as the precondition of pleasure, remains only in complete externality, in which all essential relations between man and man are silenced. Happiness is thus situated at the antipode of internalization and inwardness.

Plato's earlier solution of the problem of true pleasure takes another direction. In the *Gorgias* he proceeds directly to the question of the social order within which the individual is to fulfill himself. This order itself as the highest norm against which individual pleasures are to be measured is not a subject of discussion; it is accepted in its given form. Bad wants and bad pleasures are those which destroy the just order of the soul and which prevent the individual from attaining his true potentialities. It is the community, however, within which individuals live and through which alone "the heavens and the earth, gods and men are bound together" (508a) that decides these potentialities and thus the truth and falsehood of wants and pleasures. The concept of the order of the soul turns into that of the order of the community and the concept of the individually "just" into that of justice (504). Whether the individuals enjoy the right pleasure depends on the right ordering of the polis. The generality of happiness is posed as a problem. Only those wants may be satisfied which make the individual a good citizen. They are true wants, and the pleasure associated with their gratification is true pleasure. The others are not to be fulfilled. It is the task of the statesman to look after the general interest and to bring the satisfaction of particular interests into accord with it. The possibility of such harmony, the authentic social question, is not pursued further in the *Gorgias* (although the critique of major Greek statesmen at least suggests social criticism).

Inasmuch as true and false pleasure are contraposed, happiness is subjected to the criterion of truth. If human existence is to come in pleasure to its highest fulfillment, to felicity, then not every sensation of pleasure can in itself be happiness. Plato's critique of hedonism traces the givens of wants and of pleasures back to the individuals who "have" them. This conceptual regress is made necessary by the fact that both the sick and the healthy, the good and the bad, the crazy and the normal feel pleasure in like manner (at least with respect to the fact of pleasure). What is common to all of these cannot be the highest. There must be a truth of happiness on the basis of which the happiness of the individual can be judged. Pleasure must be susceptible to distinction according to truth and falsehood and to justice and injustice if (in case pleasure is happiness) the happiness of men is not to be inseparably associated with unhappiness. The basis of such a distinction, however, cannot lie in the individual sensation of pleasure as such, for both the sick and the healthy and the bad and the good feel real pleasure. Nevertheless, just as an idea can be false even though it be a real idea, so too a pleasure can be false without the reality of the sensation of pleasure being denied (*Philebus* 36). This is more than a mere analogy. Here a cognitive function in the strictest sense is attributed to pleasure, for it reveals beings as objects of enjoyment. On the basis of its "intentional" character, pleasure is thus made accessible to the question of truth. A pleasure is untrue when the object that it intends is not "in itself" pleasurable (according to the exposition of the *Philebus*, when it can only be encountered mixed with pain).

But the question of truth does not regard only the object but also the subject of pleasure. This is made possible through Plato's interpretation of pleasure as belonging not merely to sensuousness (*aesthesis*) alone but also to the psyche (*Philebus* 33 f.). Psychic forces (such as desire, expectation, memory) are necessary for every sensation of pleasure, so that in pleasure the whole man is involved. With respect to the latter the question of truth arrives at the same point that had been reached in the *Gorgias:* that "good" men have true pleasure and "bad" men have false pleasure (*Philebus* 40 b, c).

The essential connection of the good of man with the truth of pleasure at which Plato's discussion of hedonism arrives makes of pleasure a moral problem. For it is the concrete form of the "community" that ultimately decides on this connection. Pleasure is subject to the claim of society and enters the realm of duty—duty to oneself and to others. The truth of the particular interest and its gratification is determined by the truth of the general interest. The agreement of the two is not immediate. Rather, it is mediated through the subjection of the particular to the requirements of generality. Within a society that requires morality (as an objective, general code of ethics opposed to the subjective wants and interests of individuals) for its existence, an amoral attitude is intolerable, for the latter destroys the bases of communal order. The amoral man violates the law of a society that, even if in a bad form, guarantees the preservation of social life. He does so, furthermore, without linking himself to a better, true society. For he remains in the given, "corrupted" structure of instincts and wants. Morality is the expression of the antagonism between the particular and the general interest. It is the code of these demands which are a matter of life and death for the society's self-preservation. Insofar as particular interests are not really incorporated into and fulfilled in the society, such demands appear to the individual as commands coming from outside himself. If left to itself, pleasure as the immediate gratification of the merely particular interest must come into conflict with the interest of the hypostatized social community. In contrast to the isolated individual, society represents what is historically right. It demands the repression of all pleasure that violates the decisive social taboo. It forbids the satisfaction of those wants which would shatter the foundations of the established order.

The moralization of pleasure is called for by the existence of antagonistic society. It is the historical form in which this society unites the satisfaction of particular wants and instincts with the general interest, and it has had a progressive function in the development of the social labor process. The hedonistic protest of the individual who is isolated in his particular interest is amoral. The amoral, beyond-good-and-evil attitude can be progressive only within a historical practice that leads beyond the already attained form of this process and fights for a new, true community against the established one. Only then does this attitude represent more than a merely particular interest. Isolated from the historical struggle for a better organization of the conditions of life, in which the individual has to engage himself in concrete social groups and tasks and thus gives up his amorality, amoral thought and action can, of course, escape from morality (if its subject is economically independent enough). But the ruling social law maintains its power over the amoral individual both in his wants and in the objects of their satisfaction. They originated under this law, and only the latter's transformation could overcome morality. Amoral rebellion, however, stops short of this decisive sphere. It wants to avoid morality as well as its social basis within the given order. Dodging the latter's contradictions, this amoral rebellion really remains beyond good and evil. It puts itself beyond the bounds of even that morality which links the established order with a more rational and happy society.

The attempt to save the objectivity of happiness, expressed for the first time in Plato's critique of hedonism, takes two directions in the advance toward an objective formulation of the concept of happiness. On the one hand, the gratification of the individual, his best possible existence, is measured against the "essence of man" in such a way that the highest potentialities open to man in his historical situation take precedence in development and gratification over all others in which man is not free but rather dependent on what is "external." On the other hand, the essence of man can develop only within society, whose actual organization participates in determining the realization of those potentialities and therefore also determines happiness. In Platonic and Aristotelian ethics both aspects, the personal and the social, are still joined. In the ethics of the modern period, in the form in which they have become prevalent since the Reformation, society is to a great extent relieved of responsibility for human potentialities. The latter are supposed to subsist exclusively in the individual himself, in his autonomy. The unconditioned freedom of the person becomes the measure of the "highest good." Since, however, this freedom is only abstract in the real world and coexists with social unfreedom and unhappiness, it becomes, in idealist ethics, programmatically separated from happiness. The latter increasingly takes on the character of irrational, bodily gratification, of mere enjoyment and therefore of inferiority:

> . . . reason can never be persuaded that the existence of a man who merely lives for *enjoyment* . . . has a worth in itself. . . . Only through what he does without reference to enjoyment, in full freedom and independently of what nature can procure for him passively, does he give an absolute worth to his being, as the existence of a person; and happiness, with the whole abundance of its pleasures, is far from being an unconditioned good.[8]

The duress of the disciplining process of modern society comes to expression: the happiness of the individual is at best a worthless accident of his life. In the determination of the highest good, happiness is completely subordinated to virtue. Happiness may be only the "morally conditioned although necessary consequence" of morality. A "necessary connection" between the ethics of conviction and happiness becomes possible only through the assumption of a "purely intellectual determining principle" of human action and of an "intelligible author of nature." The harmony of virtue and happiness belongs to those beautiful relations for whose realization the world beyond is necessary.

The unconditional manner, however, in which German idealism adhered to the principle of freedom as the condition of the highest good serves to emphasize more than ever the inner connection between happiness and freedom. The concrete form of human freedom determines the form of human happiness. Comprehension of the connection between happiness and freedom was already expressed in the ancient critique of hedonism. Happiness, as the fulfillment of all potentialities of the individual, presupposes freedom: at root, it is freedom. Conceptual analysis reveals them to be ultimately identical. Because freedom does not reign in the material conditions of the external world, because there happiness and contingency are almost identical, and because on the other hand the individual's freedom was maintained as a condition of the "highest good," felicity could not be made to reside in the external world. This motive is at work in Platonic and Aristotelian ethics. In the moral critique of the bourgeois period, too, hedonism is rejected from the standpoint of the concept of freedom. Kant rejected the

---

8. Kant, *Critique of Judgment.* J. H. Bernhard, trans. New York: Macmillan, 1892, p. 52.

principle of pleasure as something merely contingent which contradicted the autonomy of the person. And Fichte called pleasure essentially "involuntary" since it presupposes an agreement of the "external world" with the instincts and wants of the subject, whose realization does not fall within the range of the subject's freedom. In the happiness of pleasure, the individual is thus "alienated from himself." This position presupposes that the subject's unfreedom in relation to the good things of the external world cannot be abolished and that the free person is therefore necessarily debased if his happiness is located in this relation. For the ancient critique the highest good was still supposed really to be the highest happiness. But now factual unfreedom is ontologized, and both freedom and happiness are so internalized that in the process happiness is excluded. The attempt to include happiness in the autonomous development of the person is abandoned, and a virtue is made out of the abstract freedom that accompanies social unfreedom.

The gratification of instincts and wants falls into ill repute; in any case, it lies beneath the human sphere with which philosophy is to concern itself. Moral commands can be followed without one's wants having been fulfilled to more than the physiological minimum; with this proposition, to be sure, a decisive achievement of modern society receives philosophical recognition. Man educated to internalization will not be easily induced, even under extreme wretchedness and injustice, to struggle against the established order.

In the moral concept of the highest good an untruth of hedonism is supposed to be eliminated: the mere subjectivity of happiness. Happiness remains an "element" of the highest good, but it stays subject to the universality of the moral law. This law is a law of reason: happiness is linked to knowledge and taken out of the dimension of mere feeling. Real happiness presupposes knowledge of the truth: that men know what they can attain as the highest potential of their existence, that they know their true interest. Individuals can feel happy and yet not be happy, because they do not even know real happiness. How, though, is one to judge of the reality of happiness? What is the criterion of its truth? In the ancient critique of hedonism this question became the political question of the right organization of the polis. The Christian ethics of the Middle Ages saw the answer to it in divine justice. The rigoristic morality of the bourgeois period made freedom the criterion of truth. But this was defined as the abstract freedom of the rational being and, in contrast to it, happiness remained external and contingent. The moral interpretation of happiness, its subjection to a universal law of reason, tolerated both the essential isolation of the autonomous person and his actual limitation.

Critical theory comes to the question of the truth and universality of happiness in the elucidation of the concepts with which it seeks to determine the rational form of society. One of these determinations circumscribing the association of free men contains the explicit demand that each individual share in the social product according to his needs. With the comprehensive development of individuals and of the productive forces, society can inscribe on its banner, "From each according to his abilities, to each according to his needs." Here reappears the old hedonistic definition which seeks happiness in the comprehensive gratification of needs and wants. The needs and wants to be gratified should become the regulating principle of the labor process. But the wants of liberated men and the enjoyment of their satisfaction will have a different form from wants and satisfaction in a state of unfreedom, even if they are physiologically the same. In a social organization that opposes atomized individuals to one another in classes and leaves their particular freedom to the mechanism of an uncontrolled economic system, unfreedom is already operative in the needs and wants themselves: how much more so in enjoyment. The way want and enjoyment appear here, they do not even require general freedom. The development of the productive forces, the growing domination of nature, the extension and refinement of the production of commodities, money, and universal reification have created, along with new needs, new possibilities for enjoyment. But these given possibilities for enjoyment confront men who objectively, due to their economic status, as well as subjectively, due to their education and disciplining, are largely incapable of enjoyment. From the discrepancy between what exists as objects of possible enjoyment and the way in which these objects are understood, taken, and used arises the question of the truth of the condition of happiness in this society. Acts intending enjoyment do not achieve the fulfillment of their own intention; even when they fulfill themselves, they remain untrue.

Enjoyment is an attitude or mode of conduct toward things and human beings. The former, unless they have been made generally available by nature or by social regulation, are commodities accessible to corresponding purchasing power. For the great majority of humanity, only the very cheapest portion of these commodities is available. They become objects of enjoyment as commodities, and their origin is preserved within them—even enjoyment has a class character. The cheap is not as good as the dear. Precisely insofar as they lie outside the labor process, relations between men are essentially relations between members of the same class. For the majority, one's partner in pleasure will also be one's partner in the poverty of the same class. These conditions of life are a paltry showplace for happiness. The continual pressure under which the great masses must be kept for the reproduction of this society has only been augmented by the monopolistic accumulation of wealth. Any growth of enjoyment would endanger necessary discipline and make difficult the punctual and reliable coordination of the masses who keep the apparatus of the whole in operation. The economic regulation of enjoyment is supplemented by the police and the administration of justice. Pleasure wants essentially its own augmentation and refinement. The unfolding of the personality must not be merely spiritual. Industrial society has differentiated and intensified the objective world in such a manner that only an extremely differentiated and intensified sensuality can respond adequately to it. Modern technology contains all the means necessary to extract from things and bodies their mobility, beauty, and softness in order to bring them closer and make them available. Both the wants corresponding to these potentialities and the sensual organs through which they can be assimilated have been developed. What man can perceive, feel, and do in the midst of advanced civilization corresponds to the newly opened-up wealth of the world. But only those groups with the greatest purchasing power can take advantage of the expanded capacities and their gratification. The development of sensuality is only one part of the development of the productive forces; the need to fetter them is rooted in the antagonistic social system within which this development has taken place. There are many ways in which the ruled strata can be educated to diversion and substitute gratification. Here sports and a wide variety of permitted popular entertainment fulfill their historical function. In authoritarian states sadistic terror against enemies of the regime has found unforeseen modes of organized discharge. At the movies the common man can regularly participate in the glamour of the world of the stars and yet be aware at the same time that it is only a film and that there, too, there is splendor, bitterness, trouble, guilt, atonement, and the triumph of the good. The labor process, in which the laborer's organs atrophy and are coarsened, guarantees that the sensuousness of the lower strata does not develop beyond the technically necessary minimum. What is allowed beyond this as immediate enjoyment is circumscribed by the penal code.

It is not only the masses, however, in whom enjoyment cannot achieve the fulfillment of all subjective and objective potentialities, as it intends. Where the prevailing social relationship is the relation of men to one another as owners of commodities and where the value of every commodity is determined by the abstract labor time applied to it, enjoyment has no value in itself. For all that it is in this society, it is in separation from labor. In enjoyment the individual expends no labor power, nor does he reproduce labor power. He behaves as and acknowledges himself to be a private person. When value, the standard of the equity of exchange, is created only by abstract labor, then pleasure may not be a value. For if it were, social justice would be called into question. Indeed, it would reveal itself as striking injustice. The legitimation of pleasure as a value would, in fact, invert what is "all the news that's fit to print."

> For every modern man the value of a thing is the value of the labor that was necessary to produce it. Value is thus coated with the laborer's sweat, which pastes up the flaming sword that separates culture from paradise. It is dangerous to associate conceptually pleasure and pain with value. For the question then arises whether those who produce values have more pleasure or more pain. And one could come upon the thought that value may be in inverse proportion to pleasure.[9]

The danger of this conceptual association was recognized as early as at the origins of bourgeois society. The worthlessness of mere pleasure was inculcated by all means into the consciousness of individuals.

Nowhere does the connection between the devaluation of enjoyment and its social justification manifest itself as clearly as in the interpretation of sexual pleasure. The latter—pragmatically or morally—is rationalized and appears as a mere means to an end lying outside of itself, in the service of a smooth subordination of the individual to the established form of the labor process. As a hygienic value sexual pleasure is supposed to contribute to physical and mental health, which promotes the normal functioning of man within the given order. According to Spinoza, "sensual pleasure" may only "be sought as means," and above all as hygienic means. We may "indulge ourselves with pleasures only insofar as they are

---

9. Herman Cohen, *Ethik des reinen Willens*. Berlin 1931, p. 163.

necessary for preserving health." Leibniz declares that "voluptuousness of the senses must be used, according to the rules of reason, as a nourishment, medication, or tonic." Fichte brings sexuality into immediate conjunction with the renovation of the social labor process:

> The real station, the honor and worth of the human being, and quite particularly of man in his morally natural existence, consists without doubt in his capacity as original progenitor to produce out of himself new men, new commanders of nature: beyond his earthly existence and for all eternity to establish new masters of nature. . . . It would consequently be absolute dishonor, the abnegation of authentic human and manly honor, if the capacity bestowed for the exercise of that privilege were made into a means of sensual pleasure. What is above all of nature and intended to reproduce dominion over her would become secondary and subject to one of nature's urges: pleasure. . . . [This absolute worthlessness is] lewdness—the use of the faculty of generation for mere pleasure, without intending its purpose or consciously willing it.[10]

Only when sexual relations are placed under the express purpose of the production of new labor power for the process of the social domination of nature is their enjoyment worthy of a human being and sanctioned. Later representatives of idealist ethics turned away from such frankness. Hermann Cohen considers the mere procreation of men an "animalistic" process and demands the purification of sexual pleasure by means of a truly ethical purpose. Only in love based on fidelity is sexual intercourse raised to the sphere of morality, making "sexual love" into a "characteristic of the pure will to the formation of ethical self-consciousness." In the authoritarian phase of the bourgeois order, the attachment of love to the form of marriage comes into open contradiction to the state's need of a strong military and economic reserve army. The "experience of love" is "not unconditionally bound to marriage." But love should be "the presupposition and condition of marriage and of childbearing in marriage." Not the begetting of children as such, but the procreation of industrious and useful children is decisive. "Racial hygiene, social anthropology, and other medical-anthropological disciplines [give consideration] in a very meritorious way to valuable aspects even of human procreation."

The unpurified, unrationalized release of sexual relationships would be the strongest release of enjoyment as such and the total

---

10. Fichte, *Die Staatslehre Werke VI*, pp. 523–24.

devaluation of labor for its own sake. No human being could tolerate the tension between labor as valuable in itself and the freedom of enjoyment. The dreariness and injustice of work conditions would penetrate explosively the consciousness of individuals and make impossible their peaceful subordination to the social system of the bourgeois world.

The function of labor within this society determines its attitude with respect to enjoyment. The latter may not be meaningful in itself or remain unrationalized. Instead it must receive its value from elsewhere. "Pleasure . . . and pain are withdrawn from any justification or motivation by the will to labor; rather, they provide this will with the stimulus to labor," which would then be subsumed under the principle of the satisfaction of wants. "Hedonism is the limit of a self-justification of the will to labor" and contradicts the basic interest of the established order. The internalization and spiritualization by means of which enjoyment is refined to the level of culture, which helps reproduce the whole and thus proves its social value, is subject to this conviction. For the immediate producer the restriction of enjoyment operates immediately, without any moral mediation, through the working day, which leaves only a brief period of "leisure time" for enjoyment and puts it in the service of relaxation and the recreation of energy or labor power. The usufructuaries of the labor process are affected by the same valuation. That their enjoyment consists of doing and having what actually produces no value, creates a kind of social guilt feeling that leads to a rationalization of enjoyment. As representation, relaxation, and display of the splendor of those who are on top and bear the greatest responsibility, this enjoyment is discharged almost as a burden or duty.

The creation of social guilt feeling is a decisive achievement of education. The prevailing law of value is mirrored in the continually renewed conviction that everyone, left completely to himself, must earn a living in the general competitive struggle, if only in order to be enabled to continue to earn it in the future, and that everyone is rewarded in proportion to the labor power he has expended. Happiness, however, cannot be earned in this fashion. The goal of labor is not supposed to be happiness, and its remuneration is not enjoyment but profit or wages, i.e. the possibility of working more in the future. For the perpetuation of this labor process, those instincts and wants which could undermine the normal relation of labor and enjoyment (as the extent of the absence of labor) and the institutions that secure it (such as the family or marriage) must be diverted or repressed. This diversion and repression is not always linked to cultural progress. Many instincts and wants first become false and destructive due to the false forms into which their satisfaction is channeled, while the attained level of objective development would permit their true gratification—true because they could fulfill themselves in their original intention of "unmixed" pleasure. Such are the repressed cruelty that leads to sadistic terror and the repressed self-abandon that leads to masochistic subjection. In their authentic intention as forms of the sexual instinct they can result in augmented pleasure not only for the subject but for the object as well. They are then no longer connected with destruction. But precisely the increased differentiation of pleasure is intolerable in a society that requires such wants to be gratified in a repressed form. Augmented pleasure would represent immediately increased liberation of the individual, for it would demand freedom in the choice of object, in the knowledge and in the realization of his potentialities, and freedom of time and of place. All these demands violate the law of life of the established society. The taboo on pleasure has been most stubbornly maintained due to the innermost connection of happiness and freedom. This taboo has extended far into the ranks of the historical opposition to the given order, distorting the problem and its solutions.

The designation of happiness as the condition of the comprehensive gratification of the individual's needs and wants is abstract and incorrect as long as it accepts needs and wants as ultimate data in their present form. For as such they are beyond neither good and evil nor true and false. As historical facts they are subject to questioning as to their "right": Are they of such a sort that their gratification can fulfill the subjective and objective potentialities of individuals? For many forms of want characteristic of the prevailing human condition, this question would have to be answered in the negative in view of the already attained stage of social development. For the latter makes possible a truer happiness than that which men attain for themselves today. Pleasure in the abasement of another as well as self-abasement under a stronger will, pleasure in the manifold surrogates for sexuality, in meaningless sacrifices, in the heroism of war, are false pleasures because the drives and needs that fulfill themselves in them make men less free, blinder, and more wretched than they have to be. They are the drives and needs of individuals who were raised in an antagonistic society. To the extent to which they do not completely disappear in a new form of social organization, modes of their gratification are conceivable in which the most extreme potentialities of men can really unfold happiness. This liberation of potentialities is a matter of social practice. What men, with their developed sensuous and psychic organs and the wealth created by their work, can undertake to attain the highest measure of happiness rests with this practice. Understood in this way, happiness can no longer or in any way be merely subjective: it enters the realm of men's communal thought and action.

Where society utilizes the developed productive forces only in fettered form, it is not just the gratifications but the very wants themselves that are falsified. Insofar as they extend beyond the subsistence minimum, they come to expression only in proportion to their effective demand. Class situation, especially the situation of the individual in the labor process, is active in them, for this situation has formed the (bodily and spiritual) organs and capacities of men and the horizon of their demands. Since these appear as wants only in their stunted form, with all their repressions, renunciations, adaptations, and rationalizations, they can normally be satisfied within the given social framework. Because they are themselves already unfree, the false happiness of their fulfillment is possible in unfreedom.

In critical theory, the concept of happiness has been freed from any ties with bourgeois conformism and relativism. Instead, it has become a part of general, objective truth, valid for all individuals insofar as all their interests are preserved in it. Only in view of the historical possibility of general freedom is it meaningful to designate as untrue even actual, really perceived happiness in the previous and present conditions of existence. It is the individual's interest that expresses itself in his wants, and their gratification corresponds to this interest. That there is any happiness at all in a society governed by blind laws is a blessing. Through this happiness, the individual in this society can feel secure and protected from ultimate desperation. Rigoristic morality sins against the cheerless form in which humanity has survived. All hedonism is right in opposing it. Only today, at the highest stage of development of the established order, when the objective forces making for a higher order of humanity have become mature, and only in connection with the theory and practice linked to such a transformation, may the critique of the totality of the established order also take as its object the happiness that this order provides. It appears that individuals reared to be integrated into the antagonistic labor process cannot be judges of their own happiness. They have been prevented from knowing their true interest. Thus it is possible for them to designate their condition as happy and, without external compulsion, embrace the system that oppresses them. The results of modern plebiscites prove that men separated from possible truth can be brought to vote against themselves. As long as individuals see their interests only as getting along within the given order, such plebiscites pose no problems for the authoritarian apparatus. Terror merely supplements the delusions of the governed. Appeal to interest is untrue.

In view of the possibility of a happier real state of humanity the interest of the individual is no longer an ultimate datum. There are true and false interests even with regard to the individual. His factual, immediate interest is not in itself his true interest. It is not as though the true interest were that which demanded, on the grounds of lesser risk and greater chance of enjoyment, the sacrifice of an immediate interest. Such calculation of happiness stays within the general framework of false interest and can at best facilitate the choice of the better false happiness. It cannot be in the true interest of the individual to want his own and others' vitiation—not even in the true interest of those whose power can only be maintained at the cost of such vitiation. At the attained level of development power can no longer enjoy the world which it dominates. For if it were to cease working and continually renewing the bloody and destructive process of its mere reproduction, it would be instantly lost. Even the powers that be have something to gain.

That the true interest of individuals is the interest of freedom, that true individual freedom can coexist with real general freedom and, indeed, is possible only in conjunction with it, that happiness ultimately consists in freedom—these are not propositions of philosophical anthropology about the nature of man but descriptions of a historical situation which humanity has achieved for itself in the struggle with nature. The individuals whose happiness is at stake in making good use of this situation have grown up in the school of capitalism. To the high intensification and differentiation of their abilities and of their world corresponds the social shackling of this development. Insofar as unfreedom is already present in wants and not just in their gratification, they must be the first to be liberated—not through an act of education or of the moral renewal of man but through an economic and political process encompassing the disposal over the means of production by the community, the reorientation of the productive process toward the needs and wants of the whole society, the shortening of the working day, and the active participation of the individuals in the administration of the whole.

When all present subjective and objective potentialities of development have been unbound, the needs and wants themselves will change. Those based on the social compulsion of repression, on injustice, and on filth and poverty would necessarily disappear. There may still be the sick, the insane, and the criminal. The realm of necessity persists; struggle with nature and even among men continues. Thus the reproduction of the whole will continue to be associated with privations for the individual. Particular interest will not coincide immediately with true interest. The difference between particular and true interest, nevertheless, is something other than the difference between particular interest and a hypostatized general interest that suppresses the individuals. In his relation to an authentic general interest, the individual would relate to truth; the demands and decisions of the whole would then preserve the individual interest and eventually promote his happiness. If the true interest, furthermore, must be represented by a general law forbidding specific wants and gratifications, such a law will no longer be a front for the particular interest of groups that maintain their power against the general interest through usurpation. Rather, it will express the rational decision of free individuals. Having come of age, men themselves will have to confront and deal with their wants. Their responsibility will be infinitely greater, because they will no longer have the false pleasure of masochistic security in the strong protection of a heteronomous power. The internal, real union of duty and happiness (and not a union effected in the world beyond), which idealist ethics had doubted, is possible only in freedom. This was Kant's intention when he founded the concept of duty on the autonomy of the person. Through its limitation to the freedom of the pure will, autonomy limits itself in favor of a social order that it could only admit in an abstract form.

If individuals, having attained majority, reject particular wants or a particular pleasure as bad, this would occur on the basis of the autonomous recognition of their true interest: the preservation of general freedom. Consequently it would occur in the interest of happiness itself, which can only exist in general freedom as the fulfillment of all developed potentialities. It was the ancient desideratum of hedonism to join in thought both happiness and truth. The problem was insoluble. For as long as an anarchic, unfree society determined the truth, the latter could only manifest itself either in the particular interest of the isolated individual or in the necessities of the hypostatized general interest, the society. In the first case its form (generality) was lost; in the second, its content (particularity).

The truth to which the liberated individual relates in happiness is both general and particular. The subject is no longer isolated in its interest against others. His life can be happy beyond the contingency of the moment, because his conditions of existence are no longer determined by a labor process which creates wealth only through the perpetuation of poverty and privation. Instead they are regulated through the rational self-administration of the whole in which the subject participates actively. The individual can relate to others as equals and to the world as his world, no longer alienated from him. Mutual understanding will no longer be permeated by unhappiness, since insight and passion will no longer come into conflict with a reified form of human relationship.

General happiness presupposes knowledge of the true interest: that the social life-process be administered in a manner which brings into harmony the freedom of individuals and the preservation of the whole on the basis of given objective historical and natural conditions. With the development of social antagonisms the connection of happiness with knowledge was obscured. The abstract reason of isolated individuals is certainly powerless over a happiness abandoned to contingency. But this very social development has also brought forth the forces which can once again bring about that connection. For the immediate producers, isolating individuation has already been abolished extensively within unfreedom: the individual has no property to preserve that can only be enjoyed at the expense of others. His interest drives him not to competition or into interest groups based in turn upon competition but rather to militant solidarity. The first goal of struggle is only a particular social group's interest in better, more humane conditions of life. But this particular interest cannot be pursued without bettering and making more humane the conditions of life of the whole and liberating the entire society. In the monopolistic phase of bourgeois society, when the preservation of the general interest on the part of the groups fighting for transformation is obvious enough, the efforts of the beneficiaries of the Establishment are directed toward splitting that solidarity. Bureaucratization, increase of wage differentials, and immediate corruption of the workers are intended to root contradictions even among these strata. Their true interest requires not piecemeal change but the reconstruction of the productive process. When this has been achieved, general reason can no longer outwit the particular interest behind the backs of the individuals. To the contrary, the particular interest becomes the active and cognitive force of the process through which generality, embodied in the community, is advanced. Only at this point in society is "the truth of *particular* satisfactions . . . the *general* satisfaction that, as happiness, the thinking will sets itself as goal."[11]

Hegel pointed out that general progress comes about in history only through particular interests, for only particular interest can stir the individual to the passion of historical struggle. "The particular interest of passion is therefore inseparable from the activity of the universal; for it is from the particular and determinate and from its negation, that the universal results." When this inseparability rests on the cunning of reason, it entails the unhappiness of individuals. In the passion with which they pursue their particular interests, they wear themselves out and are destroyed. Hegel called it a "horrible comfort" that "historical men have not been what is called happy." If no higher form of historical reason is possible than the antagonistic organization of humanity, then this horror cannot be thought away. It is true, of course, that men intend not happiness but, in each case, specific ends whose fulfillment then brings happiness. In the specific goals which are aimed at in solidary struggle for a rational society, happiness is no longer merely an attendant contingency. It is built into the very structure of the new order of the conditions of existence that have been demanded. Happiness ceases to be a mere subjective state of feeling when general concern for the potentialities of individuals is effective at the level of the liberated needs and wants of the subjects.

For Hegel, then, the struggle for the higher generality, or form of society, of the future becomes in the present the cause of particular individuals and groups, and this constitutes the tragic situation of world-historical persons. They attack social conditions in which— even if badly—the life of the whole reproduces itself. They fight against a concrete form of reason without empirical proof of the practicability of the future form which they represent. They offend against that which, within limits at least, has proven true. Their rationality necessarily operates in a particular, irrational, explosive form, and their critique of decadence and anarchy appears anarchic and destructive. Individuals who hold so fast to the Idea that it permeates their existence are unyielding and stubborn. Common sense cannot distinguish between them and criminals, and in fact in the given order they are criminals like Socrates in Athens. Universality and reason have become their own passion. The formalistic conformist, for whom one want is just as valid as another, knows of them as selfish characters who are dangerous. He sees how the critique of the appearance of freedom in the present and the knowl-

---

11. Hegel, *Enzyklopädie,* ß *478.*

edge of the future reality of freedom already constitute their happiness, because in them the blunt separation of here and there, today and tomorrow, the exclusive, defensive ego-feeling of bourgeois existence is overcome—but he cannot understand it. Whatever he may say, they are to him exalted, at best religious. For of themselves, thinks the conformist, people have only their own advantage in mind. Their paradoxical situation is apparent only to few.

Just as the attainable form of happiness can only be realized through the particular interest of only those social strata whose liberation leads not to the domination of particular interests over the community but to the general liberation of humanity, the same holds for the correct knowledge required by this form. This interest requires its ideology as a veil over the structure of truth in order to justify itself as a general interest. This interest, by its very nature, implies thinking to the end all realizable potentialities (which in the bourgeois period found their social limit in the danger of a material transformation of the whole) and keeping to the goal of their realization. The loss of correct knowledge would entail the loss of happiness as well, for the compulsion and necessity of an uncontrollable situation would once again win its contingent power over men. Freedom of knowledge is a part of real freedom, which can only exist together with common decision and action on the basis of what is known to be true. The essential role of truth for the happiness of individuals makes the characterization of happiness as pleasure and enjoyment appear insufficient. When knowledge of truth is no longer linked to knowledge of guilt, poverty, and injustice, it is no longer forced to remain external to a happiness ceded to immediate, sensual relationships. Even the most personal human relations can be opened to happiness in a really guiltless knowledge. Perhaps they would thereby become, in fact, that free community in life of which idealist morality had expected the highest unfolding of individuality. Knowledge will no longer disturb pleasure. Perhaps it can even become pleasure, which the ancient idea of *nous* had dared to see as the highest determination of knowledge. The bogey of the unchained voluptuary who would abandon himself only to his sensual wants is rooted in the separation of intellectual from material productive forces and the separation of the labor process from the process of consumption. Overcoming this separation belongs to the preconditions of freedom. The development of material wants must go together with the development of psychic and mental wants. The organization of technology, science, and art changes with their changed utilization and changed content. When they are no longer under the compulsion of a system of production based on the unhappiness of the majority, and of the pressures of rationalization, internalization, and sublimation, then mind and spirit can only mean an augmentation of happiness. Hedonism is both abolished and preserved in critical theory and practice. If freedom prevails in the spiritual and mental side of life, i.e. in culture, and if culture is no longer subject to the compulsion of internalization, then it becomes meaningless to restrict happiness to sensual pleasure.

The reality of happiness is the reality of freedom as the self-determination of liberated humanity in its common struggle with nature. "The truth of particular satisfactions is the *general* [*allgemeine*] satisfaction that, as happiness, the thinking will sets itself as goal." But this happiness is at first "generality of content only as representation, as abstraction, only as something that *should* be." Its truth is "the *universal* [*allegemeine*] determinacy of the will in itself, i.e., its own self-determination: *freedom*." For idealism, freedom was also reason: "the substance of" and "that alone which is true of spirit." In their completed form both, happiness and reason, coincide. Hegel did not believe that the realization of this form by bringing about a new form of social organization of humanity could become the task of historical practice. Under the title of the "ideal," however, he represented happiness as a "stage of world development" that is simultaneously one of reason and freedom: as the abolition of the antithesis, characteristic of the bourgeois stage of development, between individuals isolated in their particular interests, on the one hand, and the hypostatized general interests as the state that perpetuates itself through the sacrifice of individuals, on the other.

> In the ideal . . . particular individuality is supposed to remain precisely in undissolved harmony with the substantial; and insofar as the ideal partakes of the freedom and independence of subjectivity, to that extent the surrounding world of conditions and developmental structures may not possess any essential objectivity belonging to itself quite apart from the subjective and the individual. For the ideal individual should be self-contained. The objective world should still be part of what is incontestably his and not move or develop by itself, detached from the individuality of subjects. Otherwise the subject becomes merely subordinate to a world that is complete in itself.[12]

Translated by Jeremy J. Shapiro

---

12. Hegel, *Vorlesungen über die Ästhetik*. Werke X, pp. 227–28.

SOLIDARITY

My attempt to analyze the present opposition to the society organized by corporate capitalism was focused on the striking contrast between the radical and total character of the rebellion on the one hand, and the absence of a class basis for this radicalism on the other. This situation gives all efforts to evaluate and even discuss the prospects for radical change in the domain of corporate capitalism their abstract, academic, unreal character. The search for specific historical agents of revolutionary change in the advanced capitalist countries is indeed meaningless. Revolutionary forces emerge in the process of change itself; the translation of the potential into the actual is the work of political practice. And just as little as critical theory can political practice orient itself on a concept of revolution which belongs to the nineteenth and early twentieth century, and which is still valid in large areas of the Third World. This concept envisages the "seizure of power" in the course of a mass upheaval, led by a revolutionary party acting as the avantgarde of a revolutionary class and setting up a new central power which would initiate the basic social changes. Even in industrial countries where a strong Marxist party has organized the exploited masses, strategy is no longer guided by this notion—witness the long-range Communist policy of "popular fronts." And the concept is altogether inapplicable to those countries in which the integration of the working class is the result of structural economic-political processes (sustained high productivity; large markets; neo-colonialism; administered democracy) and where the masses themselves are forces of conservatism and stabilization. It is the very power of this society which contains new modes and dimensions of radical change.

The dynamic of this society has long since passed the stage where it could grow on its own resources, its own market, and on normal trade with other areas. It has grown into an imperialist power which, through economic and technical penetration and outright military intervention, has transformed large parts of the Third World into dependencies. Its policy is distinguished from classical imperialism of the preceding period by effective use of economic and technical conquests on the one hand, and by the political-strategic character of intervention on the other: the requirements of the global fight against communism supersede those of profitable investments. In any case, by virtue of the evolution of imperialism, the developments in the Third World pertain to the dynamic of the First World, and the forces of change in the former are not extraneous to the latter; the "external proletariat" is a basic factor of potential change within the dominion of corporate capitalism. Here is the coincidence of the historical factors of revolution: this predominantly agrarian proletariat endures the dual oppression exercised by the indigenous ruling classes and those of the foreign metropoles. A liberal bourgeoisie which would ally itself with the poor and lead their struggle does not exist. Kept in abject material and mental privation, they depend on a militant leadership. Since the vast majority outside the cities is unable to mount any concerted economic and political action which would threaten the existing society, the struggle for liberation will be a predominantly military one, carried out with the support of the local population, and exploiting the advantages of a terrain which impedes traditional methods of suppression. These circumstances, of necessity, make for guerrilla warfare. It is the great chance, and at the same time the terrible danger, for the forces of liberation. The powers that be will not tolerate a repetition of the Cuban example; they will employ ever more effective means and weapons of suppression, and the indigenous dictatorships will be strengthened with the ever more active aid from the imperialist metropoles. It would be romanticism to underrate the strength of this deadly alliance and its revolution to contain subversion. It seems that not the features of the terrain, nor the unimaginable resistance of the men and women of Vietnam, nor considerations of "world opinion," but fear of the other nuclear powers has so far prevented the use of nuclear or seminuclear weapons against a whole people and a whole country.

Under these circumstances, the preconditions for the liberation and development of the Third World must emerge in the advanced capitalist countries. Only the internal weakening of the superpower can finally stop the financing and equipping of suppression in the backward countries. The National Liberation Fronts threaten the life and line of imperialism; they are not only a material but also an ideological catalyst of change. The Cuban revolution and the Viet Cong have demonstrated: it can be done; there is a morality, a humanity, a will, and a faith which can resist and deter the gigantic technical and economic force of capitalist expansion. More than the "socialist humanism" of the early Marx, this violent solidarity in defense, this elemental socialism in action, has given form and substance to the radicalism of the New Left; in this ideological respect too, the external revolution has become an essential part of the opposition within the capitalist metropoles. However, the exemplary force, the ideological power of the external revolution, can come to fruition only if the internal structure and cohesion of the capitalist system begin to disintegrate. The chain of exploitation must break at its strongest link.

Corporate capitalism is not immune against economic crisis. The huge "defense" sector of the economy not only places an increasingly heavy burden on the taxpayer, it also is largely responsible for the narrowing margin of profit. The growing opposition against the war in Vietnam points up the necessity of a thorough conversion of the economy, risking the danger of rising unemployment, which is a by-product of technical progress in automation. The "peaceful" creation of additional outlets for the productivity of the metropoles would meet with the intensified resistance in the Third World, and with the contesting and competitive strength of the Soviet orbit. The absorption of unemployment and the maintenance of an adequate rate of profit would thus require the stimulation of demand on an ever larger scale, thereby stimulating the rat race of the competitive struggle for existence through the multiplication of waste, planned obsolescence, parasitic and stupid jobs and services. The higher standard of living, propelled by the growing parasitic sector of the economy, would drive wage demands toward capital's point of no return. But the structural tendencies which determine the development of corporate capitalism do not justify the assumption that aggravated class struggles would terminate in a socialist revolution through organized political action. To be sure, even the most advanced capitalist welfare state remains a class society and therefore a state of conflicting class interests. However, prior to the disintegration of the state power, the apparatus and the suppressive force of the system would keep the class struggle within the capitalist framework. The translation of the economic into the radical political struggle would be the consequence rather than the cause of change. The change itself could then occur in a general, unstructured, unorganized, and diffused process of disintegration. This process may be sparked by a crisis of the system which would activate the resistance not only against the political but also against the mental repression imposed by the society. Its insane features, expression of the ever more blatant contradiction between the available resources for liberation and their use for the perpetuation of servitude, would undermine the daily routine, the repressive conformity, and rationality required for the continued functioning of the society.

The dissolution of social morality may manifest itself in a collapse of work discipline, slowdown, spread of disobedience to rules and regulations, wildcat strikes, boycotts, sabotage, gratuitous acts of noncompliance. The violence built into the system of repression may get out of control, or necessitate ever more totalitarian controls.

Even the most totalitarian technocratic-political administration depends, for its functioning, on what is usually called the "moral fiber": a (relatively) "positive" attitude among the underlying population toward the usefulness of their work and toward the necessity of the repressions exacted by the social organization of work. A society depends on the relatively stable and calculable sanity of the people, sanity defined as the regular, socially coordinated functioning of mind and body—especially at work, in the shops and offices, but also at leisure and fun. Moreover, a society also demands to a considerable extent, belief in one's beliefs (which is part of the required sanity); belief in the operative value of society's values. Operationalism is indeed an indispensable supplement to want and fear as forces of cohesion.

Now it is the strength of this moral fiber, of the operational values (quite apart from their ideational validity), which is likely to wear off under the impact of the growing contradictions within the society. The result would be a spread, not only of discontent and mental sickness, but also of inefficiency, resistance to work, refusal to perform, negligence, indifference—factors of dysfunction which would hit a highly centralized and coordinated apparatus, where breakdown at one point may easily affect large sections of the whole. To be sure, these are subjective factors, but they may assume material force in conjunction with the objective economic and political strains to which the system will be exposed on a global scale. Then, and only then, that political climate would prevail which could provide a mass basis for the new forms of organization required for directing the struggle.

We have indicated the tendencies which threaten the stability of the imperialist society and emphasized the extent to which the liberation movements in the Third World affect the prospective development of this society. It is to an even greater extent affected by the dynamic of "peaceful coexistence" with the old socialist societies, the Soviet orbit. In important aspects, this coexistence has contributed to the stabilization of capitalism: "world communism" has been the Enemy who would have to be invented if he did not exist— the Enemy whose strength justified the "defense economy" and the mobilization of the people in the national interest. Moreover, as the common Enemy of *all* capitalism, communism promoted the organization of a common interest superseding the intercapitalist differences and conflicts. Last but not least, the opposition within the advanced capitalist countries has been seriously weakened by the repressive Stalinist development of socialism, which made socialism not exactly an attractive alternative to capitalism.

More recently, the break in the unity of the communist orbit, the triumph of the Cuban revolution, Vietnam, and the "cultural revolution" in China have changed this picture. The possibility of constructing socialism on a truly popular base, without the Stalinist bureaucratization and the danger of a nuclear war as the imperialist answer to the emergence of this kind of socialist power, has led to some sort of common interest between the Soviet Union on the one side and the United States on the other.

In a sense, this is indeed the community of interests of the "haves" against the "have nots," of the Old against the New. The "collaborationist" policy of the Soviet Union necessitates the pursuance of power politics which increasingly reduces the prospect that Soviet society, by virtue of its basic institutions alone (abolition of private ownership and control of the means of production: planned economy) is still capable of making the transition to a free society. And yet, the very dynamic of imperialist expansion places the Soviet Union in the other camp: would the effective resistance in Vietnam, and the protection of Cuba be possible without Soviet aid?

However, while we reject the unqualified convergence thesis, according to which—at least at present—the assimilation of interests prevails upon the conflict between capitalism and Soviet socialism, we cannot minimize the essential difference between the latter and the new historical efforts to construct socialism by developing and creating a genuine solidarity between the leadership and the liberated victims of exploitation. The actual may considerably deviate from the ideal, the fact remains that, for a whole generation, "freedom," "socialism," and "liberation" are inseparable from Fidel and Che and the guerrillas—not because their revolutionary struggle could furnish the model for the struggle in the metropoles, but because they have recaptured the truth of these ideas, in the day-to-day fight of men and women for a life as human beings: for a new life.

What kind of life? We are still confronted with the demand to state the "concrete alternative." The demand is meaningless if it asks for a blueprint of the specific institutions and relationships which would be those of the new society: they cannot be determined a priori; they will develop, in trial and error, as the new society develops. If we could form a concrete concept of the alternative today, it would not be that of an alternative; the possibilities of the new society are sufficiently "abstract," i.e., removed from and incongruous with the established universe to defy any attempt to identify them in terms of this universe. However, the question cannot be brushed aside by saying that what matters today is the destruction of the old, of the powers that be, making way for the emergence of the new. Such an answer neglects the essential fact that the old is not simply bad, that it delivers the goods, and that people have a real stake in it. There can be societies which are much worse—there are such societies today. The system of corporate capitalism has the right to insist that those who work for its replacement justify their action.

But the demand to state the concrete alternatives is justified for yet another reason. Negative thinking draws whatever force it may have from its empirical basis: the actual human condition in the given society, and the "given" possibilities to transcend this condition, to enlarge the realm of freedom. In this sense, negative thinking is by virtue of its own internal concepts "positive": oriented toward, and comprehending a future which is "contained" in the present. And in this containment (which is an important aspect of the general containment policy pursued by the established societies), the future appears as possible liberation. It is not the only alternative: the advent of a long period of "civilized" barbarism, with or without the nuclear destruction, is equally contained in the present. Negative thinking, and the praxis guided by it, is the positive and positing effort to prevent this utter negativity.

The concept of the primary, initial institutions of liberation is familiar enough and concrete enough: collective ownership, collective control and planning of the means of production and distribution. This is the foundation, a necessary but not sufficient condition for the alternative: it would make possible the usage of all available resources for the abolition of poverty, which is the prerequisite for the turn from quantity into quality: the creation of a reality in accordance with the new sensitivity and the new consciousness. This goal implies rejection of those policies of reconstruction, no matter how revolutionary, which are bound to perpetuate (or to introduce) the pattern of the unfree societies and their needs. Such false policy is perhaps best summed up in the formula "to catch up with, and to overtake the productivity level of the advanced capitalist countries." What is wrong with this formula is not the emphasis on the rapid improvement of the material conditions but on the model guiding their improvement. The model denies the alternative, the qualitative difference. The latter is not, and cannot be, the result of the fastest possible attainment of capitalist productivity, but rather the development of new modes and ends of production—"new" not only (and perhaps not at all) with respect to technical innovations and production relations, but with respect to the different human needs and the different human relationships in working for the satisfaction of these needs. These new relationships would be the result of a "biological" *solidarity* in work and purpose, expressive of a true harmony between social and individual needs and goals, between recognized necessity and free development—the exact opposite of the administered and enforced harmony organized in the advanced capitalist (and socialist?) countries. It is the image of this solidarity as elemental, instinctual, creative force which the young radicals see in Cuba, in the guerillas, in the Chinese cultural revolution.

Solidarity and cooperation: not all their forms are liberating. Fascism and militarism have developed a deadly efficient solidarity. Socialist solidarity is autonomy: self-determination begins at home—and that is with every I, and the We whom the I chooses. And this end must indeed appear in the means to attain it, that is to say, in the strategy of those who, within the existing society, work for the new one. If the socialist relationships of production are to be a new way of life, a new Form of life, then their existential quality must show forth, anticipated and demonstrated, in the fight for their realization. Exploitation in all its forms must have disappeared from this fight: from the work relationships among the fighters as well as from their individual relationships. Understanding, tenderness toward each other, the instinctual consciousness of that which is evil, false, the heritage of oppression, would then testify to the authenticity of the rebellion. In short, the economic, political, and cultural features of a classless society must have become the basic needs of those who fight for it. This ingression of the future into the present, this depth dimension of the rebellion accounts, in the last analysis, for the incompatibility with the traditional forms of the political struggle. The new radicalism militates against the centralized bureaucratic communist as well as against the semi-democratic liberal organization. There is a strong element of spontaneity, even anarchism, in this rebellion, expression of the new sensibility, sensitivity against domination: the feeling, the awareness, that the joy of freedom and the need to be free must precede liberation. Therefore the aversion against preestablished Leaders, apparatchiks of all sorts, politicians no matter how leftist. The initiative shifts to small groups, widely diffused, with a high degree of autonomy, mobility, flexibility.

To be sure, within the repressive society, and against its ubiquitous apparatus, spontaneity by itself cannot possibly be a radical and revolutionary force. It can become such a force only as the result of enlightenment, education, political practice—in this sense indeed, as a result of organization. The anarchic element is an essential factor in the struggle against domination: preserved but disciplined in the preparatory political action, it will be freed and *aufgehoben* in the goals of the struggle. Released for the construction of the initial revolutionary institutions, the antirepressive sensibility, allergic to domination, would militate against the prolongation of the "First Phase," that is, the authoritarian bureaucratic development of the productive forces. The new society could then reach relatively fast the level at which poverty be abolished (this level could be considerably lower than that of advanced capitalist productivity, which is geared to obscene affluence and waste). Then the development could tend toward a sensuous culture, tangibly contrasting with the gray-on-gray culture of the socialist societies of Eastern Europe. Production would be redirected in defiance of all the rationality of the Performance Principle; socially necessary labor would be diverted to the construction of an aesthetic rather than repressive environment, to parks and gardens rather than highways and parking lots, to the creation of areas of withdrawal rather than massive fun and relaxation. Such redistribution of socially necessary labor (time), incompatible with any society governed by the Profit and Performance Principle, would gradually alter society in all its dimensions—it would mean the ascent of the Aesthetic Principle as Form of the Reality Principle: a culture of receptivity based on the achievements of industrial civilization and initiating the end of its self-propelling productivity.

Not regression to a previous stage of civilization, but return to an imaginary *temps perdu* in the real life of mankind: progress to a stage of civilization where man has learned to ask for the sake of whom or of what he organizes his society; the stage where he checks and perhaps even halts his incessant struggle for existence on an enlarged scale, surveys what has been achieved through centuries of misery and hecatombs of victims, and decides that it is enough, and that it is time to enjoy what he has and what can be reproduced and refined with a minimum of alienated labor: not the arrest or reduction of technical progress, but the elimination of those of its features which perpetuate man's subjection to the apparatus and the intensification of the struggle for existence—to work harder in order to get more of the merchandise that has to be sold. In other words, electrification indeed, and all technical devices which alleviate and protect life, all the mechanization which frees human energy and time, all the standardization which does away with spurious and parasitarian "personalized" services rather than multiplying them and the gadgets and tokens of exploitative affluence. In terms of the latter (and only in terms of the latter), this would certainly be a regression—but freedom from the rule of merchandise over man is a precondition of freedom.

The construction of a free society would create new incentives for work. In the exploitative societies, the so-called work instinct is mainly the (more or less effectively) introjected necessity to perform productively in order to earn a living. But the life instincts themselves strive for the unification and enhancement of life; in nonrepressive sublimation they would provide the libidinal energy for work on the development of a reality which no longer demands the exploitative repression of the Pleasure Principle. The "incentives" would then be built into the instinctual structure of men. Their sensibility would register, as biological reactions, the difference between the ugly and the beautiful, between calm and noise, tenderness and brutality, intelligence and stupidity, joy and fun, and it would correlate this distinction with that between freedom and servitude. Freud's last theoretical conception recognizes the erotic instincts as work instincts—work for the creation of a sensuous environment. The social expression of the liberated work instinct is *cooperation*, which, grounded in solidarity, directs the organization of the realm of necessity and the development of the realm of freedom. And there is an answer to the question which troubles the minds of so many men of good will: what are the people in a free society going to do? The answer which, I believe, strikes at the heart of the matter was given by a young black girl. She said: for the first time in our life, we shall be free to think about what we are going to do.

THE CATASTROPHE OF LIBERATION

Positive thinking and its neo-positivist philosophy counteract the historical content of rationality. This content is never an extraneous factor or meaning which can or cannot be included in the analysis; it enters into conceptual thought as constitutive factor and determines the validity of its concepts. To the degree to which the established society is irrational, the analysis in terms of historical rationality introduces into the concept the negative element—critique, contradiction, and transcendence.

This element cannot be assimilated with the positive. It changes the concept in its entirety, in its intent and validity. Thus, in the analysis of an economy, capitalist or not, which operates as an "independent" power over and above the individuals, the negative features (overproduction, unemployment, insecurity, waste, repression) are not comprehended as long as they appear merely as more or less inevitable by-products, as "the other side" of the story of growth and progress.

True, a totalitarian administration may promote the efficient exploitation of resources; the nuclear-military establishment may provide millions of jobs through enormous purchasing power; toil and ulcers may be the by-product of the acquisition of wealth and responsibility; deadly blunders and crimes on the part of the leaders may be merely the way of life. One is willing to admit economic and political madness—and one buys it. But this sort of knowledge of "the other side" is part and parcel of the solidification of the state of affairs, of the grand unification of opposites which counteracts qualitative change, because it pertains to a thoroughly hopeless or thoroughly preconditioned existence that has made its home in a world where even the irrational is Reason.

The tolerance of positive thinking is enforced tolerance—enforced not by any terroristic agency but by the overwhelming, anonymous power and efficiency of the technological society. As such it permeates the general consciousness—and the consciousness of the critic. The absorption of the negative by the positive is validated in the daily experience, which obfuscates the distinction between rational appearance and irrational reality. Here are some banal examples of this harmonization:

(1) I ride in a new automobile. I experience its beauty, shininess, power, convenience—but then I become aware of the fact

that in a relatively short time it will deteriorate and need repair; that its beauty and surface are cheap, its power unnecessary, its size idiotic; and that I will not find a parking place. I come to think of *my* car as a product of one of the Big Three automobile corporations. The latter determine the appearance of my car and make its beauty as well as its cheapness, its power as well as its shakiness, its working as well as its obsolescence. In a way, I feel cheated. I believe that the car is not what it could be, that better cars could be made for less money. But the other guy has to live, too. Wages and taxes are too high; turnover is necessary; we have it much better than before. The tension between appearance and reality melts away and both merge in one rather pleasant feeling.

(2) I take a walk in the country. Everything is as it should be: Nature at its best. Birds, sun, soft grass, a view through the trees of the mountains, nobody around, no radio, no smell of gasoline. Then the path turns and ends on the highway. I am back among the billboards, service stations, motels, and roadhouses. I was in a National Park, and I now know that this was not reality. It was a "reservation," something that is being preserved like a species dying out. If it were not for the government, the billboards, hot dog stands, and motels would long since have invaded that piece of Nature. I am grateful to the government; we have it much better than before. . . .

(3) The subway during evening rush hour. What I see of the people are tired faces and limbs, hatred and anger. I feel someone might at any moment draw a knife—just so. They read, or rather they are soaked in their newspaper or magazine or paperback. And yet, a couple of hours later, the same people, deodorized, washed, dressed-up or down, may be happy and tender, really smile, and forget (or remember). But most of them will probably have some awful togetherness or aloneness at home.

These examples may illustrate the happy marriage of the positive and the negative—the *objective* ambiguity which adheres to the data of experience. It is objective ambiguity because the shift in my sensations and reflections responds to the manner in which the experienced facts are actually interrelated. But this interrelation, if comprehended, shatters the harmonizing consciousness and its false realism. Critical thought strives to define the irrational character of the established rationality (which becomes increasingly obvious) and to define the tendencies which cause this rationality to generate its own transformation. "Its own" because, as historical totality, it has developed forces and capabilities which themselves become projects beyond the established totality. They are possibilities of the advancing technological rationality and, as such, they involve the whole of society. The technological transformation is at the same time political transformation, but the political change would turn into qualitative social change only to the degree to which it would alter the direction of technical progress—that is, develop a new technology. For the established technology has become an instrument of destructive politics.

Such qualitative change would be transition to a higher stage of civilization if technics were designed and utilized for the pacification of the struggle for existence. In order to indicate the disturbing implications of this statement, I submit that such a new direction of technical progress would be the catastrophe of the established direction, not merely the quantitative evolution of the prevailing (scientific and technological) rationality but rather its catastrophic transformation, the emergence of a new idea of Reason, theoretical and practical.

The new idea of Reason is expressed in Whitehead's proposition: "The function of Reason is to promote the art of life." In view of this end, Reason is the "direction of the attack on the environment" which derives from the "threefold urge: (1) to live, (2) to live well, (3) to live better."[1]

Whitehead's propositions seem to describe the actual development of Reason as well as its failure. Or rather they seem to suggest that Reason is still to be discovered, recognized, and realized, for hitherto the historical function of Reason has also been to repress and even destroy the urge to live, to live well, and to live better—or to postpone and put an exorbitantly high price on the fulfillment of this urge.

In Whitehead's definition of the function of Reason, the term "art" connotes the element of determinate negation. Reason, in its application to society, has thus far been opposed to art, while art was granted the privilege of being rather irrational—not subject to scientific, technological, and operational Reason. The rationality of domination has separated the Reason of science and the Reason of

---

1. A. N. Whitehead, *The Function of Reason* (Boston: Beacon Press, 1959).

art, or, it has falsified the Reason of art by integrating art into the universe of domination. It was a separation because, from the beginning, science contained the aesthetic Reason, the free play and even the folly of imagination, the fantasy of transformation; science indulged in the rationalization of possibilities. However, this free play retained the commitment to the prevailing unfreedom in which it was born and from which it abstracted; the possibilities with which science played were also those of liberation—of a higher truth.

Here is the original link (within the universe of domination and scarcity) between science, art, and philosophy. It is the consciousness of the discrepancy between the real and the possible, between the apparent and the authentic truth, and the effort to comprehend and to master this discrepancy. One of the primary forms in which this discrepancy found expression was the distinction between gods and men, finiteness and infinity, change and permanence. Something of this mythological interrelation between the real and the possible survived in scientific thought, and it continued to be directed toward a more rational and true reality. Mathematics was held to be real and "good" in the same sense as Plato's metaphysical Ideas. How then did the development of the former become *science*, while that of the latter remained metaphysics?

The most obvious answer is that, to a great extent, the *scientific* abstractions entered and proved their truth in the actual conquest and transformation of nature, while the *philosophic* abstractions did not—and could not. For the conquest and transformation of nature occurred within a law and order of life which philosophy transcended, subordinating it to the "good life" of a different law and order. And this other order, which presupposed a high degree of freedom from toil, ignorance, and poverty, was *unreal*, at the origins of philosophic thought and throughout its development, while scientific thought continued to be applicable to an increasingly powerful and universal *reality*. The final philosophic concepts remained indeed metaphysical; they were not and could not be verified in terms of the established universe of discourse and action.

But if this is the situation, then the case of metaphysics, and especially of the meaningfulness and truth of metaphysical propositions, is a historical case. That is, historical rather than purely epistemological conditions determine the truth, the cognitive value of such propositions. Like all propositions that claim truth, they must be verifiable; they must stay within the universe of possible experience. This universe is never co-extensive with the established one but extends to the limits of the world which can be created by transforming the established one, with the means which the latter has provided or withheld. The range of verifiability in this sense grows in the course of history. Thus, the speculations about the Good Life, the Good Society, Permanent Peace obtain an increasingly realistic content; on technological grounds, the metaphysical tends to become physical.

Moreover, if the truth of metaphysical propositions is determined by their historical content (i.e., by the degree to which they define historical possibilities), then the relation between metaphysics and science is strictly historical. In our own culture, at least, that part of Saint-Simon's Law of the Three Stages is still taken for granted which stipulates that the metaphysical *precedes* the scientific stage of civilization. But is this sequence a final one? Or does the scientific transformation of the world contain its own metaphysical transcendence?

At the advanced stage of industrial civilization, scientific rationality, translated into political power, appears to be the decisive factor in the development of historical alternatives. The question then arises: does this power tend toward its own negation—that is, toward the promotion of the "art of life"? Within the established societies, the continued application of scientific rationality would have reached a terminal point with the mechanization of all socially necessary but individually repressive labor ("socially necessary" here includes all performances which can be exercised more effectively by machines, even if these performances produce luxuries and waste rather than necessities). But this stage would also be the end and limit of the scientific rationality in its established structure and direction. Further progress would mean the *break*, the turn of quantity into quality. It would open the possibility of an essentially new human reality—namely, existence in free time on the basis of fulfilled vital needs. Under such conditions, the scientific project itself would be free for trans-utilitarian ends, and free for the "art of living" beyond the necessities and luxuries of domination. In other words, the completion of the technological reality would be not only the prerequisite, but also the rationale for *transcending* the technological reality.

This would mean reversal of the traditional relationship between science and metaphysics. The ideas defining reality in terms other than those of the exact or behavioral sciences would lose their metaphysical or emotive character as a result of the scientific transformation of the world; the scientific concepts could project and define the possible realities of a free and pacified existence. The elaboration of such concepts would mean more than the evolution of the prevailing sciences. It would involve the scientific rationality as a whole, which has thus far been committed to an unfree existence and would mean a new idea of science, of Reason.

If the completion of the technological project involves a break with the prevailing technological rationality, the break in turn depends on the continued existence of the technical base itself. For it is this base which has rendered possible the satisfaction of needs and the reduction of toil—it remains the very base of all forms of human freedom. The qualitative change rather lies in the reconstruction of this base—that is, in its development with a view of different ends.

I have stressed that this does not mean the revival of "values," spiritual or other, which are to supplement the scientific and technological transformation of man and nature. On the contrary, the historical achievement of science and technology has rendered possible the *translation of values into technical tasks*—the materialization of values. Consequently, what is at stake is the redefinition of values in *technical terms,* as elements in the technological process. The new ends, as technical ends, would then operate in the project and in the construction of the machinery, and not only in its utilization. Moreover, the new ends might assert themselves even in the construction of scientific hypotheses—in pure scientific theory. From the quantification of secondary qualities, science would proceed to the quantification of values.

For example, what is calculable is the minimum of labor with which, and the extent to which, the vital needs of all members of a society could be satisfied—provided the available resources were used for this end, without being restricted by other interests, and without impeding the accumulation of capital necessary for the development of the respective society. In other words, quantifiable is the available range of freedom from want. Or, calculable is the degree to which, under the same conditions, care could be provided for the ill, the infirm, and the aged—that is, quantifiable is the possible reduction of anxiety, the possible freedom from fear.

The obstacles that stand in the way of materialization are definable political obstacles. Industrial civilization has reached the point where, with respect to the aspirations of man for a human existence, the scientific abstraction from final causes becomes obsolete in science's own terms. Science itself has rendered it possible to make final causes the proper domain of science. Society, through a raising and enlarging of the technical sphere, must treat *as technical* problems, questions of finality considered wrongly as ethical and sometimes religious. The *incompleteness* of technics makes a fetish of problems of finality and enslaves man to ends which he thinks of as absolutes (Gilbert Simondon).

Under this aspect, "neutral" scientific method and technology become the science and technology of a historical phase which is being surpassed by its own achievements—which has reached its determinate negation. Instead of being separated from science and scientific method, and left to subjective preference and irrational, transcendental sanction, formerly metaphysical ideas of liberation may become the proper object of science. But this development confronts science with the unpleasant task of becoming *political*—of recognizing scientific consciousness as political consciousness, and the scientific enterprise as political enterprise. For the transformation of values into needs, of final causes into technical possibilities is a new stage in the conquest of oppressive, unmastered forces in society as well as in nature. It is an act of *liberation:*

> Man liberates himself from his situation of being subjected to the finality of everything by learning to create finality, to organise a "finalised" whole, which he judges and evaluates. Man overcomes enslavement by organising consciously finality. (Simondon)

However, in constituting themselves *methodically* as political enterprise, science and technology would *pass beyond* the stage at which they were, because of their neutrality, *subjected* to politics and against their intent functioning as political instrumentalities. For the technological redefinition of the technical mastery of final causes *is* the construction, development, and utilization of resources (material and intellectual) *freed* from all *particular* interests which impede the satisfaction of human needs and the evolution of human faculties. In other words, it is the rational enterprise of man as man, of mankind. Technology thus may provide the historical correction of the premature identification of Reason and Freedom, according to which man can become and remain free in the progress of self-perpetuating productivity on the basis of oppression. To the extent to which technology has developed on this basis, the correction can never be the result of technical progress per se. It involves a political reversal.

Industrial society possesses the instrumentalities for transforming the metaphysical into the physical, the inner into the outer, the adventures of the mind into adventures of technology. The terrible phrases (and realities of) "engineers of the soul," "head shrinkers," "scientific management," "science of consumption," epitomize (in a miserable form) the progressing rationalization of the irrational, of the "spiritual"—the denial of the idealistic culture. But the consummation of technological rationality, while translating ideology into reality, would also transcend the materialistic antithesis to this culture. For the translation of values into needs is the twofold process of (1) material satisfaction (materialization of freedom) and (2) the free development of needs on the basis of satisfaction (non-repressive sublimation). In this process, the relation between the material and intellectual faculties and needs undergoes a fundamental change. The free play of thought and imagination assumes a rational and directing function in the realization of a pacified existence of man and nature. And the ideas of justice, freedom, and humanity then obtain their truth and good conscience on the sole ground on which they could even have truth and good conscience—the satisfaction of man's material needs, the rational organization of the realm of necessity.

"Pacified existence." The phrase conveys poorly enough the intent to sum up, in one guiding idea, the tabooed and ridiculed *end* of technology, the repressed final cause behind the scientific enterprise. If this final cause were to materialize and become effective, the Logos of technics would open a universe of qualitatively different relations between man and man, and man and nature.

But at this point, a strong caveat must be stated—a warning against all technological fetishism. Such fetishism has recently been exhibited mainly among Marxist critics of contemporary industrial society—ideas of the future omnipotence of technological man, of a "technological Eros," etc. The hard kernel of truth in these ideas demands an emphatic denunciation of the mystification which they express. Technics, as a universe of instrumentalities, may increase the weakness as well as the power of man. At the present stage, he is perhaps more powerless over his own apparatus than he ever was before.

The mystification is not removed by transferring technological omnipotence from particular groups to the new state and the central plan. Technology retains throughout its dependence on other than technological ends. The more technological rationality, freed from its exploitative features, determines social production, the more will it become dependent on political direction—on the collective effort to attain a pacified existence, with the goals which the free individuals may set for themselves.

"Pacification of existence" does not suggest an accumulation of power but rather the opposite. Peace and power, freedom and power, Eros and power may well be contraries! I shall presently try to show that the reconstruction of the material base of society with a view to pacification may involve a qualitative as well as quantitative *reduction* of power, in order to create the space and time for the development of productivity under self-determined incentives. The notion of such a reversal of power is a strong motive in dialectical theory.

To the degree to which the goal of pacification determines the Logos of technics, it alters the relation between technology and its primary object, Nature. Pacification presupposes mastery of Nature, which is and remains the object opposed to the developing subject. But there are two kinds of mastery: a repressive and a liberating one. The latter involves the reduction of misery, violence, and cruelty. In Nature as well as in History, the struggle for existence is the token of scarcity, suffering, and want. They are the qualities of blind matter, of the realm of immediacy in which life passively suffers its existence. This realm is gradually mediated in the course of the historical transformation of Nature; it becomes part of the human world, and to this extent, the qualities of Nature are historical qualities. In the process of civilization, Nature ceases to be mere Nature to the degree to which the struggle of blind forces is comprehended and mastered in the light of freedom.

History is the negation of Nature. What is only natural is overcome and recreated by the power of Reason. The metaphysical notion that Nature comes to itself in history points to the unconquered limits of Reason. It claims them as historical limits—as a task yet to be accomplished, or rather yet to be undertaken. If Nature is in itself a rational, legitimate object of science, then it is the legitimate object not only of Reason as power but also of Reason as freedom; not only of domination but also of liberation. With the emergence of man as the *animal rationale*—capable of transforming Nature in accordance with the faculties of the mind and the capacities of matter—the merely natural, as the sub-rational, assumes negative status. It becomes a realm to be comprehended and organized by Reason.

And to the degree to which Reason succeeds in subjecting matter to rational standards and aims, all sub-rational existence appears to be want and privation, and their reduction becomes the historical task. Suffering, violence, and destruction are categories of the natural as well as human reality, of a helpless and heartless universe. The terrible notion that the sub-rational life of nature is destined to remain forever such a universe, is neither a philosophic nor a scientific one; it was pronounced by a different authority:

> When the Society for the Prevention of Cruelty to Animals asked the Pope for his support, he refused it, on the ground that human beings owe no duty to lower animals, and that ill-treating animals is not sinful. This is because animals have no souls. (Bertrand Russell)

Materialism, which is not tainted by such ideological abuse of the soul, has a more universal and realistic concept of salvation. It admits the reality of Hell only at one definite place, here on earth, and asserts that this Hell was created by Man (and by Nature). Part of this Hell is the ill-treatment of animals—the work of a human society whose rationality is still the irrational.

All joy and all happiness derive from the ability to transcend nature—a transcendence in which the mastery of Nature is itself subordinated to liberation and pacification of existence. All tranquillity, all delight is the result of conscious *mediation*, of autonomy and contradiction. Glorification of the natural is part of the ideology which protects an unnatural society in its struggle against liberation. The defamation of birth control is a striking example. In some backward areas of the world, it is also "natural" that black races are inferior to white, and that the dogs get the hindmost, and that business must be. It is also natural that big fish eat little fish—though it may not seem natural to the little fish. Civilization produces the means for freeing Nature from its own brutality, its own insufficiency, its own blindness, by virtue of the cognitive and transforming power of Reason. And Reason can fulfill this function only as post-technological rationality, in which technics is itself the instrumentality of pacification, organon of the "art of life." The function of Reason then converges with the function of *Art*.

The Greek notion of the affinity between art and technics may serve as a preliminary illustration. The artist possesses the ideas which, as final causes, guide the construction of certain things—just as the engineer possesses the ideas which guide, as final causes, the construction of a machine. For example, the idea of an abode for human beings determines the architect's construction of a house; the idea of wholesale nuclear explosion determines the construction of the apparatus which is to serve this purpose. Emphasis on the essential relation between art and technics points up the specific *rationality* of art.

Like technology, art creates another universe of thought and practice against and within the existing one. But in contrast to the technical universe, the artistic universe is one of illusion, semblance, *Schein*. However, this semblance is resemblance to a reality which exists as the threat and promise of the established one. In various forms of mask and silence, the artistic universe is organized by the images of a life without fear—in mask and silence because art is without power to bring about this life, and even without power to represent it adequately. Still, the powerless, illusory truth of art (which has never been more powerless and more illusory than today, when it has become an omnipresent ingredient of the administered society) testifies to the validity of its images. The more blatantly irrational the society becomes, the greater the rationality of the artistic universe.

Technological civilization establishes a specific relation between art and technics. I mentioned above the notion of a reversal of the Law of the Three Stages and of a "revalidation" of metaphysics *on the basis* of the scientific and technological transformation of the world. The same notion may now be extended to the relation between science-technology and art. The rationality of art, its ability to "project" existence, to define yet unrealized possibilities could then be envisaged as *validated by and functioning in the scientific-technological transformation of the world.* Rather than being the handmaiden of the established apparatus, beautifying its business and its misery, art would become a technique for destroying this business and this misery.

The technological rationality of art seems to be characterized by an aesthetic "reduction":

> Art is able to reduce the apparatus which the external appearance requires in order to preserve itself—reduction to the limits in which the external may become the manifestation of spirit and freedom.

According to Hegel, art reduces the immediate contingency in which an object (or a totality of objects) exists, to a state in which the object takes on the form and quality of freedom. Such transformation is reduction because the contingent situation suffers requirements which are external, and which stand in the way of its free realization. These requirements constitute an "apparatus" inasmuch as they are not merely natural but rather subject to free, rational change and development. Thus, the artistic transformation violates the natural object, but the violated is itself oppressive; thus the aesthetic transformation is liberation.

The aesthetic reduction appears in the technological transformation of Nature where and if it succeeds in linking mastery and liberation, directing mastery toward liberation. In this case, the conquest of Nature reduces the blindness, ferocity, and fertility of Nature—which implies reducing the ferocity of man against Nature. Cultivation of the soil is qualitatively different from destruction of the soil, extraction of natural resources from wasteful exploitation, clearing of forests from wholesale deforestation. Poverty, disease, and cancerous growth are natural as well as human ills—their reduction and removal is liberation of life. Civilization has achieved this "other," liberating transformation in its gardens and parks and reservations. But outside these small, protected areas, it has treated Nature as it has treated man—as an instrument of destructive productivity.

In the technology of pacification, aesthetic categories would enter to the degree to which the productive machinery is constructed with a view of the free play of faculties. But against all "technological Eros" and similar misconceptions, "labor cannot become play . . ." Marx's statement precludes rigidly all romantic interpretation of the "abolition of labor." The idea of such a millennium is as ideological in advanced industrial civilization as it was in the Middle Ages, and perhaps even more so. For man's struggle with Nature is increasingly a struggle with his society, whose powers over the individual become more "rational" and therefore more necessary than ever before. However, while the realm of necessity continues, its organization with a view of qualitatively different ends would change not only the mode, but also the extent of socially necessary production. And this change in turn would affect the human agents of production and their needs:

> free time transforms its possessor into a different Subject, and as different Subject he enters the process of immediate production. (Marx)

I have recurrently emphasized the historical character of human needs. Above the animal level even the necessities of life in a free and rational society will be other than those produced in and for an irrational and unfree society. Again, it is the concept of "reduction" which may illustrate the difference.

In the contemporary era, the conquest of scarcity is still confined to small areas of advanced industrial society. Their prosperity covers up the Inferno inside and outside their borders; it also spreads a repressive productivity and "false needs." It is repressive precisely to the degree to which it promotes the satisfaction of needs which require continuing the rat race of catching up with one's peers and with planned obsolescence, enjoying freedom from using the brain, working with and for the means of destruction. The obvious comforts generated by this sort of productivity, and even more, the support which it gives to a system of profitable domination, facilitate its importation in less advanced areas of the world where the introduction of such a system still means tremendous progress in technical and human terms.

However, the close interrelation between technical and political-manipulative know-how, between profitable productivity and domination, lends to the conquest of scarcity the weapons for continuing liberation. To a great extent, it is the sheer *quantity* of goods, services, work, and recreation in the overdeveloped countries which effectuates this containment. Consequently, qualitative change seems to presuppose a *quantitative* change in the advanced standard of living, namely, *reduction of overdevelopment.*

The standard of living attained in the most advanced industrial areas is not a suitable model of development if the aim is pacification. In view of what this standard has made of Man and Nature, the question must again be asked whether it is worth the sacrifices and the victims made in its defense. The question has ceased to be irresponsible since the "affluent society" has become a society of permanent mobilization against the risk of annihilation, and since the sale of its goods has been accompanied by moronization, the perpetuation of toil, and the promotion of frustration.

Under these circumstances, liberation from the affluent society does not mean return to healthy and robust poverty, moral cleanliness, and simplicity. On the contrary, the elimination of profitable waste would increase the social wealth available for distribution, and the end of permanent mobilization would reduce the social need for the denial of satisfactions that are the individual's own—denials which now find their compensation in the cult of fitness, strength, and regularity.

Today, in the prosperous warfare and welfare state, the human qualities of a pacified existence seem asocial and unpatriotic—qualities such as the refusal of all toughness, togetherness, and brutality; disobedience to the tyranny of the majority; profession of fear and weakness (the most rational reaction to this society!); a sensitive intelligence sickened by that which is being perpetrated; the commitment to the feeble and ridiculed actions of protest and refusal. These expressions of humanity, too, will be marred by necessary compromise—by the need to cover oneself, to be capable of cheating the cheaters, and to live and think in spite of them. In the totalitarian society, the human attitudes tend to become escapist attitudes, to follow Samuel Beckett's advice: "Don't wait to be hunted to hide. . . ."

Even such personal withdrawal of mental and physical energy from socially required activities and attitudes is today possible only for a few; it is only an inconsequential aspect of the redirection of energy which must precede pacification. Beyond the personal realm, self-determination presupposes free available energy which is not expended in superimposed material and intellectual labor. It must be free energy also in the sense that it is not channeled into the handling of goods and services which satisfy the individual, while rendering him incapable of achieving an existence of his own, unable to grasp the possibilities which are repelled by his satisfaction. Comfort, business, and job security in a society which prepares itself for and against nuclear destruction may serve as a universal example of enslaving contentment. Liberation of energy from the performances required to sustain destructive prosperity means decreasing the high standard of servitude in order to enable the individuals to develop that rationality which may render possible a pacified existence.

A new standard of living, adapted to the pacification of existence, also presupposes reduction in the future population. It is understandable, even reasonable, that industrial civilization considers legitimate the slaughter of millions of people in war, and the daily sacrifices of all those who have no adequate care and protection, but discovers its moral and religious scruples if it is the question of avoiding the production of more life in a society which is still geared to the planned annihilation of life in the National Interest, and to the unplanned deprivation of life on behalf of private interests. These moral scruples are understandable and reasonable because such a society needs an ever-increasing number of customers and supporters; the constantly regenerated excess capacity must be managed.

However, the requirements of profitable mass production are not necessarily identical with those of mankind. The problem is not only (and perhaps not even primarily) that of adequately feeding and caring for the growing population—it is first a problem of number, of mere quantity. There is more than poetic license in the indictment which Stefan George pronounced half a century ago: ``*Schon eure Zahl ist Frevel!*''

The crime is that of a society in which the growing population aggravates the struggle for existence in the face of its possible alleviation. The drive for more "living space" operates not only in international aggressiveness but also *within* the nation. Here, expansion has, in all forms of teamwork, community life, and fun, invaded the inner space of privacy and practically eliminated the possibility of that isolation in which the individual, thrown back on himself alone, can think and question and find. This sort of privacy—the sole condition that, on the basis of satisfied vital needs, can give meaning to freedom and independence of thought—has long since become the most expensive commodity, available only to the very rich (who don't use it). In this respect, too, "culture" reveals its feudal origins and limitations. It can become democratic only through the abolition of mass democracy, i.e., if society has succeeded in restoring the prerogatives of privacy by granting them to all and protecting them for each.

To the denial of freedom, even of the possibility of freedom, corresponds the granting of liberties where they strengthen the repression. The degree to which the population is allowed to break the peace wherever there still is peace and silence, to be ugly and to uglify things, to ooze familiarity, to offend against good form is frightening. It is frightening because it expresses the lawful and even organized effort to reject the Other in his own right, to prevent autonomy even in a small, reserved sphere of existence. In the overdeveloped countries, an ever-larger part of the population becomes one huge captive audience—captured not by a totalitarian regime but by the liberties of the citizens whose media of amusement and elevation compel the Other to partake of their sounds, sights, and smells.

Can a society which is incapable of protecting individual privacy even within one's four walls rightfully claim that it respects the individual and that it is a free society? To be sure, a free society is defined by more, and by more fundamental achievements, than private autonomy. And yet, the absence of the latter vitiates even the most conspicuous institutions of economic and political freedom—by denying freedom at its hidden roots. Massive socialization begins at home and arrests the development of consciousness and conscience. The attainment of autonomy demands conditions in which the repressed dimensions of experience can come to life again; their liberation demands repression of the heteronomous needs and satisfactions which organize life in this society. The more they have become the individual's own needs and satisfactions, the more would their repression appear to be an all but fatal deprivation. But precisely by virtue of this fatal character, it may create the primary subjective prerequisite for qualitative change—namely, the *redefinition of needs.*

To take an (unfortunately fantastic) example: the mere absence of all advertising and of all indoctrinating media of information and entertainment would plunge the individual into a traumatic void where he would have the chance to wonder and to think, to know himself (or rather the negative of himself) and his society. Deprived of his false fathers, leaders, friends, and representatives, he would have to learn his ABCs again. But the words and sentences which he would form might come out very differently, and so might his aspirations and fears.

To be sure, such a situation would be an unbearable nightmare. While the people can support the continuous creation of nuclear weapons, radioactive fallout, and questionable foodstuffs, they cannot (for this very reason!) tolerate being deprived of the entertainment and education which make them capable of reproducing the arrangements for their defense and/or destruction. The nonfunctioning of television and the allied media might thus begin to achieve what the inherent contradictions of capitalism did not achieve—the disintegration of the system. The creation of repressive needs has long since become part of socially necessary labor—necessary in the sense that without it, the established mode of production would not be sustained. Neither problems of psychology nor of aesthetics are at stake, but the material base of domination.

Norbert Elias

THE CIVILIZING PROCESS: INTRODUCTION

1

In thinking and theorizing about the structure and controls of human affects nowadays, we are usually content to use as evidence observations from the more developed societies of today. We thus proceed from the tacit assumption that it is possible to construct theories about the affect structures of man in general on the basis of studies of people in a specific society that can be observed here and now—our own. However, there are numerous relatively accessible observations which point to the conclusion that the standard and pattern of affect controls in societies at different stages of development, and even in different strata of the same society, can differ. Whether we are concerned with the development of European countries, which has lasted for centuries, or with the so-called developing countries in other parts of the world, we are constantly confronted by observations which give rise to the following question: how and why, in the course of the overall transformations of society which take place over long time spans and in a particular direction—for which the term "development" has been adopted—is the affectivity of human behavior and experience, the control of individual affects by external and internal constraints, and in this sense the structure of all forms of human expression altered in a particular direction? Such changes are indicated in everyday speech by such statements as that the people of our own society are more "civilized" than they were earlier, or that those of other societies are more "uncivilized" (or even more "barbaric") than those of our own. The value judgments contained in such statements are obvious; the facts to which they relate are less so. This is partly because empirical investigations of long-term transformations of personality structures, and especially of affect controls, give rise at the present stage of sociological research to very considerable difficulties. At the forefront of sociological interest at present are relatively short-term processes, and usually only problems relating to a given state of society. Long-term transformations of social structures, and therefore of personality structures as well, have by and large been lost to view.

The present study is concerned with these long-term processes. Understanding of it may be aided by a brief indication of the various kinds of such processes. To begin with, two main directions in the structural changes of societies may be distinguished: those tending toward increased differentiation and integration, and those tending toward decreased differentiation and integration. In addition, there is a third type of social process, in the course of which the structure of a society or of its particular aspects is changed, but without a tendency toward either an increase or a decrease in the level of differentiation and integration. Finally, there are countless changes in a society which do not involve a change in its structure. This account does not do justice to the full complexity of such changes, for there are numerous hybrid forms, and often several types of change, even in society. But for the present, this brief outline of the different types of change suffices to indicate the problems with which this study is concerned.

This first volume addresses itself above all to the question of whether the supposition, based on scattered observations, that there are long-term changes in the affect and control structures of people in particular societies—changes which follow one and the same direction over a large number of generations—can be confirmed by reliable evidence and proved to be factually correct. This volume therefore contains an account of sociological procedures and findings, the best-known counterpart of which in the physical sciences is the experiment and its results. It is concerned with the discovery and elucidation of what actually takes place in the as yet unexplored field of inquiry to which our questions relate: the discovery and definition of factual connections.

The demonstration of a change in human affect and control structures taking place over a large number of generations in the same direction—to state it briefly, the increased tightening and differentiation of controls—gives rise to a further question. Is it possible to relate this long-term change in personality structures with long-term structural changes in society as a whole, which likewise tend in a particular direction, toward a higher level of social differentiation and integration? The second volume is concerned with these problems.

For these long-term structural changes of society, empirical evidence is likewise lacking. It has therefore been necessary to devote a part of the second volume to the discovery and elucidation of factual connections in this second area. The question is whether a structural change of society as a whole, tending toward a higher level of differentiation of integration, can be demonstrated with the aid of reliable empirical evidence. This proves possible. The process of the formation of nation states, discussed in the second volume, is an example of this kind of structural change.

Finally, in a provisional sketch of a theory of civilization, a model is evolved to show the possible connections between the long-term change in human personality structures toward a consolidation and differentiation of affect controls, and the long-term change in the social structure toward a higher level of differentiation and integration—for example, toward a differentiation and prolongation of the chains of interdependence and a consolidation of "state controls."

2

It can readily be seen that in adopting an approach directed at factual connections and their explanation (that is, an empirical and theoretical approach concerned with long-term structural changes of a specific kind, or "developments"), we take leave of the metaphysical ideas which connect the concept of development either to the notion of a mechanical necessity or to that of a teleological purpose. The concept of civilization, as the first chapter of this volume shows, has often been used in a semimetaphysical sense and has remained highly nebulous until today. Here, the attempt is made to isolate the factual core to which the current prescientific notion of the civilizing process refers. This core consists primarily of the structural change in people toward an increased consolidation and differentiation of their affect controls, and therefore both of their experience (e.g., in the form of an advance in the threshold of shame and revulsion) and of their behavior (e.g., in the differentiation of the implements used at table). The next task posed by the demonstration of such a change in a specific direction over many generations is to provide an explanation. A sketch of one is to be found, as already mentioned, at the end of the second volume.

But with the aid of such an investigation we likewise take leave of the theories of social change predominant today, which in the course of time have taken the place in sociological inquiry of an earlier one centered on the old, semimetaphysical notion of development. As far as can be seen, these current theories scarcely ever distinguish in an unambiguous way between the different types of social change briefly mentioned earlier. In particular, there is still a lack of theories based on empirical evidence to explain the type of long-term social changes which take the form of a process and, above all, of a development.

When I was working on this book it seemed quite clear to me that I was laying the foundation of an undogmatic, empirically based sociological theory of social processes in general and of social development in particular. I believed it quite obvious that the investigation, and the concluding model of the long-term process of state formation to be found in the second volume, could serve equally as a model of the long-term dynamic of societies in a particular direction, to which the concept of social development refers. I did not believe at that time that it was necessary to point out explicitly that this study was neither of an "evolution" in the nineteenth-century sense of an automatic progress, nor of an unspecific "social change" in the twentieth-century sense. At that time this seemed so obvious that I omitted to mention these theoretical implications explicitly. The introduction to the second edition gives me the opportunity to make good this omission.

3

The comprehensive social development studied and presented here through one of its central manifestations—a wave of advancing integration over several centuries, a process of state formation with the complementary process of advancing differentiation—is a figurational change which, in the to-and-fro of contrary movements, maintains, when surveyed over an extended time span, a constant direction through many generations. This structural change in a specific direction can be demonstrated as a fact, regardless of how it is evaluated. The factual proof is what matters here. The concept of social change by itself does not suffice, as an instrument of research, to take account of such facts. A mere change can be of the kind observable in clouds or smoke rings: now they look like this, now like that. A concept of social change that does not distinguish clearly between changes that relate to the structure of a society and those that do not—and, further, between structural changes without a specific direction and those which follow a particular direction over many generations, e.g., toward greater or lesser complexity—is a very inadequate tool of sociological inquiry.

The situation is similar with a number of other problems dealt with here. When, after several preparatory studies which enabled me both to investigate documentary evidence and to explore the gradually unfolding theoretical problems, the way to a possible solution became clearer, I was made aware that this study brings somewhat nearer to resolution the intractable problem of the connection between individual psychological structures (so-called personality structures) and figurations formed by large numbers of interdependent individuals (social structures). It does so because it approaches both types of structure not as fixed, as usually happens, but as changing, and as interdependent aspects of the same long-term development.

4

If the various academic disciplines whose subject matter is touched on by this study—including, above all, the discipline of sociology—had already reached the stage of scientific maturity at present enjoyed by many of the natural sciences, it might have been expected that a carefully documented study of long-term processes, such as those of civilization or state formation, with the theoretical proposals developed from it, would be assimilated, either in its entirety or in some of its aspects, after thorough testing and discussion, after critical sifting of all unsuitable or disproved content, to that discipline's stock of empirical and theoretical knowledge. Since the advance of scholarship depends in large measure on interchange and cross-fertilization between numerous colleagues and on the continuous development of the common stock of knowledge, it might have been expected that thirty years later this study would either have become a part of the standard knowledge of the discipline or have been more or less superseded by the work of others and laid to rest.

Instead, I find that a generation later this study still has the character of a pioneering work in a problematic field which today is hardly less in need than it was thirty years ago, of the simultaneous investigation on the empirical and theoretical plane that is to be found here. Understanding of the urgency of the problems discussed here has grown. Everywhere gropings in the direction of these problems are observable. There is no lack of later attempts to solve problems to whose solution the empirical documentation in these two volumes, and the concluding sketch of a theory of civilization, endeavor to contribute. I do not believe these later attempts to have been successful.

To exemplify this, it must suffice to discuss the way in which the man who at present is widely regarded as the leading theoretician of sociology, Talcott Parsons, attempts to pose and solve some of the problems dealt with here. It is characteristic of Parson's theoretical approach to attempt to dissect analytically into their elementary components, as he once expressed it, the different types of society in his field of observation. He called one particular type of elementary component "pattern variables." These pattern variables include the dichotomy of "affectivity" and "affective neutrality." His conception can best be understood by comparing society to a game of cards: every type of society, in Parson's view, represents a different "hand." But the cards themselves are always the same; and their number is small, however diverse their faces may be. One of the cards with which the game is played is the polarity between affectivity and affective neutrality. Parsons originally conceived this idea, he tells us, in analysing Tönnies's society types *Gemeinschaft* (community) and *Gesellschaft* (society). "Community," Parsons appears to believe, is in determining the differences between different types of society, and between different types of relationship within one and the same society, he attributes to this "pattern variable" in the card game, as to the others, a wholly general meaning. In the same context, Parsons addresses himself to the problem of the relation of social structure to personality. He indicates that while he had previously seen them merely as closely connected and interacting "human action systems," he can now state with certainty that in a theoretical sense they are different phases or aspects of one and the same fundamental action system. He illustrates this by an example, explaining that what may be considered on the sociological plane as an institutionalization of affective neutrality is essentially the same as what may be regarded on the level of personality as "the imposition of renunciation of immediate gratification in the interests of disciplined organization and the longer-run goals of the personality."

It is perhaps useful for an understanding of this study to compare this later attempt to solve such problems with the earlier one reprinted in unchanged form here. The decisive difference in scientific approach, and in the conception of the objectives of sociological theory, is evident from even this short example of Parson's treatment of similar problems. What in this book is shown with the aid of extensive empirical documentation to be a process, Parsons, by the static nature of his concepts, reduces retrospectively, and it seems to me quite unnecessarily, to states. Instead of a relatively complex process whereby the affective life of people is gradually moved toward an increased and more even control of affects—but certainly not toward a state of total affective neutrality—Parsons presents a simple opposition between two states, affectivity and affective neutrality, which are supposed to be present to different degrees in different types of society, like different quantities of chemical substances. By reducing to two different states what was shown empirically in *The Civilizing Process* to be a process and interpreted theoretically as such, Parsons deprives himself of the possibility of discovering how the distinguishing peculiarities of different societies to which he refers are actually to be explained. So far as is apparent, he does not even raise the question of explanation. The different states denoted by the antitheses of the "pattern variables" are, it seems, simply given. The subtly articulated structural change toward increased and more even affect control that may be observed in reality disappears in this kind of theorizing. Social phenomena in reality can only be observed as evolving and having evolved; their dissection by means of pairs of concepts which restrict the analysis to two antithetical states represents an unnecessary impoverishment of sociological perception on both empirical and theoretical levels.

Certainly, it is the task of every sociological theory to clarify the characteristics that all possible human societies have in common. The concept of the social process, like many others used in this study, has precisely this function. But the basic categories selected by Parsons seem to me arbitrary to a high degree. Underlying them is the tacit, untested, and seemingly self-evident notion that the objective of every scientific theory is to reduce everything variable to something invariable, and to simplify all complex phenomena by dissecting them into their individual components.

The example of Parsons's theory suggests, however, that theorizing in the field of sociology is complicated rather than simplified by a systematic reduction of social processes to social states, and of complex, heterogeneous phenomena to simpler, seemingly homogeneous components. This kind of reduction and abstraction could be justified as a method of theorizing only if it led unambiguously to a clearer and deeper understanding by men of themselves as societies and as individuals. Instead of this we find that the theories formed by such methods, like the epicycle theory of Ptolemy, require needlessly complicated auxiliary constructions to make them agree with the observable facts. They often appear like dark clouds from which here and there a few rays of light touch the earth.

5

One example of this, which will be discussed more fully later, is Parsons's attempt to develop a theoretical model of the relation between personality structures and social structures. In this undertaking two not very compatible ideas are frequently thoroughly confused: the notion that individual and society—"ego" and "social system"—are two entities existing independently of each other, with the individual regarded as the actual reality and society treated as an epiphenomenon; and the notion that the two are different but inseparable planes of the universe formed by men. Furthermore, concepts like "ego" and "social system" and all those related to them, which refer to men as individuals and as societies, are applied by Parsons—except when he is using psychoanalytical categories—as if the normal condition of both could be considered as an unalterable state. This study cannot be properly understood if the view of what is actually observable in human beings is blocked by such notions. It cannot be understood if we forget that concepts such as "individual" and "society" do not relate to two objects existing separately but to different yet inseparable aspects of the same human beings, and that both aspects (and human beings in general) are normally involved in a structural transformation. Both have the character of processes, and there is not the slightest necessity, in forming theories about human beings, to abstract from this process-character. Indeed, it is indispensable that the concept of process be included in sociological and other theories relating to human beings. As is shown in this study, the relation between individual and social structures can only be clarified if both are investigated as changing, evolving entities. Only then is it possible to develop models of their relationship, as is done here, which are in some agreement with the demonstrable facts. It can be stated with complete certainty that the relations between what is referred to conceptually as the "individual" and as "society" will remain incomprehensible so long as these concepts are used as if they represented two separate bodies, and even bodies normally at rest, which only come into contact with one another afterward as it were. Without ever saying so clearly and openly, Parsons's and all sociologists of the same persuasion undoubtedly envisage those things to which the concepts "individual" and "society" refer as existing separately. Thus—to give only one example—Parsons adopts the notion already developed by Emile Durkheim that the relation between "individual" and "society" is an "interpenetration" of the individual and the social system. However such an "interpenetration" is conceived, what else can this metaphor mean than that we are concerned with two different entities that first exist separately and then subsequently "interpenetrate"?

This makes clear the difference between the two sociological approaches. In this study the possibility of discerning more precisely the connection between individual structures and social structures results from a refusal to abstract from the process of their evolution as from something incidental or "merely historical." For the structures of personality and of society evolve in an indissoluble interrelationship. It can never be said with certainty that the people of a society *are* civilized. But on the basis of systematic investigations referring to demonstrable evidence, it can be said with a high degree of certainty that some groups of people have *become* more civilized, without necessarily implying that it is better or worse, has a positive or negative value, to become more civilized. Such a change in personality structures can, however, be shown without difficulty to be a specific aspect of the development of social structures. This is attempted in what follows.

It is not particularly surprising to encounter in Parsons, and in many other contemporary sociological theoreticians, a tendency to reduce processes to states even when these writers are explicitly concerned with the problem of social change. In keeping with the predominant trend in sociology, Parsons takes as his starting point the hypothesis that every society normally exists in a state of unchanging equilibrium which is homeostatically preserved. It changes, he supposes, when this normal state of social equilibrium is disturbed by, for example, a violation of the social norms, a breach of conformity. Social change thus appears as a phenomenon resulting from the accidental, externally activated malfunction of a normally well-balanced social system. Moreover, the society thus disturbed strives, in Parsons's view, to regain its state of rest. Sooner or later, as he sees it, a different "system" with a different equilibrium is established, which once again maintains itself more or less automatically, despite oscillations, in the given state. In a word, the concept of social change refers here to a transitional state between two normal states of changelessness, brought about by malfunction. Here, too, the difference between the theoretical approaches represented by this study and by Parsons and his school emerges very distinctly. The present study upholds the idea, based on abundant documentary material, that change is a normal characteristic of society. A structured sequence of continuous change serves here as the frame of reference for investigating states located at particular points in time. In prevailing sociological opinion, conversely, social situations treated as if they normally existed in a state of rest serve as the frame of reference for all change. Thus a society is regarded as a "social system," and a "social system" as a "system in a state of rest." Even when a relatively differentiated, "highly developed" society is involved, the attempt is often made to consider it as at rest and self-contained. It is not regarded as an integral part of the inquiry to ask how and why this highly developed society has developed to this state of differentiation. In keeping with the static frame of reference of the predominant system-theories, social changes, processes, and developments, which include the development of a state or a civilizational process, appear merely as something additional, a mere "historical introduction" the investigation and explanation of which may very well be dispensed with in coming to an understanding of the "social system" and its "structure" and "functions," as they may be observed here and now from a short-term viewpoint. These conceptual tools themselves—including concepts like "structures" and "function," which serve as the badge of the contemporary sociological school of "structural functionalists"—bear the stamp of this specific mode of thinking, which reduces processes to states. Of course, their originators cannot entirely dismiss the idea that the "structures" and "functions" of the social "unit" or its "parts," which they picture as states, move and change. But the problems which thus come into view are reconciled with the static mode of thought by encapsulating them in a special chapter with the title "Social Change," as though the phenomenon were supplementary to the problems of the normally unchanging system. In this way "social change" itself is treated as an attribute of a state of rest. In other words, the basic, state-orientated attitude is reconciled with empirical observations of social change by introducing into the theoretical waxworks of motionless social phenomena a few more equally motionless figures with labels like "social change" or "social process." In this way the problems of social change are in a sense frozen and rendered innocuous to state-oriented sociology. So it happens that the concept of "social development" has almost completely vanished from the sight of contemporary sociological theorists—paradoxically, in a phase of social development when, in actual social life and partly also in empirical sociological research, people are concerning themselves more intensely and consciously than ever before with problems of social development.

6

In writing an introduction to a book that on both the theoretical and the empirical side is squarely opposed to widespread tendencies in contemporary sociology, one has a certain obligation to tell the reader clearly and unequivocally how and why the problems posed here, and the steps taken to solve them, differ from those of the predominant type of sociology, and particularly from those of theoretical sociology. To do this, one cannot entirely evade the question how it is to be explained that sociology, for whose leading nineteenth-century representatives the problems of long-term social processes were of primordial interest, should in the twentieth century have become a sociology of states to such an extent that the investigation of long-term social processes has as much as disappeared from its research activity. Within the scope of this introduction I cannot presume to discuss this displacement of the center of interest of sociological research, and the radical change in the entire sociological manner of thinking connected with it, with the thoroughness they deserve. But the problem is too important for an understanding of what follows, and beyond that for the further development of sociology, to be passed over in complete silence. I shall therefore confine myself to picking out a few elements from the complex of conditions responsible for this regression in the intellectual apparatus of sociology and the concomitant narrowing of its field of inquiry.

The most obvious reason why awareness of the significance of problems of long-term social change, of the sociogenesis and development of social formations of all kinds has been largely lost to sociologists, and why the concept of development has fallen into disrepute among them, is to be found in the reaction of many sociologists—above all, the leading theoreticians of the twentieth century—to certain aspects of the outstanding sociological theories of the nineteenth century. It has been shown that the theoretical models of long-term social development elaborated in the nineteenth century by men like Comte, Spencer, Marx, Hobhouse, and many others rested in part on hypotheses determined primarily by the political and philosophical ideals of these men and only secondarily by their relation to facts. Later generations had a much larger and constantly increasing supply of facts at their disposal. Reexamination of the classical nineteenth-century theories of development in light of the more comprehensive findings of subsequent generations made many aspects of the earlier process-models appear questionable or at any rate in need of revision. Many of the sociological pioneers' articles of faith were no longer accepted by twentieth-century sociologists. These included, above all, the belief that the development of society is necessarily a development for the better, a movement in the direction of progress. This belief was emphatically rejected by many later sociologists in accordance with their own social experience. They could see more clearly in retrospect that the earlier models of development comprised a mixture of relatively fact-based and of ideological notions.

In a mature discipline one might, first of all, have set about the task of revising and correcting the earlier models of development. One might have tried, in this situation, to ascertain which aspects of the old theories could be used as a basis for further research in light of the more comprehensive factual knowledge now available, and which should find their place as expressions of time-bound political or philosophical prejudice, with a suitable tombstone, in the graveyard of dead doctrines.

Instead, an extremely sharp reaction against the type of sociological theory concerned with long-term social processes set in. The study of the long-term development of society was almost universally decried, and the center of sociological interest moved, in a radical reaction against the older type of theory, to the investigation of data on society conceived as normally existing in a state of rest and equilibrium. Hand in hand with this went the hardening of a collection of stereotyped arguments against the older sociological theories and many of their central concepts, particularly that of social development. As these sociologists did not trouble to distinguish between the fact-based and the ideological elements in the concept of development, the whole discussion of long-term social processes, particularly developmental processes, was henceforth associated with one or another of the nineteenth-century systems of belief, and so, above all, with the notion that social development, whether proceeding in a straight line without conflict or dialectically with conflict, must automatically be a change for the better, a movement in the direction of progress. From then on it appeared almost old-fashioned to occupy oneself with questions of social development. It is sometimes said that generals, in planning strategy for a new war, take the strategy of the old one as their model. To assume without question that concepts like "social development" or "long-term social processes" inevitably include the old idea of progress is to proceed in a similar way.

We find, therefore, in the framework of sociology, an intellectual development involving a radical swing of the pendulum from a one-sided position to an opposite position no less one-sided. A phase in which sociological theorists primarily sought models of long-term social development has been succeeded by one in which they are primarily concerned with models of societies in a state of rest and immutability. If research was once founded on a Heraclitean kind of basic assumption that all is in flux (with the difference that it was taken almost for granted that the flow was in the direction of improvement), it is based now on an Eleatic idea. The Eleatics, it is said, imagined the flight of an arrow as a series of states of rest; actually, it seemed to them, the arrow does not move at all. For at every given moment it is in a particular place. The assumption of many present-day sociological theorists that societies are usually to be found in a state of equilibrium, so that the long-term social development of mankind appears as a chain of static social types, is strongly reminiscent of the Eleatic conception of the flight of an arrow. How can this swing of the pendulum from one extreme to the other in the development of sociology be explained?

At first sight, it seems that the decisive reason for the change in the theoretical orientation of sociology is a reaction of scientists protesting in the name of the scientific character of their research against the interference of political and philosophical ideas in the theory of their subject. Exponents of contemporary sociological theories of state are themselves often inclined to this interpretation. On closer examination, however, it is found to be inadequate. The reaction against the sociology of development predominant in the nineteenth century was not directed simply against the primacy of ideals, the dominance of preconceived social doctrines, in the name of scientific objectivity. It was not simply the expression of a concern to pull aside the veil of short-lived notions of what society ought to be, in order to perceive the real dynamics and functioning of society itself. In the last analysis it was a reaction against the primacy of *particular* ideals in sociological theory, in the name of others partly opposed to them. If in the nineteenth century specific conceptions of what ought to be or of what was desired—specific ideological conceptions—led to a central interest in the development of society, in the twentieth century other conceptions of what ought to be or is desirable—other ideological conceptions—led to the pronounced interest among leading sociological theorists in the state of society as it is, to their neglect of problems of the dynamics of social formations, and to their lack of interest in problems of long-term processes and in all the opportunities of explanation that the investigation of such problems provides.

This sharp change in the character of social ideals, encountered here in the development of sociology, is not an isolated phenomenon. It is symptomatic of a more comprehensive change in the ideals predominant in the countries in which the main work of sociology is concentrated. This change points, in turn, to a specific transformation that has been taking place in the nineteenth and twentieth centuries in the internal and external relations of the older, developed industrial states. It must suffice here—as a summary of a more extensive inquiry—to indicate briefly the main outline of this transformation. This will facilitate understanding of sociological studies which, like the present one, give a central place to the investigation of long-term processes. The purpose is not to attack other ideals in the name of one's own, but to seek a better understanding of the structure of such processes themselves and to emancipate the theoretical framework of sociological research from the primacy of social ideals and doctrines. For we can only elicit sociological knowledge which is sufficiently adequate to be of use in solving the acute problems of society if, when posing and solving sociological problems, we cease giving precedence to preconceived notions of what the solutions ought to be over the investigation of what is.

7

In the industrializing countries of the nineteenth century in which the first great pioneering works of sociology were written, the voices expressing the social beliefs, ideals, hopes, and long-term goals of the rising industrial classes gradually gained the advantage over those seeking to preserve the existing social order in the interests of the established courtly-dynastic, aristocratic, or patrician power elites. It was the former who, in keeping with their situation as the rising classes, had high expectations of a better future. And as their ideal lay not in the present but in the future, they were particularly interested in the dynamics, the development of society. In conjunction with one or another of these rising industrial classes, the sociologists of the time sought confirmation that the development of mankind would move in the direction of their wishes and hopes. They did so by exploring the direction and the driving forces of social development hitherto. In this activity they undoubtedly brought to light a very considerable amount of adequate knowledge on the problems of social development. But it is often very difficult in retrospect to distinguish between specific heteronomous doctrines filled with short-lived, time-bound ideals and those conceptual models which have significance independently of these ideals, solely with regard to verifiable facts.

On the other side, in the nineteenth century, were to be heard the voices of those who for one reason or another opposed the transformation of society through industrialization, whose social faith was oriented toward conservation of the existing heritage, and who held up, against what they took to be the deteriorating present, their ideal of a better past. They represented not only the preindustrial elites of the dynastic states but also broader working groups—above all, those engaged in agriculture and handicrafts, whose traditional livelihoods were being eroded by advancing industrialization. They were the opponents of all those who spoke from the standpoint of the two rising industrial classes, the industrial and commercial bourgeoisie and the industrial working class, and who, in keeping with the rising situation of these classes, drew their inspiration from a belief in a better future, the progress of mankind. Thus, in the nineteenth century, the chorus of voices was split between those extolling a better past and those celebrating a better future.

Among the sociologists whose image of society was oriented toward progress and a better future are to be found, as we know, spokesmen of the two industrial classes. They include men like Marx and Engels, who identified themselves with the industrial working class; and they include bourgeois sociologists like Comte at the beginning of the nineteenth century or Hobhouse at the end. The spokesmen for the two rising industrial classes took confidence in the thought of the future improvement of the human condition, even if what they envisaged as improvement and progress varied widely depending on their class. It is of no small importance to realize how intense the interest in the problems of social development in the nineteenth century was, and to ask on what this interest was founded, if one is to understand why the belief in progress waned in the twentieth century and why, correspondingly, interest among sociologists in the problems of long-term social development declined.

But to understand this shift it is not sufficient, as has already been indicated, to consider only class figurations, the social relationships within states. The rise of industrial classes within the industrializing states of Europe in the nineteenth century went hand in hand with the continuing rise of these nations themselves. In that century these nations drove each other by constant rivalry to a greater increase of their predominance over less developed nations than ever before. Not only the classes within them but also these state-societies in their totality were rising, expanding social formations.

One might be tempted to attribute the belief in progress in European writing in the centuries preceding the twentieth primarily to the progress in science and technology. But that is an insufficient explanation. How little the experience of scientific and technological progress alone gives rise to an idealization of progress, to a confident faith in the continuous improvement of the human condition, is shown clearly enough by the twentieth century. The actual degree and tempo of progress in science and technology in this century exceed that in the preceding centuries very considerably. Likewise, the standard of living of the masses in the countries of the first wave of industrialization has been higher in the twentieth century than in preceding centuries. The state of health has improved; life expectancy has increased. But in the total chorus of the time, the voices of those who affirm progress as something valuable, who see in the improvement of the condition of men the centerpiece of a social ideal, and who believe confidently in the better future of mankind, have become appreciably fewer than in preceding centuries. On the other side of the choir, the voices of those who cast doubt on all these developments, who see no great promise of a better future for mankind or even for their own nation, and whose central social faith concentrates instead on the present as the highest value, on the conservation of their own nation, on the idealization of its existing social form or even of its past, its heritage and its traditional order, are increasing in the twentieth century and gradually becoming louder. In the preceding centuries, in which actual progress was already very palpable yet still slow and relatively limited, the idea of further, future progress had the character of an ideal toward which its adherents were striving and which possessed high value precisely as an ideal. In the twentieth century, when actual progress in science, technology, health, the standard of living, and not least in the reduction of inequality between people exceeds by far, in the older industrial nations, the progress in all previous centuries, progress has ceased for many people to be an ideal. The voices of those who doubt all this actual progress are growing more numerous.

The reasons for this change are manifold. Not all need be considered here. The recurrent wars, the incessant danger of war, and the threat of nuclear and other new scientific weapons certainly contribute to this coincidence of accelerating progress, particularly in the scientific and technical fields, with diminishing confidence in the value of this progress and of progress in general.

But the contempt heaped in the twentieth century on the preceding centuries' "shallow" belief in progress or their notion of a progressive development of human society; the obstructions blocking sociologists' view of problems of long-term social processes; the almost complete disappearance of the concept of social development from sociological texts—these and other symptoms of an extreme swing of the intellectual pendulum are not sufficiently explained by the upheavals of war and related phenomena. To understand them, we must also take account of specific changes in the twentieth century in the overall internal structure and international position of the great industrial nations of the nineteenth century.

Within these nations the representatives of the two industrial classes, the industrial bourgeoisie and the industrial working class, now establish themselves firmly against the earlier dynastic-aristocratic military power elites as the ruling groups in their states. The two industrial classes hold each other in an often precarious and always unstable balance of tensions, with the established working class still in the weaker position, but slowly gaining strength. The rising classes of the nineteenth century, who still had to fight within their states against the traditional dynastic elite, and for whom development, progress, a better future was not only a fact but also an ideal of great emotional significance, have become in the course of the twentieth century the more or less established industrial classes whose representatives are installed institutionally as the ruling or co-ruling groups. Partly as partners, partly as opponents, the representatives of the industrial bourgeoisie and the established industrial working class now form the primary elite in the nations of the first wave of industrialization. Accordingly, alongside class-consciousness and class ideals, and partly as a disguise for them, national consciousness and the ideal of their own nation as the highest value play an increasing role within the two industrial classes—first of all in the industrial bourgeoisie, but increasingly in the industrial working class as well.

Seen as an ideal, however, the nation turns attention to what already exists. Since representatives of the two powerful and populous industrial classes now have access to positions of power in the state, the nation, organized as a state, appears emotionally and ideologically as the highest value in its present condition. Moreover, it appears—emotionally and ideologically—as eternal, immutable in its essential features. Historical changes affect only externals; the people, the nation, so it appears, do not change. The English, German, French, Italian, and all other nations are, for those who constitute them, everlasting. In their "essence" they are always the same, whether we are speaking of the tenth or the twentieth century.

Furthermore, it was not only the two industrial classes within the older industrial nations which changed, once and for all, in the course of the twentieth century. The rise of the European nations and of their offshoots in other parts of the world, which had gone on for centuries, also came slowly to a standstill in our own. To be sure, their actual lead over non-European nations (with few exceptions) at first remained large; for a time it even increased. But the idea had formed and established itself in the age of the unchallenged ascendancy of the European nations, as among all powerful and ruling groups in the world, that the power they were able to wield over other nations was the expression of an eternal mission bestowed on them by God or nature or historical destiny, the expression of a superiority over those less powerful which was founded in their very essence. This idea of their own self-evident superiority, deeply rooted in the self-image of the older industrial nations, has been profoundly shaken by the actual course of development in the twentieth century. The reality-shock suffered when a national ideal collides with social reality has been absorbed by each nation in a different way, according to its own development and the specific nature of its national self-image. For Germany the more comprehensive significance of this collision was first concealed by the more direct shock of the military defeats. But it is indicative both of the solidity of the old national ideals and of the relative autonomy of this development as a whole that even in the victorious countries of the second European-American war there were, at first, immediately after the victory had been won, as far as can be determined, only very few people who realized how radically and fundamentally the military conflicts between two groups of relatively highly developed countries would reduce the power of this class of countries as a whole over the less developed countries, a reduction which had been prepared for some time. As is often the case, this sudden diminution in their power found the previously mighty countries unprepared and bewildered.

The actual opportunities for progress, for a better future, are— leaving aside the regressive possibilities of war—still very great for the older industrial nations. But in relation to their traditional national self-images, in which the idea of their own national civilization or culture is usually ensconced as the highest value of mankind, the future is disappointing. The idea of the unique nature and value of one's own nation often serves as legitimation for that nation's claim to lead all other nations. It is this self-image, this claim to leadership by the older industrial nations, that has been shaken in the second half of the twentieth century by what is still a very limited increase in power among the poorer, previously dependent and partly subjugated pre-industrial societies in other parts of the world.

In other words, this reality-shock, insofar as it affects the emotive value of the present state of a nation in regard to its future possibilities, merely reinforces a tendency already present in national feeling. What the nation is and always has been, its eternal, unalterable heritage, possesses a far greater emotive value, as a means of self-legitimation and as an expression of the national scale of values and the national ideal, than any promise or ideal located in the future. The "national ideal" draws attention away from what changes to the enduring and the immutable.

This aspect of the transformation taking place in the European states, and in a number of closely related non-European states as well, has been matched by specific changes in the realm of ideas and in the modes of thought of intellectuals. In the eighteenth and nineteenth centuries, philosophers and sociologists who spoke of "society" were usually thinking of "bourgeois society"—that is, aspects of social life that seemed to lie beyond the dynastic and military aspects of the state. In keeping with their situation and their ideals as spokesmen for groups which were by and large excluded from access to the central positions of state power, these men, when talking of society, usually had in mind a human society transcending all state frontiers. With the extensive assumption of state power by representatives of the two industrial classes, and with the corresponding development of national ideals in these two classes and particularly in their representative ruling elites, this conception of society was changed in sociology as well.

In society at large, the various class ideals of the industrial classes increasingly mingle and interpenetrate with national ideals. Certainly, conservative and liberal national ideals show a different nuance of nationalism than do socialist or communist ones. But such nuances influenced only marginally, if at all, the broad outline of the change that took place in the attitude toward state and nation of the established industrial classes, including their political and intellectual spokesmen, when these classes, ceasing to be groups excluded from central state power, became groups truly constituting the nation, whose leaders themselves represented and exercised state power. It accords with this development that many twentieth-century sociologists, when speaking of "society," no longer have in mind (as did their predecessors) a "bourgeois society" or a "human society" beyond the state, but increasingly the somewhat diluted ideal image of a nation–state. Within their general conception of society as something abstracted from the reality of the nation–state, the above-mentioned political and ideological nuances are again to be found. Among the leading sociological theorists of the twentieth century, conservative and liberal as well as socialist and communist shades are to be found in the image of society. Since, in the twentieth century, American sociology has taken over for a time the leading role in the development of theoretical sociology, the dominant type of sociological theory of this period reflects the specific character of its predominant national ideal, within which conservative and liberal features are not so sharply divided, or felt to be so antithetical, as in some European nation-states, particularly Germany.

In sociological discussion, and in philosophical debates as well, the rejection of certain aspects of the sociological theories of the nineteenth century—above all, their orientation toward social development and the concept of progress—is often presented as based solely on the factual inadequacy of these theories. The short survey that has been given here of one of the main structural tendencies of the development of relations within and between the older industrial nations throws into sharper relief certain ideological aspects of this rejection. In accordance with the concept of ideology developed within the Marxian tradition, one might seek to explain the ideological aspects of the neglect of social development, and the preoccupation with the state of social systems, dominant in recent sociological theories solely by reference to the ideals of classes whose hopes, wishes, and ideals are related not to the future but to the conservation of the existing order. But this class-explanation of the social beliefs and ideals implicit in sociological theory is no longer sufficient in the twentieth century. In this period we must also take account of the development of national ideals transcending social classes in order to understand the ideological aspects of sociological theories. The integration of the two industrial classes into a state structure previously ruled by numerically very small preindustrial minorities; the rise of both classes to a position in which their representatives play a more or less dominant role in the state, and in which even the weaker sectors of the industrial workers can no longer be ruled without their consent; and the resulting stronger identification of both classes with the nation—all these factors give special impetus, in the social attitudes of this time, to the belief in one's own nation as one of the highest values in human life. The lengthening and multiplication of chains of interdependence between states, and the heightening of specific tensions and conflicts between states resulting from this, the momentous national wars and the very-present danger of war—all these factors contribute to the growth of nation-centered patterns of thought.

It is the convergence of these two intrastate and interstate lines of development in the older industrial nations that has weakened the ideal of progress, the orientation of faith and desire toward a better future and therefore also toward an image of the past considered as development. Combined, the two lines of development cause this type of ideal to be replaced by others directed at conserving and defending the existing order. They relate to something that is felt to be immutable and realized in the present—the eternal nation. The voices proclaiming belief in a better future and the progress of mankind as their ideal make way, as the dominant section in the mixed social chorus of the time, for the voices of those who give precedence to the value of what exists and, above all, to the timeless value of their own nations, for which, in the succession of great and small wars, many people have lost their lives. This is—sketched in its main outline—the overall structural development which is reflected in the development of theories of society. Theories which reflect the ideals of rising classes in expanding industrial societies are replaced by theories dominated by the ideals of more or less established classes in highly developed societies whose growth has reached or passed its peak.

As an example of this type of sociological theory, it may suffice to cite one of its representative concepts, that of the "social system," as used by Parsons, but certainly not by him alone. It expresses very clearly the way in which a "society" is now conceived. A "social system" is a society "in equilibrium." Small oscillations of this equilibrium do occur, but normally society exists in a state of rest. All its parts, in this conception, are normally harmoniously attuned to one another. All individuals belonging to it are normally attuned by the same kind of socialization to the same norms. All are normally well-integrated, respect the same values in their actions, fulfill their prescribed roles without difficulty. Conflicts between them do not normally occur; these, like changes in the system, are manifestations of malfunction. In short, the image of society represented theoretically by this concept of the social system reveals itself on closer inspection to be the ideal image of a nation: all the people belonging to it obey the same norms on the basis of the same socialization, uphold the same values, and thus live normally in well-integrated harmony with one another. In the conception of the "social system" that we have before us, in other words, the image of the nation as community can be discerned. It is tacitly assumed that within such a "system" there is a relatively high degree of equality between people, for integration rests on the same socialization of people, on the uniformity of their values and norms throughout the entire system. Such a "system" is therefore a construction abstracted from a democratically conceived nation–state. From whatever side this construction is considered, the distinction between what the nation is and what the nation ought to be is blurred. Just as in the nineteenth-century sociological models of development the desired social process was presented (mingled with realistic observations) as a fact, so in the twentieth-century sociological models of a normally unchanging "social system" the desired ideal of a harmonious integration of all parts of the nation is also represented (mingled with realistic observations) as something that exists, a fact. But in the former case it is the future, in the latter the present, the nation–state existing here and now, that is idealized.

A mixture of "is" and "ought," of factual analyses and normative postulates, relating primarily to a society of a very definite type, a nation–state conceived in broadly egalitarian fashion, thus presents itself as the centerpiece of a theory which claims to be capable of serving as a model for the scientific investigation of societies in all times and places. One need only raise the question of whether and how far such sociological theories—derived primarily from present-day, more or less democratic nation-state societies which presuppose a high degree of integration of people into the "social system" as something both self-evident and desirable, and which therefore, imply a relatively advanced stage of social democratization—are applicable to societies at different stages of development, and which are less centralized and democratized, in order to perceive the weakness of a general theory of society from the church-steeple perspective of the present state of our own society. If such models of a "social system" are tested for their suitability as theoretical tools for the scientific investigation of a society with a high percentage of slaves or unfree subjects, or of feudal or hierarchical states—that is, societies in which not even the same laws apply to all people, not to speak of the same norms and values—it is quickly seen how present-centered these sociological models of systems conceived as states actually are.

What has been illustrated here by the "social" system example could be shown without difficulty to apply to other concepts of dominant contemporary sociology. Concepts like "structure," "function," "norm," "integration," and "role" all represent in their current forms attempts to conceptualize certain aspects of human societies by abstracting from their dynamics, their genesis, their character as a process, their development. The rejection of the nineteenth-century ideological understanding of these dynamic aspects of society that has taken place can therefore be seen not only as a criticism of these ideological aspects in the name of a scientific concern with fact, but above all as a criticism of earlier ideals that no longer correspond to present social conditions and experience and have therefore been rejected in the name of later ideals. This replacement of one ideology by another explains the fact that it is not simply the ideological elements in the nineteenth-century sociological concept of development that have been called into question, but the concept of development itself, the very consideration of problems of long-term social development, of sociogenesis and psychogenesis. In a word, the baby has been thrown out with the bathwater.

The present study, which concerns itself once again with social processes, may be better understood if this development of theoretical sociology is kept in mind. The tendency to condemn the social ideologies of the nineteenth century from the standpoint of those of the twentieth appears to preclude the idea that long-term processes might be made the object of investigation without an ideological motive—that is, without the author, under the pretense of speaking of what is or was, speaking in reality of what he believes and wishes ought to be. If the present study has any significance at all, this results not least from its opposition to this mingling of what is and what ought to be, of scientific analysis and ideal. It points to the possibility of freeing the study of society from its bondage to social ideologies. This is not to say that an investigation of social problems which excludes political and philosophical ideas means renouncing the possibility of influencing the course of political events through the results of sociological research. The opposite is the case. The usefulness of sociological research as a tool of social practice is increased if the researcher does not deceive himself by projecting what he desires, what he believes ought to be, into his investigation of what is and has been.

8

To understand the blockage which the predominant modes of thinking and feeling place in the way of the investigation of long-term changes of social structure and personality structure—and thus in the way of an understanding of this book—it is not enough to trace the development of the image of men as societies, the image of society. It is also necessary to keep in mind the development of the image of men as individuals, the image of the personality. As has been mentioned, one of the peculiarities of the traditional image of man is that people often speak and think of individuals and societies as if these were two phenomena existing separately—of which, moreover, one is often considered "real" and the other "unreal"—instead of two different aspects of the same human being.

This curious aberration of thinking, too, cannot be understood without a glance at its implicit ideological content. The splitting of the image of humanity into an image of man as individual and an image of men as societies has widely ramifying roots. One branch is a very characteristic split in the values and ideals encountered, on close inspection, in all the more developed nation-states, and perhaps most pronounced in nations with a strong liberal tradition. In the development of the value systems of all such nation-states, one finds, on the one hand, a strand which sees society as a whole, the nation, as the highest value; and, on the other, a strand which posits the wholly self-sufficient, free individual, the "closed personality," as the highest value. It is not always easy to harmonize these two "highest values" with one another. There are situations in which the two ideals are plainly irreconcilable. But usually this problem is not squarely faced. People talk with great warmth of the freedom and independence of the individual, and with equal warmth of the freedom and independence of their own nation. The first ideal arouses the expectation that the individual member of a nation-state, despite his community and interdependence with others, can reach his decisions in an entirely self-sufficient way, without regard to others; the second arouses the expectation—fulfilled particularly in war but often enough in peacetime, too—that the individual should and must subordinate everything belonging to him, even his life, to the survival of the "social whole."

This split in the ideals, this contradiction in the ethos by which people are brought up, finds expression in the theories of sociology.

Some of these theories take as their starting point the independent, self-sufficient individual as the "true" reality, and therefore as the true object of social science; others start with the independent social totality. Some theories attempt to harmonize the two conceptions, usually without indicating how it is possible to reconcile the idea of an absolutely independent and free individual with that of an equally independent and free "social totality," and often without clearly perceiving the problem. The reflection of this unresolved inner division between the two ideals is seen above all in the theories of sociologists whose national ideal has a conservative-liberal tinge. Max Weber's theoretical work—if not his empirical work—and the theories of his successor Talcott Parsons are examples of this.

It may suffice as illustration to return once more to what has already been said about Parsons's conception of the relation of individual and society, of the "individual actor" and the "social system." One description of their relation is contained in the metaphor of "interpenetration," which shows clearly the important role played by the idea of the separate existence of the two human aspects. The reification of the ideal therefore finds expression in this conceptual edifice not only in the notion of the social system as a specific ideal image of the nation, but also in that of the individual actor, the "ego," as an ideal image of the free individual existing independently of all others. In both cases the theorist's ideal image is changed unawares under his hands into a fact, something that actually exists. For with regard to the image of the individual, too, what in the mind of the theorist ought to be, the image of the absolutely free and independent individual, is treated as if it were the image of what the individual actually is.

Now this is certainly not the place to fathom the reasons for this widely disseminated split in thinking about human beings. But the concern of the present study cannot properly be understood so long as the problems of the civilizing process are approached with the notions of the individual that have just been mentioned. In the course of this process the structures of the individual human being are changed in a particular direction. This is what the concept of "civilization," in the factual sense in which it is used here, actually means. The image current today of the individual as an absolutely independent and self-sufficient being is difficult to reconcile with the facts adduced here. It obstructs understanding of the long-term processes which people undergo on both the individual and social planes. Parsons uses on occasion, to illustrate his image of the personality, the old metaphor of the personality of the human actor as a "black box," i.e., a closed container "inside" which certain individual processes take place. The metaphor is taken from the toolbox of psychology. It basically means that all that can be observed scientifically in a human being is his behavior. We can observe what the "black box" does. But what goes on inside the box, what is also termed the "soul" or "mind"—the "ghost in the machine," as an English philosopher called it—is not an object of scientific investigation. One cannot avoid, in this context, exploring in more detail an image of the individual which plays a considerable role in the human sciences today and thus also contributes to the neglect of long-term changes in human beings in the course of social development as a subject of research.

The image of the individual as an entirely free, independent being, a "closed personality" who is "inwardly" quite self-sufficient and separate from all other people, has behind it a long tradition in the development of European societies. In classical philosophy this figure comes onto the scene as the epistemological subject. In this role, as *homo philosophicus*, the individual gains knowledge of the world "outside" him in a completely autonomous way. He does not need to learn, to take this knowledge from others. The fact that he came into the world as a child, the whole process of his development to adulthood and as an adult, is neglected as immaterial by this image of man. In the development of mankind it took many thousands of years for people to learn to understand the relations between natural events, the course of the stars, rain and sun, thunder and lightning, as manifestations of a blind, impersonal, purely mechanical and regular sequence of causal connections. But the "closed personality" of *homo philosophicus* apparently perceives this mechanical and regular causal chain as an adult simply by opening his eyes, without needing to learn anything about it from others, and quite independently of the stage of knowledge reached by society. The process—the individual human being as a process in growing up, human beings together as a process in the development of mankind—is reduced in thought to a state. The individual opens his eyes as an adult and not only recognizes autonomously here and now, without learning from others, what all these objects are that he perceives; he not only knows immediately what he is to classify as animate and inanimate, as mineral, vegetable, or animal; but he also knows directly here and now that they are linked causally in accordance with natural laws. The question for philosophers is merely whether he gains this knowledge of causal connections here and now on the basis of his experience—whether, in other words, these connections are a property of the observable facts "outside" him—or the connections are something rooted in the nature of human reason and superadded from "inside" the human being to what flows into him from "outside" through the sense organs. If we start from this image of man, from the *homo philosophicus* who was never a child and seemingly came into the world an adult, there is no way out of the epistemological impasse. Thought steers helplessly back and forth between the Scylla of positivism and the Charybdis of apriorism. It does so precisely because what is actually observable as a process, a development of the social macrocosm within which the development of the individual microcosm can also be observed, is reduced in thought to a state, an act of perception taking place here and now. We have here an example of how closely the inability to conceive long-term social processes (i.e., structured changes in the figurations formed by large numbers of interdependent human beings) or to understand the human beings forming such figurations is connected to a certain type of image of man and of self-perception. People to whom it seems self-evident that their own self (or their ego, or whatever else it may be called) exists, as it were, "inside" them, isolated from all the other people and things "outside," have difficulty assigning significance to all those facts which indicate that individuals live from the first in interdependence with others. They have difficulty conceiving people as relatively but not absolutely autonomous and interdependent individuals forming changeable figurations with one another. Since the former self-perception seems self-evident to those subscribing to it, they cannot easily take account of facts which show that this kind of perception is itself limited to particular societies, that it comes into being in conjunction with certain kinds of interdependencies, of social bonds between people—in short, that it is a structural peculiarity of a specific stage in the development of civilization, corresponding to a specific stage of differentiation and individualization of human groups. If one grows up in the midst of such a group, one cannot easily imagine that there could be people who do not experience themselves in this way as entirely self-sufficient individuals cut off from all other beings and things. This kind of self-perception appears as obvious, a symptom of an eternal human state, simply the normal, natural, and universal self-perception of all human beings. The conception of the individual as *homo clausus*, a little world in himself who ultimately exists quite independently of the great world outside, determines the image of man in general. Every other human being is likewise seen as a *homo clausus;* his core, his being, his true self appears likewise as something divided within him by an invisible wall from everything outside, including every other human being.

But the nature of this wall itself is hardly ever considered and never properly explained. Is the body the vessel which holds the true self locked within it? Is the skin the frontier between "inside" and "outside"? What in man is the capsule, and what the encapsulated? The experience of "inside" and "outside" seems so self-evident that such questions are scarcely ever posed; they seem to require no further examination. One is satisfied with the spatial metaphor of "inside" and "outside," but one makes no serious attempt to locate the "inner" in space; and although this omission to investigate one's own presuppositions is hardly appropriate to scientific procedure, this preconceived image of *homo clausus* commands the stage not only in society at large but also in the human sciences. Its derivatives include not only the traditional *homo philosophicus,* the image of man of classical epistemology, but also *homo oeconomicus, homo psychologicus, homo historicus,* and not least *homo sociologicus* in his present-day version. The images of the individual of Descartes, of Max Weber, and of Parsons and many other sociologists are of the same provenance. As philosophers did before them, many sociological theorists today accept this self-perception, and the image of the individual corresponding to it, as the untested basis of their theories. They do not detach themselves from it in order to confront it and call its aptness into question. Consequently, this kind of self-perception and image of the individual often coexists unchanged with attempts to abolish the reduction to states. In Parsons, for example, the static image of the ego, the individual actor, the adult abstracted from the process of growing up, coexists unmediated with the psychoanalytical ideas that he has taken over in his theory—ideas which relate to the state of adulthood but to the process of becoming adult, to the individuals as an open process in indissoluble interdependence with other individuals. As a result, the ideas of social theorists constantly find themselves in blind alleys from which there seems no way out. The individual—or, more precisely, what the present concept of the individual refers to—appears again and again as something existing "outside" society. What the concept of society refers to appears again and again as something existing outside and beyond individuals. One seems to have the choice only between theoretical approaches which present the individual as the truly existent beyond society, the truly "real" (society being seen as an abstraction, something not truly existing), and other theoretical approaches which posit society as a "system," a "social fact sui generis," a reality of a peculiar type beyond individuals. At most one can—as is occasionally done in an apparent solution to the problem—juxtapose the two conceptions unconnectedly, that of the individual as *homo clausus*, as ego, as individual beyond society, and that of society as a system outside and beyond individuals. But the incompatibility of these two conceptions is not thereby disposed of. In order to pass beyond this dead end of sociology and the social sciences in general, it is necessary to make clear the inadequacy of both conceptions, that of the individual outside society and, equally, that of a society outside individuals. This is difficult as long as the sense of the encapsulation of the self within itself serves as the untested basis of the image of the individual, and as long as, in conjunction with this, the concepts "individual" and "society" are understood as if they related to unchanging states.

The conceptual trap in which one is continually being caught by these static notions of "individual" and "society" can only be pried open if, as is done here, these notions are developed further, in conjunction with empirical investigations, in such a way that the two concepts are made to refer to processes. But this development is initially blocked by the extraordinary conviction carried in European societies since roughly the Renaissance by the self-perception of human beings in terms of their own isolation, the severance of their own "inside" from everything "outside." In Descartes the perception of the isolation of the individual, who finds himself confronted as a thinking ego within his own head by the entire external world, is somewhat weakened by the idea of God. In contemporary sociology the same basic experience finds theoretical expression in the acting ego, which finds itself confronted with people "outside" as "others." Apart from Leibnizian monadology, there is in this philosophico-sociological tradition scarcely a single approach to the problem that sets out from the basis of a multiplicity of interdependent human beings. Leibniz, who did just that, only managed to do so by bringing his version of *homo clausus*, the "windowless monads," in relation to one another by a metaphysical construction. All the same, monadology represents an early advance in the direction of precisely the kind of model that is urgently in need of further development in sociology today. The decisive step Leibniz took was an act of self-distantiation, which enabled him to entertain the idea that one might experience oneself not as an "ego" confronting all other people and things, but as a being among others. It was characteristic of the prevalent kind of experience in that whole period that the geocentric world-picture of the preceding age was superseded only in the area of inanimate nature by a world-picture demanding from the subject of experience a higher degree of self-detachment, a removal of oneself from the center. In men's reflection on themselves the geocentric world-picture was to a large extent preserved in the egocentric one that replaced it. At the center of the human universe, or so it appeared, stood each single human being as an individual completely independent of all others.

Nothing is more characteristic of the unquestioning way in which even today, in thinking about human beings, the separate individual is taken as the starting point than the fact that one does not speak of *homines sociologiae* or *oeconomiae* when talking of the image of man in the social sciences, but always of the image of the single human being, the *homo sociologicus* or *oeconomicus*. From this conceptual starting point, society presents itself finally as a collection of individuals completely independent of each other, whose true essence is locked within them and who therefore communicate only externally and from the surface. One must call on the help of a metaphysical solution, as Leibniz did, if, starting from windowless, closed, human and extrahuman monads, one is to justify the notion that interdependence and communication between them, or the perception by human beings of interdependence and communications, are possible. Whether we are dealing with human beings in their role as "subject" confronting the "object," or in their role as "individual" confronting "society," in both cases the problem is presented as if an adult human being, completely isolated and self-sufficient—that is, in a form reflecting the prevalent self-perception of people in the modern age crystallized in an objectifying concept—constitutes the frame of reference. What is discussed is his relation to something "outside" himself conceived (like the isolated human being) as a state, to "nature" or to "society." Does this something exist? Or is it only produced by a mental process, or at any rate founded primarily on a mental process?

9

Let us try to make clear what the problem actually is that is being discussed here. We are not concerned with calling into doubt the authenticity of the self-perception that finds expression in the image of man as *homo clausus* and its many variations. The question is whether this self-perception, and the image of man in which it is usually crystallized quite spontaneously and without reflection, can serve as a reliable starting point for an attempt to gain adequate understanding of human beings—and therefore also of oneself—regardless of whether this attempt is philosophical or sociological. Is it justified—that is the question—to place at the foundation of philosophical theories of perception and knowledge, and of sociological and other theories in the human sciences, as a self-evident assumption incapable of further explanation, the sharp dividing line between what is "inside" man and the "external world," a division which often appears directly given in self-awareness, and furthermore has put down deep roots in European intellectual and linguistic traditions, without a critical and systematic examination of its validity?

This conception has had, for a certain period of human development, an extraordinary persistence. It is found in the writings of all groups whose powers of reflection and whose self-awareness have reached the stage at which people are in a position not only to think but also to be conscious of themselves, and to reflect on themselves, as thinking beings. It is already found in Platonic philosophy and in a number of other schools of philosophy in antiquity. The idea of the "self in a case," as already mentioned, is one of the recurrent *leitmotivs* of modern philosophy, from the thinking subject of Descartes, Leibniz's windowless monads, and the Kantian subject of knowledge (who from his aprioristic shell can never quite break through to the "thing in itself") to the more recent extension of the same basic idea of the entirely self-sufficient individual: beyond the perspective of thought and perception as reified into "understanding" *(Verstand)* and "reason" *(Vernunft)*, to the whole "being" of man, his "existence" in the various versions of existentialist philosophy; or to his action as the starting point of the social theory of Max Weber, for example, who—entirely in keeping with the above-mentioned split—made the not wholly successful attempt to distinguish between "social action" and "nonsocial action," i.e., presumably "purely individual action."

But one would gain only a very inadequate idea of the nature of this self-perception and this image of man if they were understood merely as ideas set forth in scholarly writings. The windowlessness of the monads, the problems surrounding *homo clausus*, which a man like Leibniz tries to make at least more bearable by a speculative solution showing the possibility of relationships between monads, is today accepted as self-evident not only by scholars. Expressions of this self-perception are found in a less reflected form in imaginative literature—for example, in Virginia Woolf's lament over the incommunicability of experience as the cause of human solitude. Its expression is found in the concept of "alienation," used more and more frequently within and outside literature in the most diverse variation in recent decades. It would not be uninteresting to ascertain more systematically whether and how far gradations and variations of this type of self-perception extend to the various elite groups and the broader strata of more developed societies. But the examples cited suffice to indicate how persistent and how much taken for granted in the societies of modern Europe is the feeling of people that their own "self," their "true identity," is something locked away "inside" them, severed from all other people and things "outside"—although, as has been mentioned, no one finds it particularly simple to show clearly where and what the tangible walls or barriers are which enclose this inner self as a vessel encloses its contents, and separate it from what is "outside." Are we here concerned, as it often appears, with an eternal, fundamental experience of all human beings accessible to no further explanation, or with a type of self-perception which is characteristic of a certain stage in the development of the figurations formed by people, and of the people forming these figurations?

In the context of this book the discussion of this complex of problems has a twofold significance. On the one hand, the civilizing process cannot be understood so long as one clings to this type of self-perception and regards the image of man as *homo clausus* as self-evident, not open to discussion as a source of problems. On the other hand, the theory of civilization developed in this study offers a procedure for solving these problems. The discussion of this image of man serves in the first place to improve understanding of the ensuing study of the civilizing process. It is possible, however, that one might gain a better understanding of this introductory discussion from the vantage point of the end of the book, from a more comprehensive picture of the civilizing process. It will suffice here to indicate briefly the connection between the problems arising from the concept of *homo clausus* and the civilizing process.

One can gain a clear idea of this connection relatively simply by first looking back at the change in people's self-perception that was influenced by the abandonment of the geocentric world-picture. Often this transition is presented simply as a revision and extension of knowledge about the movements of the stars. But it is obvious that this changed conception of the figurations of the stars would not have been possible had not the prevailing image of man been seriously shaken on its own account, had not people become capable of perceiving themselves in a different light than before. Of primary importance for human beings everywhere is a mode of experience by which they place themselves at the center of public events, not just as individuals but as groups. The geocentric world-picture is the expression of this spontaneous and unreflecting self-centeredness of men, which is still encountered unequivocally today in the ideas of people outside the realm of nature, e.g., in natiocentric sociological modes of thought or those centered on the isolated individual.

The geocentric experience is still accessible to everyone as a plane of perception even today. It merely does not constitute the dominant plane of perception in public thought. When we say, and indeed "see," that the sun rises in the east and goes down in the west, we spontaneously experience ourselves and the earth on which we live as the center of the cosmos, as the frame of reference for the movements of the stars. It was not simply new discoveries, a cumulative increase in knowledge about the objects of human reflection, that were needed to make possible the transition from a geocentric to a heliocentric world-picture. What was needed above all was an increased capacity in men for self-detachment in thought. Scientific modes of thought cannot be developed and become generally accepted unless people renounce their primary, unreflecting, and spontaneous attempt to understand all their experience in terms of its purpose and meaning for themselves. The development that led to more adequate knowledge and increasing control of nature was therefore, considered from one aspect, also a development toward greater self-control by men.

It is not possible to go into more detail here about the connections between the development of the scientific manner of acquiring knowledge of objects, on the one hand, and the development of new attitudes of men toward themselves, new personality structures, and especially shifts in the direction of greater affect control and self-detachment, on the other. Perhaps it will contribute to an understanding of these problems if one recalls the spontaneous, unreflecting self-centeredness of thought that can be observed at any time among children in our own society. A heightened control of the affects, developed in society and learned by the individual, and above all a heightened degree of autonomous affect control, was needed in order for the world-picture centered on the earth and the people living on it to be overcome by one which, like the heliocentric world-picture, agreed better with the observable facts but was at first far less satisfying emotionally; for it removed man from his position at the center of the universe and placed him on one of many planets circling about the center. The transition from an understanding of nature legitimized by a traditional faith to one based on scientific research, and the shift in the direction of greater affect control that this transition involved, thus represents one aspect of the civilizing process examined from other aspects in the following study.

But at that particular stage in the development of these more object-related than self-related conceptual instruments for exploring extra-human nature, it was apparently not possible to include in the investigation, and to reflect upon, this civilizational shift itself, the move toward stronger and more "internalized" self-control that was taking place within man himself. What was happening to human beings as they increased their understanding of nature remained at first inaccessible to scientific insight. It is not a little characteristic of this stage of self-consciousness that the classical theories of knowledge representing it are concerned far more with the problems of the object of knowledge than with the subject of knowledge, with object-perception than with self-perception. But if the latter is not included from the start in posing epistemological problems, then this very posing leads to an impasse of equally inadequate alternatives.

The development of the idea that the earth circles round the sun in a purely mechanical way in accordance with natural laws—that is, in a way not in the least determined by any purpose relating to mankind, and therefore no longer possessing any great emotional significance for men—presupposed and demanded at the same time a development in human beings themselves toward increased emotional control, a greater restraint of their spontaneous feeling that everything they experience and everything that concerns them takes its stamp from them, is the expression of an intention, a destiny, a purpose relating to themselves. Now, in the age that we call "modern," men reach a stage of self-detachment that enables them to conceive of natural processes as an autonomous sphere operating without intention or purpose or destiny in a purely mechanical or causal way, and having a meaning or purpose for themselves only if they are in a position, through objective knowledge, to control it and thereby give it a meaning and a purpose. But at this stage they are not yet able to detach themselves sufficiently from themselves to make their own self-detachment, their own affect restraint—in short, the conditions of their own role as the subject of the scientific understanding of nature—the object of knowledge and scientific enquiry.

Herein lies one of the keys to the question of why the problem of scientific knowledge took on the form of classical European epistemology familiar today. The detachment of the thinking subject from his objects in the act of cognitive thought, and the affective restraint that is demanded, did not appear to those thinking about it at this stage as an act of distancing but as a distance actually present, as an eternal condition of spatial separation between a mental apparatus apparently locked "inside" man, an "understanding" or "reason," and the objects "outside" and divided from it by an invisible wall.

If we saw earlier how ideals can turn unawares in thought into something actually existing, how "ought" becomes "is," we are here confronted with a reification of a different kind. The act of conceptual distancing from the objects of thought that any more emotionally controlled reflection involves—which scientific observations and thought demand in particular,.and which at the same time makes them possible—appears to self-perception at this stage as a distance actually existing between the thinking subject and the objects of his thought. And the greater restraint of affect-charged impulses in the face of the objects of thought and observation, which accompanies every step toward increased conceptual distancing, appears here in people's self-perception as an actually existing cage which separates and excludes the "self" or "reason" or "existence," depending on the point of view, from the world "outside" the individual.

The fact that, and in part the reason why, from the late Middle Ages and the early Renaissance on, there was a particularly strong shift in individual self-control—above all, in self-control acting independently of external agents as a self-activating automatism, revealingly said today to be "internalized"—is presented in more detail from other perspectives in the following study. The transformation of interpersonal external compulsion into individual internal compulsion, which now increasingly takes place, leads to a situation in which many affective impulses cannot be lived out as spontaneously as before. The autonomous individual self-controls produced in this way in social life, such as "rational thought" or the "moral conscience," now interpose themselves more sternly than ever before between spontaneous and emotional impulses, on the one hand, and the skeletal muscles, on the other, preventing the former with greater severity from directly determining the latter (i.e., action) without the permission of these control mechanisms.

That is the core of the structural change and the structural peculiarities of the individual which are reflected in self-perception, from about the Renaissance onward, in the notion of the individual "ego" in its locked case, the "self" divided by an invisible wall from what happens "outside." It is these civilization self-controls, functioning in part automatically, that are now experienced in individual self-perception as a wall, either between "subject" and "object" or between one's own "self" and other people ("society").

The shift in the direction of greater individualization that took place during the Renaissance is well enough known. This study gives a somewhat more detailed picture of this development in terms of personality structure. At the same time, it points to connections that have not yet been properly clarified. The transition from the experience of nature as landscape standing opposed to the observer, from the experience of nature as a perceptual object separated from its subject as if by an invisible wall; the transition from the intensified self-perception of the individual as an entirely self-sufficient entity independent and cut off from other people and things—these and many other phenomena of the time bear the structural characteristics of the same civilizational shift. They all show marks of the transition to a further stage of self-consciousness at which the inbuilt self-control of the affects grows stronger and reflective detachment greater, while the spontaneity of affective action diminishes, and at which people feel these peculiarities of themselves but do not yet detach themselves sufficiently from them in thought to make themselves the object of investigation.

We thus come somewhat closer to the center of the structure of the individual personality underlying the self-experience of *homo clausus*. If we ask once again what really gives rise to this concept of the individual as encapsulated "inside" himself, severed from everything existing outside him, and what the capsule and the encapsulated really stand for in human terms, we can now see the direction in which the answer must be sought. The firmer, more comprehensive and uniform restraint of the affects characteristic of this civilizational shift, together with the increased internal compulsions that, more implacably than before, prevent all spontaneous impulses from manifesting themselves directly and motorically in action, without the intervention of control mechanisms—these are what is experienced as the capsule, the invisible wall dividing the "inner world" of the individual from the "external world" or, in different versions, the subject of cognition from its object, the "ego" from the "other," the "individual" from "society." What is encapsulated are the restrained instinctual and affective impulses denied direct access to the motor apparatus. They appear in self-perception as what is hidden from all others, and often as the true self, the core of individuality. The term "the inner man" is a convenient metaphor, but it is a metaphor that misleads.

There is good reason for saying that the human brain is situated within the skull and the heart within the rib cage. In these cases we can say clearly what is the container and what is contained, what is located within walls and what outside, and of what the dividing walls consist. But if the same figures of speech are applied to personality structures they become inappropriate. The relation of instinct controls to instinctive impulses, to mention only one example, is not a spatial relationship. The former do not have the form of a vessel containing the latter within it. There are schools of thought that consider the control mechanisms, conscience or reason, as more important, and there are others which attach greater importance to instinctual or emotional impulses. But if we are not disposed to argue about values, if we restrict our efforts to the investigation of what is, we find that there is no structural feature of man that justifies our calling one thing the core of man and another the shell. Strictly speaking, the whole complex of tensions, such as feeling and thought, or spontaneous behavior and controlled behavior, consists of human activities. If instead of the usual substance-concepts like "feeling" and "reason" we use activity-concepts, it is easier to understand that while the image of "outside" and "inside," of the shell of a receptacle containing something inside it, is applicable to the physical aspects of a human being mentioned above, it cannot apply to the structure of the personality, to the living human being as a whole. On this level there is nothing that resembles a container—nothing that could justify metaphors like that of the "inside" of a human being. The intuition of a wall, of something "inside" man separated from the "outside" world, however genuine it may be as an intuition, corresponds to nothing in man having the character of a real wall. One recalls that Goethe once expressed the idea that nature has neither core nor shell and that in her there is neither inside nor outside. This is true of human beings as well.

On the one hand, therefore, the theory of civilization which the following study attempts to develop helps us to see the misleading image of man in what we call the modern age as less self-evident, and to detach ourselves from it, so that work can begin on an image of man oriented less by one's own feelings and the value judgments attached to them than by men as the actual objects of thought and observation. On the other hand, a critique of the modern image of man is needed for an understanding of the civilizing process. For in the course of this process the structure of individual human beings changes; they become "more civilized." And so long as we see the individual human being as by nature a closed container with an outer shell and a core concealed within it, we cannot comprehend how a civilizing process embracing many generations is possible, in the course of which the personality structure of the individual human being changes without the nature of human beings changing.

This must suffice here as an introduction to the reorientation of individual self-consciousness and to the resulting development of the image of man, without which any ability to conceive a civilizing process or a long-term process involving social and personality structures is largely blocked. So long as the concept of the individual is linked with the self-perception of the "ego" in a closed case, we can hardly conceive "society" as anything other than a collection of windowless monads. Concepts like "social structure," "social process," or "social development" then appear at best as artificial products of sociologists, as "ideal-typical" constructions needed by scientists to introduce some order, at least in thought, into what appears in reality to be a completely disordered and structureless accumulation of absolutely independent individual agents.

As can be seen, the actual state of affairs is the exact converse. The notion of individuals deciding, acting, and "existing" in absolute independence of one another is an artificial product of men which is characteristic of a particular stage in the development of their self-perception. It rests partly on a confusion of ideals and facts, and partly on a reification of individual self-control mechanisms—of the severance of individual affective impulses from the motor apparatus, from the direct control of bodily movements and actions.

This self-perception in terms of one's own isolation, of the invisible wall dividing one's own "inner" self from all the people and things "outside," takes on for a large number of people in the course of the modern age the same immediate force of conviction that the movement of the sun around an earth situated at the center of the cosmos possessed in the Middle Ages. Like the geocentric picture of the physical universe earlier, the egocentric image of the social universe is certainly capable of being conquered by a more realistic, if emotionally less appealing picture. The emotion may or may not remain: it is an open question how far the feeling of isolation and alienation is attributable to ineptitude and ignorance in the development of individual self-controls, and how far to structural characteristics of advanced societies. Just as the public predominance of emotionally less appealing images of a physical universe not centered on the earth did not entirely efface the more private self-centered experience of the sun as circling around the earth, the ascendancy of a more objective image of man in public thinking may not necessarily efface the more private ego-centered experience of an invisible wall dividing one's own "inner world" from the world "outside." But it is certainly not impossible to dislodge this experience, and the image of man corresponding to it, from its self-evident acceptance in research in the human sciences. Here and in what follows one can see at least the beginnings of an image of man that agrees better with unhindered observations of human beings, and for this reason facilitates access to problems which, like those of the civilizing process or the state-building process, remain more or less inaccessible from the standpoint of the old image of man, or which, like the problem of the relation of individuals to society, continually give rise from that standpoint to unnecessarily complicated and never entirely convincing solutions.

The image of man as a "closed personality" is here replaced by the image of man as an "open personality" who possesses a greater or lesser degree of relative (but never absolute and total) autonomy vis-a-vis other people and who is, in fact, fundamentally oriented toward and dependent on other people throughout his life. The network of interdependencies among human beings is what binds them together. Such interdependencies are the nexus of what is here called the figuration, a structure of mutually oriented and dependent people. Since people are more or less dependent on each other first by nature and then through social learning, through education, socialization, and socially generated reciprocal needs, they exist, one might venture to say, only as pluralities, only in figurations. That is why, as was stated earlier, it is not particularly fruitful to conceive of men in the image of the individual man. It is more appropriate to envisage an image of numerous interdependent people forming figurations (i.e., groups or societies of different kinds) with each other. Seen from this basic standpoint, the rift in the traditional image of man disappears. The concept of the figuration has been introduced precisely because it expresses what we call "society" more clearly and unambiguously than the existing conceptual tools of sociology, as neither an abstraction of attributes of individuals existing without a society, nor a "system" or "totality" beyond individuals, but the network of interdependencies formed by individuals. It is certainly quite possible to speak of a social system formed of individuals. But the undertones associated with the concept of the social system in contemporary sociology make such an expression seem forced. Furthermore, the concept of the system is prejudiced by the associated notion of immutability.

What is meant by the concept of the figuration can be conveniently explained by reference to social dances. They are, in fact, the simplest example that could be chosen. One should think of a mazurka, a minuet, a polonaise, a tango, or rock'n'roll. The image of the mobile figurations of interdependent people on a dance floor perhaps makes it easier to imagine states, cities, families, and also capitalist, communist, and feudal systems as figurations. By using this concept we can eliminate the antithesis, resting finally on different values and ideals, immanent today in the use of the words "individual" and "society." One can certainly speak of a dance in general, but no one will imagine a dance as a structure outside the individual or as a mere abstraction. The same dance figurations can certainly be danced by different people; but without a plurality of reciprocally oriented and dependent individuals, there is no dance. Like every other social figuration, a dance figuration is relatively independent of the specific individuals forming it here and now, but not of individuals as such. It would be absurd to say that dances are mental constructions abstracted from observations of individuals considered separately. The same applies to all other figurations. Just as the small dance figurations change—becoming now slower, now quicker—so too, gradually or more suddenly, do the large figurations which we call societies. The following study is concerned with such changes. Thus, the starting point of the study of the process of state formation is a figuration made up of numerous relatively small social units existing in free competition with one another. The investigation shows how and why this figuration changes. It demonstrates at the same time that there are explanations which do not have the character of causal explanations. For a change in a figuration is explained partly by the endogenous dynamic of the figuration itself, the immanent tendency of figuration of freely competing units to form monopolies. The investigation therefore shows how in the course of centuries the original figuration changes into another, in which such great opportunities of monopoly power are linked with a single social position—kingship—that no occupant of any other social position within the network of interdependencies can compete with the monarch. At the same time, it indicates how the personality structures of human beings also change in conjunction with such figurational changes.

Jürgen Habermas

ADORNO–THE PRIMAL HISTORY
OF SUBJECTIVITY

When we were together a few weeks ago, Adorno told me this story about Charlie Chaplin. At a party in Hollywood for the producer of *The Best Years of Our Lives* there was a man who had lost both his hands in the war. Adorno extended his hand to the celebrated hero but drew back when he felt the metal claws of the prosthesis. Chaplin, reacting with lightning speed, translated into pantomime Adorno's perceptibly upset state and his hopeless attempts to cover it up. The story about Chaplin is also about Adorno.

Adorno had called coldness the principle of bourgeois subjectivity without which Auschwitz would not have been possible. He had deciphered in even the most unsuspect normality a vitality grown cold. This sensitivity developed to the point of virtuosity does not (as Bloch had supposed) evince the malicious gaze of the experienced misanthrope, but instead a bit of unexpressed, constantly arousable, and repeatedly disconcerted naivete. In the midst of the sociability, which was surely put on for a look at the artificial body part, the coldness of the metal had caught Adorno completely off guard. What the speechless mimesis of the great clown had made possible for that fleeting moment—the release of tension on the part of the onlookers and of Adorno seeking to take hold—may have remained a motif of Adorno's language and of his enchanting analyses.

In Adorno's last philosophical work, *Negative Dialectics*, there is a difficult statement that draws together in one breath the central idea of the "dialetic of enlightenment":

> That reason is something different from nature and yet a moment within it—this is its prehistory, which has become part of its immanent determination. As the psychic force branching out for the purposes of self-preservation, it is nature; however, once it has been split

off and contrasted with nature, it also becomes the other of nature. Reason, cutting nature down to size in an ephemeral way, is identical and nonidentical with nature, dialectical in accord with its own concept. Yet the more unrestrainedly reason is made into an absolute over against nature within that dialectic and becomes oblivious of itself in this, the more it regresses, as self-assertion gone wild, into nature; only as nature's reflection would it be supernature.

Adorno had used *The Odyssey* to secure the almost lost traces of a primal history of subjectivity. The episodes in the wanderings of the one beaten in a double sense reveal the crises that the self, in the process of forming its own identity, experiences in itself and within itself. The cunning Odysseus escapes animistic charms and mythological forces; he evades ritually prescribed sacrifices by apparently subjecting himself to them. The intelligent deception of those institutions that uphold the connection between an overpowering nature and a mimetic, self-adapting, still diffuse self is the original Enlightenment. With this act a permanently identical I is formed and power is gained over a desouled nature. The I acquires its inner organizational form in the measure that, in order to coerce external nature, it coerces the amorphous element in itself, its inner nature. Upon this relationship of autonomy and mastery of nature is perched the triumphant self-consciousness of the Enlightenment. Adorno calls into question its undialectical self-certitude.

If the subjection of outer nature is successful only in the measure of the repression of inner nature, mounting technological mastery strikes back at the subjectivity that gets shaped in these conquests. The constitution of an I permanently identifying with itself already results, according to Adorno's surmise, from the dissolution of that fluid, sympathetic, and at the same time murderous connection with nature which the sacrifice of the self called for in ritual promised to maintain. The history of civilization arises, then, from an act of violence, which humans and nature undergo in the same measure. The triumphal procession of the instrumental spirit is a history of the introversion of the sacrifice (that is to say, of the renunciation) no less than it is a history of the unfolding of the forces of production. In the metaphor of the mastery of nature, this coupling of technological control and institutionalized domination still resounds: Mastery of nature is chained to the introjected violence of humans over humans, to the violence of the subject exercised upon its own nature. Thus, even the trust Marx placed in the unfolding of the forces of production as such is precipitous. The sphere of freedom of mounting technological control can no longer be deployed for the revolutionizing of forms of social interchange if, among other things, the subject is truncated by the very instrumental spirit that has created the potential for liberation. The irrationality of an Enlightenment that does not reflect on itself consists in this: "With the denial of nature within human beings, not merely does the *telos* of the outward mastery of nature turn outward, but the *telos* of one's own life becomes confused and untransparent."

In the positivist common consciousness we find mirrored today the lack of will and the incapacity to perceive the dimension in which subjectivity is transformed historically; it is as if the subjects in the caves at Altamira and in the lunar capsules were the same. The specific speechlessness of those who for the sake of rendering palpable a gigantic, outwardly oriented enterprise finally set foot on the moon, and the equally speechless echo of the spectators, could have indicated that what Hegel once called the experience of consciousness has been silenced. Astronauts, and we along with them, do not belong in the series of Odysseus's successors. His quasi-natural destiny goes on, of course, as long as the reproduction of life does not break the spell of sheer self-assertion, especially where self-assertion luxuriates. The new transcendence of a scientific-technological progress isolated from communicable needs is "self-assertion gone wild."

If the diagnosis of the age expressed by Adorno and Horkheimer in the dialectic of the enlightenment is correct, a question arises concerning the privilege of the experience to which the authors must lay claim in relation to the withered contemporary subjectivity. In his introduction to the *Minima Moralia*, which may be construed without irony as a doctrine concerning the right way to live, Adorno tried to respond. Individual experience is necessarily based on the old subject, which, historically, has already been condemned—"which is still for itself, but no longer in itself." If we wish (following Hegel) to treat what is disappearing as essential, then the bourgeois subject, apprehended in the process of disappearance, is the essence that experiences its phased-out substance today in suffering under an overwhelming objectivity of social compulsion.

In psychological terms, with our view fixed on Adorno's person, this outcome is convincing. The incomparably brilliant geniality of Adorno has constantly evinced as well something of the awkward and fragile position of a subject still for itself but no longer in itself. Adorno never accepted the alternatives of remaining childish or growing up; he wanted neither to put up with infantilism nor to pay the cost of a rigid defense against repression, even were it to be "in the service of the I." In him there remained vivid a stratum of earlier experiences and attitudes. This ground of resonance reacted hypersensitively to a resistant reality, revealing the harsh, cutting, wounding dimensions of reality itself. This primal complex was occasionally released affectively in behavior, but it was consistently in free communication with thought—opened, as it were, to intellect. The vulnerability of the senses and the unshockability of a thought free from anxiety belonged together. This gift, which was not simply an endowment, exacted its tribute in spite of everything.

Adorno was not defenseless in the sense of having been afflicted by an especially bitter fate. (This is not said lightly, in view of his very real exile and emigration in flight from anti-Semitism; and it is true that the uncurtailed primal element in him was able to flourish only inside the pacified realm preserved for him first by his mother and his aunt and later by Gretal, his wife and collaborator.) Rather, Adorno was defenseless for an altogether different reason: In the presence of "Teddy" one could play out in an uncircumspect way the role of the "proper" adult, because he was never in a position to appropriate for himslef that role's strategies of immunization and adaptation. In every institutional setting he was "out of place," and not as if he intended to be. To his university colleagues this out-of-the-ordinary man was not exactly uncanny, even if he was considered suspect. However, academic philosophy (if the term suffices in this context) never really acknowledged this unusual intellectual. Even in the sphere of the literary public, which he influenced as hardly anyone else had for a decade and a half, Adorno did not get one of the official prizes, so his joy was disproportionately great when the German Association for Sociology made him its president. Adorno was defenseless in the unqualifiedly adult situations in which the routinized types exploited his weaknesses because they either did not realize or did not want to perceive that Adorno's specific weaknesses were profoundly connected with his eminent qualities. Even among his students there were such routinized types.

In more recent times Adorno bore many other things, even insults that might have been defused with a couple of sentences. I mention only the charge that Adorno's edition of Benjamin had suppressed Benjamin the materialist who sided with the Marxist party. This objection is based especially on the fact that at one time Adorno had criticized and rejected a three-part work by Benjamin about Baudelaire. Benjamin's revised version of the middle section was published in the *Zeitschrift für Sozialforschung* in 1940 and later included in the two-volume edition of his selected writings, and the original version of "Baudelaire" is coming out this fall. Now, the letters exchanged between Benjamin and Adorno in November and December of 1938 confirm to any unbiased reader that—as Benjamin himself would never have disputed—in this debate, too, Adorno was the theoretically more reflective party and the Marxist who was more erudite and more firmly fixed in the saddle. Precisely under Marxist presuppositions, his argument is compelling. However else one may want to evaluate Adorno's arguments, the accusation of an anti-Marxist falsification of Benjamin is oversimplified and malicious agitation. According to Gershom Scholem, Benjamin had been especially close to Adorno; Adorno communicated with him, learned from him, and stimulated him in return. With his Benjamin edition and his Benjamin interpretations, and still more with the relentless recourse to Benjamin motifs in his own writings, Adorno was the first to make the thought of his friend an unfalsified and irrevocable component of German discussion. That is why the ridiculous polemic of those who came to know Benjamin through Adorno hit him so hard.

One of Adorno's students called into the master's open grave, "He practiced an irresistible critique of the bourgeois individual, and yet he was himself caught within its ruins." That is quite true. To respond that "whatever is capable of falling down ought to be knocked down" and to say that Adorno should have had the power to strip away the last layer of his "radicalized bourgeois character" and go before the parade of activists carrying a flag demonstrates not only political and psychological foolhardiness but also a lack of philosophical understanding. The figure of the bourgeois individual, now relegated to the historical past, could only be left behind, voluntarily and with good conscience and not merely sadness, if from the dissolution of the old subject a new subject had already emerged. Now, Adorno never pretended to tell stories about a "new subject," but one thing was certain for him: The freedom that would be the polemical counterimage to suffering under social compulsions would have not only to eliminate the repressivity of the I principle but also to preserve its resistance against melting into the amorphous character of one's own nature or that of the collectivity. Adorno had shown, in a text meeting the usual standards of academic philosophy, that the two belong together. In it he unfolded the aporias of the Kantian concept of the intelligible character, and he specified "freedom" in the following manner:

> On the Kantian model, subjects are free to the extent that, as they are conscious of themselves, they are identical with themselves; and within such an identity they are at once unfree to the extent that they are subject to its compulsion and perpetuate it. As nonidentical, as diffuse nature, they are unfree; and yet as such they are free, because in the impulses that overwhelm them they are rid as well of the compulsive character proper to identity. This aporia is based on the fact that the truth behind the compulsion proper to identity would not simply be something altogether different from it, but would be mediated through it.

This statement makes plain the right that the untrue bourgeois subjectivity still retains in the process of disappearing in relation to its false negation. Adorno realized this and consequently never leaped over his shadows.

In *Negative Dialectics,* which has become his philosophical testament, Adorno took up again the impetus *Dialectic of Enlightenment* had carried: to save the dimension of nonidentity that the spirit seeking identity must cut away from the object.

The concept of the nonidentical is foreshadowed in Adorno's construal of Odysseus, in which he took aim at the prehistorically amorphous self that falls prey to the disciplining of an I capable of self-identical and hence identity-seeking thought. How, however, the non-identical stands for all "the truth that is hit upon by concepts, beyond their abstract scope." "The utopia of knowledge would be to open up what is nonconceptual by means of concepts, without making it identical with them." In this way the dialectic of the universal and the particular once unfolded by Hegel is taken up again. It has been gleaned from the model of communication in everyday language and can be made plausible in relation to it.

That we can never describe concrete objects completely in explicit discourse is a trivial insight. In making a statement about a particular (a thing, an event, or a person), we always apprehend it in view of a universal determination. The significance of the particular object can never be "exhausted" by progressively subsuming it under such generalities. However, as soon as subjects speak with one another and not just about objectified states of affairs, they counter one another with the claim to be recognized as irreplaceable individuals in their absolute determinateness. This recognition requires the paradoxical achievement of grasping—with the aid of what are in principle universal determinations and by means of these, as it were—the full concreteness of that which is precisely not identical with these generalities. Adorno turns this moment of the nonidentical within inevitable acts of identification against the necessity proper to formal logic, which has to determine the relationship of universal and particular in an undialectical way.

In this respect, Adorno only revives Hegel's critique of the limitations of thought within the faculty of judgment [*Verstandesdenken*], without which thought would, of course, be impossible in principle. But Adorno turns this critique once again upon Hegel himself. Hegel's dialectic, too, is proved to be ultimately indifferent to the unique weight of the individuated singular entity. That is to say, Hegel does not grasp totality conceptually as a nexus of compulsion—for example, that of a society that mediates the particular, the individuals interacting with one another, through the universal, by means of the categories of social labor and political domination and its legitimation. Consequently, he does not see that reconstructive power of dialectic can only disclose the kinds of relationships resulting from repression of communication free from compulsion—namely, coercive relationships of systematically distorted communication, under which individuals do not know one another as an objective context renders them. In Adorno's expression, society is just as much an embodiment of subjects as it is their negation; if it were no longer so, then the nexus of coercion whose dialectic is inwardly empowered to release it would have fallen away. In this sense, for Adorno the totality that dialectical thought tries to decode counts as "the untrue," although then Hegel's category of untruth can only be thought ironically, against Hegel himself.

The key term of *Negative Dialectics* is the "primacy of the objective" [*Vorrang des Objektiven*]. Adorno connects a fourfold meaning with this. First of all, objectivity denotes the coercive character of a world-historical complex that stands under the causality of fate, can be interrupted by self-reflection, and is contingent as a whole. Next, the primacy of the objective means suffering from that which weighs upon subjects. Knowledge of the objective context thus arises out of an interest in warding off suffering. Further, the phrase means the priority of nature in relation to all subjectivity it establishes outside itself. The pure I, in Kantian terms, is mediated by the empirical I. Finally, this materialist primacy of the objective is incompatible with any absolutist claims to knowledge. Self-reflection, and precisely self-reflection, is a finite power, for it itself pertains to the objective context that penetrates it. This inherent fallibility leads Adorno to plead for an "addition of leniency": "Even the most critical person would be utterly different in a condition of freedom such as he wishes to see. A just world would probably be unbearable for every citizen of a false world; he would be too damaged for it. That should stir a pinch of tolerance in the midst of resistance into the consciousness of the intellectual who has no sympathy for the spirit of the world."

Even the faculty of knowledge is not elevated above the frail and damaged state of the subject. If this is the way things are, however, the question how critical thought can be justified recurs. Our psychological response does not meet this question; it demands that the reasons for the right of criticism be made explicit.

Adorno has stubbornly refused to give an affirmative answer. He has even contested the view that reference to the negation of experienced suffering provides such grounds for the right of critique. This reference, doubtless the most extreme, may have no implication in the sense of a determinate negation, and yet Adorno is repeatedly forced by systematic considerations to take seriously the idea of reconciliation. This Adorno cannot escape. As soon as suffering is sublimated beyond immediate physical pain, it can only be negated if at the same time we express whatever is being repressed under the objectivity of societal coercion. Adorno once did this, tying in with Eichendorff's saying about "the beautifully alien" that rises above the sentimental suffering of alienation and above Romanticism: "The reconciled state would not annex the alien with a philosophical imperialism, but would find its happiness in the fact that the alien remained distinct and remote within the preserved proximity, beyond being either heterogeneous or one's own." Whoever mediates on this assertion will become aware that the condition described, although never real, is still most intimate and familiar to us. It has the structure of a life together in communication that is free from coercion. We necessarily anticipate such a reality, at least formally, each time we want to speak what is true. The idea of truth, already implicit in the first sentence spoken, can be shaped only on the model of the idealized agreement aimed for in communication free from domination. To this extent, the truth of propositions is bound up with the intention of leading a genuine life. Critique lays claim to no more than what is implied in everyday discourse, but also to no less. Adorno, too, has to assume no more and no less than this formal anticipation of just living when, with Hegel, he criticizes the identity-seeking thought of the faculty of judgment [*Verstand*], and then in turn the compulsion to identity in Hegel's idealist reason. Adorno might just as well have not asserted to this consequence and insisted that the metaphor of reconciliation is the only one that can be spoken, and only because it satisfies the prohibition of graven images and, as it were, cancels itself out. The wholly other may only be indicated by indeterminate negation, not known.

This lack of consistency, which exposes Adorno's philosophy to an objection that can be avoided, has a deep underlying motive. If the idea of reconciliation were to "evaporate" into the idea of maturity, of a life together in communication free from coercion, and if it could be unfolded in a not-yet-determined logic of ordinary language, then this reconciliation would not be universal. [Compare my essay on a theory of linguistic communication in J. Habermas and N. Luhmann, *Theorie der Gesellschaft oder Sozialtechnologie?* (Frankfurt am Main, 1971).] It would not entail the demand that nature open up its eyes, that in the condition of reconciliation we talk with animals, plants, and rocks. Marx also fastened on this idea in the name of a humanizing of nature. Like him, Adorno (and also Benjamin, Horkheimer, Marcuse, and Bloch) entertained doubts that the emancipation of humanity is possible without the resurrection of nature. Could humans talk with one another without anxiety and repression unless at the same time they interacted with the nature around them as they would with brothers and sisters? The "dialectic of the enlightenment" remains profoundly undecided as to whether with the first act of violent self-assertion (which meant both the technological control of external nature and the repression of one's own nature) a sympathetic bond has been torn asunder that has to be reestablished through reconciliation, or whether universal reconciliation is not a rather extravagant idea.

Perhaps one can say that in a certain measure we "repress" nature in the methodical attitude of science and technology, because we only let it "have a say" in relation to our own imperatives instead of apprehending it and dealing with it from its own point of view. The pain from this has been buried over by a Judeo-Christian tradition for thousands of years, even if it is not without traces in this tradition's apocalyptic background. Uninhibited, we subdue the earth, and now the entire universe is bereft of mystery. In contrast, the "dialectic of the enlightenment" makes it clear that we ought to recall the reluctantly repressed sorrow over what we have perpetrated on technologically dominated nature in order to become aware of the repression of our own nature (that is, the deformations of subjectivity). Clearly, however, in order to eliminate avoidable social repression, we cannot refuse the exploitation of nature that is necessary for survival. The concept of a categorially different science and technology is as empty as the idea of a universal reconciliation is without basis. The latter has its ground instead in the need for consolation and solicitude in the face of death, which the most insistent critique cannot fulfill. Without theology this pain is inconsolable, although even it should not be indifferent to the possibility of a society whose reproduction would no longer require the exploitation of our repressed anxieties.

Adorno, undeviating atheist that he was, nevertheless hesitated to moderate the idea of reconciliation to that of autonomy and responsibility. He was afraid to cloud the light of the Enlightenment, since "there is no light shining on human beings and things in which transcendence is not reflected."

With this might be connected the fact that Adorno, for whom theoretic rigor was second nature, mistrusted the claims of rigorous theory. He intentionally contented himself with "models." A young critic, still sure of his Hegel, once told him that the theory that apprehended the totality of society as untrue would actually be a theory of the impossibility of theory. The material content of the theory of society would then also be relatively meager, a reprise of the Marxist doctrine. After Adorno's opening talk to the sixteenth German Congress for Sociology on "Late Capitalism or Industrial Society" one could not maintain this in the same fashion; however, the point remains.

Adorno was convinced that the principle of identity attained universal dominance in the measure that bourgeois society was subjected to the organizing principle of exchange. "In exchange [bourgeois society] finds its social model; through it nonidentical individual natures and achievements become commensurable, identical. The exploitation of the principle (of exchange) relates the whole world to what is identical, toward a totality." Exchange actuates the abstractive operation in a way that is tangibly real. In this "primordial affinity" between identity-seeking thought and the principle of exchange Adorno saw the link between the critique of the instrumental spirit and the theory of bourgeois society. This link was sufficient for him to bring in just a little too precipitously the analyses handed down from Marx. Adorno was not bothered with political economy. Albrecht Wellmer, in his recently published *Critical Theory of Society and Positivism,* has drawn attention to the danger that arises when the dialectic of the enlightenment is misunderstood as a generalization in the field of philosophy of history of the critique of political economy and tacitly substituted for it. Then, that is to say, the critique of the instrumental spirit can serve as the key to a critique of ideology, to a depth hermeneutics that starts from arbitrary objectifications of the damaged life, that is self-sufficient and no longer in need of an empirical development of social theory. Adorno never let himself fall into this misunderstanding, but the activism of some of his students leads one to suppose that the decodifying of the objective spirit by ideology critique, to which Adorno had turned all his energy in such a remarkable way, can be easily confused with a theory of late-capitalist society. That praxis miscarries may not be attributed to the historical moment alone. The added circumstance that the impatient practitioners have no correct notion of the imperfection of theory may also contribute to this impasse. They do not realize all that they are incapable of knowing in the present state of affairs.

In this situation Adorno's aid was indispensable. It has been taken away from us by his death. There is no substitute for it, however slight.

Translated by Frederick G. Lawrence

BENJAMIN–CONSCIOUSNESS-RAISING OR RESCUING CRITIQUE

Walter Benjamin is relevant even in the trivial sense: In relation to him there is a division of opinion. The battle lines drawn during the short, almost eruptive period of the influence of Benjamin's *Schriften* in Germany were presaged in Benjamin's biography. The constellation of Scholem, Adorno, and Brecht, a youthful dependence on the school reformer Gustav Wyneken, and later closer relations with the surrealists were decisive for Benjamin's life history. Scholem, his most intimate friend and mentor, is today represented by Scholem the unpolemical, sovereign, and totally inflexible advocate of the dimension in Benjamin that was captivated with the traditions of Jewish mysticism. Adorno, Benjamin's heir, partner, and forerunner all in one person, not only introduced the first wave of the posthumous reception of Benjamin but also put his lasting imprint on it. After the death of Peter Szondi (who doubtless would have stood here today in my place), Adorno's place was taken mainly by Benjamin's editors, Tiedemann and Schweppenhäuser. Brecht, who must have served as a kind of reality principle for Benjamin, brought Benjamin around to breaking with his esotericism of style and thought. In Brecht's wake, the Marxist theoreticians of art H. Brenner, H. Lethen, and M. Scharang put Benjamin's late work into the perspective of the class struggle. Wyneken, whom Benjamin (who was active in the Free School Community) repudiated as a model while still a student, signalizes ties and impulses that continue on; the youthful conservative in Benjamin has found an intelligent and valiant apologist in Hannah Arendt, who would protect the suggestible, vulnerable aesthete, collector, and private scholar against the ideological claims of his Marxist and Zionist friends. Finally, Benjamin's proximity to surrealism has again been brought to our attention with the second wave of the Benjamin reception that took its impetus from the student revolt; the works by Bohrer and Bürger, among others, document this.

Between these fronts there is emerging a Benjamin philology that relates to its subject in a scholarly fashion and respectably gives notice to the incautious that this is no longer an unexplored terrain. In relation to the factional disputes that have nearly splintered the image of Benjamin, this academic treatment furnishes a corrective, if anything, but surely not an alternative. Moreover, the competing interpretations have not been simply tacked on. It was not mere mysterymongering that led Benjamin, as Adorno reports, to keep his friends apart from one another. Only as a surrealistic scene could one imagine, say, Scholem, Adorno, and Brecht sitting around a table for a peaceful symposium, with Breton and Aragon crouching nearby, while Wyneken stands by the door, all gathered for a debate on Bloch's *Spirit of Utopia* or even Klages's *Mind as Adversary of the Soul.* Benjamin's intellectual existence had so much of the surreal about it that one should not confront it with facile demands for consistency. Benjamin brought together motifs that ordinarily run at cross-purposes, but he did not actually unite them, and had he united them he would have done so in as many unities as there are moments in which the interested gaze of succeeding interpreters breaks through the crust and penetrates to where the stones still have life in them. Benjamin belongs to those authors on whom it is not possible to gain a purchase, whose work is destined for disparate effective histories; we encounter these authors only in the sudden flash of relevance with which a thought achieves dominance for brief seconds of history. Benjamin was accustomed to explaining the nature of relevance in terms of a Talmudic legend according to which "the angels—new each moment in countless hosts—(were) created so that, after they had sung their hymn before God, they ceased to exist and passed away into nothingness (*GS II*, p. 246).[1]

I would like to start from a statement Benjamin once turned against the procedure of cultural history: "It [cultural history] increases the burden of treasures that is piled on the back of humanity. But it does not bestow upon us the power to shake it off, so as to put it at our disposal." Benjamin sees the task of criticism precisely in this. He deals with the documents of culture (which are at the same time those of barbarism) not from the historicist viewpoint of stored-up cultural goods but from the critical viewpoint (as he so obstinately expresses it) of the decline of culture into "goods that can become an object of possession for humanity." (*F*, p. 35) Benjamin says nothing, of course, about the "overcoming of culture" [*Aufhebung der Kultur*].

1

Herbert Marcuse speaks of the overcoming of culture in a 1937 essay, "The Affirmative Character of Culture." As regards classical

---

1. See Abbreviations, p. 227.

bourgeois art, he criticizes the two-sidedness of a world of beautiful illusion that has been established autonomously, beyond the struggle of bourgeois competition and social labor. This autonomy is illusory because art permits the claims to happiness by individuals to hold good only in the realm of fiction and casts a veil over the unhappiness of day-to-day reality. At the same time there is something true about the autonomy of art because the ideal of the beautiful also brings to expression the longing for a happier life, for the humanity, friendliness, and solidarity withheld from the everyday, and hence it transcends the status quo: "Affirmative culture was the historical form in which were preserved those human wants which surpassed the material reproduction of existence. To that extent, what is true of the form of social reality to which it belonged holds for it as well: Right is on its side. Certainly, it exonerated 'external relationships' from responsibility for the 'vocation of humanity,' thus stabilizing their injustice. But it also held up to them the image of a better order as a task." In relation to this art, Marcuse makes good the claim of ideology critique to take at its word the trust that is articulated in bourgeois ideals but has been reserved to the sphere of the beautiful illusion—that is, to overcome art as a sphere split off from reality.

If the beautiful illusion is the medium in which bourgeois society actually expresses its own ideals but at the same time hides the fact that they are held in suspense, then the practice of ideology critique on art leads to the demands that autonomous art be overcome and that culture in general be reintegrated into the material processes of life. The revolutionizing of bourgeois conditions of life amounts to the overcoming of culture: "To the extent that culture has transmuted fulfillable, but factually unfulfilled, longings and instincts, it will lose its object. . . . Beauty will find a new embodiment when it no longer is represented as real illusion but, instead, expresses reality and joy in reality." (*Ng*, pp. 130ff.)

In the face of the mass art of fascism, Marcuse could not have been deceived about the possibility of a false overcoming of culture. Against it he held up another kind of politicization of art, which thirty years later seemed to assume concrete shape for a moment in the flower-garlanded barricades of the Paris students. In his *Essay on Liberation* Marcuse interpreted the surrealist praxis of the youth revolt as the overcoming of art with which art passes over into life.

A year before Marcuse's essay on the affirmative character of culture, Benjamin's treatise *The Work of Art in the Age of its Technological Reproducibility* (*I*, pp. 219–51) had appeared in the same journal, *Zeitschrift für Sozialforschung.* It seems as if Marcuse only recast Benjamin's more subtle observations in terms of the critique of ideology. The theme is once again the overcoming of autonomous art. The profane cult of beauty first developed in the Renaissance and remained valid for three hundred years. (*I*, p. 224) In the measure that art becomes dissociated from its cultic basis, the illusion of its autonomy disappears. (*I*, p. 230) Benjamin grounds his thesis that "art has escaped from the realm of 'beautiful illusion' " by pointing to the altered status of the work of art and to its altered mode of reception.

With the destruction of the aura, the innermost symbolic structure of the work of art is shifted in such a way that the sphere removed from the material processes of life and counterbalancing them falls apart. The work of art withdraws its ambivalent claim to superior authenticity and inviolability. It sacrifices both historical witness and cultic trappings to the art spectator. Already in 1927 Benjamin noted that "what we used to call art only starts two meters away from the body." (*GS* II, p. 622) The trivialized work of art gains its value for exhibition at the cost of its cultural value.

To the altered structure of the work of art corresponds a changed organization of the perception and reception of art. As autonomous, art is set up for individual enjoyment; after the loss of its aura it is geared to reception by the masses. Benjamin contrasts the contemplation of the isolated, art-viewing individual with the diffusion of art within a collective, stimulated by its appeal. "In the degeneration of the bourgeoisie, meditation became a school for asocial behavior; it was countered by diversion as a variety of social behavior." (*I*, p. 238) Moreover, in this collective reception Benjamin sees an enjoyment of art that is at once instructive and critical.

I believe I can distill from these not completely consistent utterances the notion of a mode of reception that Benjamin acquired from the reactions of a relaxed, and yet mentally alert, film-viewing public:

> Let us compare the screen on which a film unfolds with the canvas of a painting. The painting invites the viewer to contemplation; before it the viewer can abandon himself to his own flow of associations. Before the movie frame, he cannot do so. . . . In fact, when a person views these constantly changing (film) images, his stream of associations is immediately disrupted. This constitutes the shock effect of the film, which like all shock effects needs to be parried by a heightened presence of mind. Because of its technical structure, the

film has liberated the physical shock effect from the moral cushion-
ing in which Dadaism had, as it were, held it. (*I*, p. 238)

In a succession of discrete shocks, the art work deprived of its aura
releases experiences that used to be enclosed within an esoteric
style. In the mentally alert elaboration of this shock Benjamin no-
tices the exoteric dissolution of a cultic spell that bourgeois culture
inflicts on the solitary spectator in virtue of its affirmative character.

Benjamin conceives the functional transformation of art, which
takes place the moment the work of art is freed "from its parasitic
dependence on ritual," as the politicizing of art. "Instead of being
based on ritual, it begins to be based on another practice—
politics." (*I*, p. 224) In the claim of fascist mass art to be political,
Benjamin, like Marcuse, sees the risk in the overcoming of autonomous art. Nazi propaganda art carries out the liquidation of arts as
pertaining to an autonomous realm, but behind the veil of politicization it really serves the aestheticizing of naked political violence.
It replaces the degraded cult value of bourgeois art with a manipu-
latively produced one. The cultic spell is broken only to be revived
synthetically; mass reception becomes mass suggestion.

Benjamin's theory of art appears to develop a notion of culture
proper to the critique of ideology, which Marcuse will take up a
year later; however, the parallels alone are deceptive. I note four
essential differences:

- Marcuse deals with the exemplary forms of bourgeois art in
  accord with ideology critique, inasmuch as he fastens on the
  contradiction between the ideal and the real. From this critique results an overcoming of autonomous art only as the
  consequence of an idea. In contrast, Benjamin does not raise
  critical demands against a culture still unshaken in its substance. Instead, he describes the factual process of the disintegration of the aura, upon which bourgeois art grounds the
  illusion of its autonomy. He proceeds descriptively. He ob-
  serves a functional change in art, which Marcuse only anticipates for the moment in which the conditions of life are
  revolutionized.
- It is thus striking that Marcuse, like most other proponents of
  idealist aesthetics, limits himself to the periods acknowledged
  within bourgeois consciousness as classical. He is oriented
  toward a notion of artistic beauty taken from the symbolic
  forms within which essence comes to appearance. The classic

works of art (in literature this means especially the novel and the bourgeois tragic drama) are suitable objects for a critique of ideology precisely because of their affirmative character, just as in the realm of political philosophy rational natural right is suitable on account of its affirmative character. Benjamin's interest, however, is in the nonaffirmative forms of art. In his investigation of the baroque tragic drama he found in the allegorical a concept that contrasted with the individual totality of the transfigurative work of art. Allegory, which expresses the experience of the passionate, the oppressed, the unreconciled, and the failed (that is, the negative), runs counter to a symbolic art that prefigures and aims for positive happiness, freedom, reconciliation, and fulfillment. Whereas the latter needs ideology critique for decodifying and overcoming, the former is itself suggestive of critique: "What has survived is the extraordinary detail of the allegorical references: an object of knowledge whose haunt lies amid the consciously constructed ruins. Criticism is the mortification of the works. This is cultivated by the essence of such production more readily than by any other." (O, p. 182)

• In this connection, it is furthermore remarkable that Marcuse spares the transformation of bourgeois art by the avant-garde from the direct grasp of ideology critique, whereas Benjamin shows the process of the elimination of autonomous art within the history of modernity. Benjamin, who regards the emergence of the metropolitan masses as a "matrix from which all traditional behavior toward works of art emerges rejuvenated," (I, p. 239); uncovers a point of contact with this phenomenon precisely in the works that seem to be hermetically closed off from it: "The masses are so interiorized by Baudelaire that one searches in vain for clarification of them by him." ("On Some Motifs in Baudelaire," I, pp. 155–200) [For this reason Benjamin opposes the superficial understanding of *l'art pour l'art:* "This is the moment to embark on a work that would illuminate as no other the crisis of the arts that we are witnessing: a history of esoteric poetry. . . . On its last page one would have to find the X-ray image of surrealism." (R, p. 184)] Benjamin pursues the traces of modernity because they lead to the point where "the realm of poetry is exploded from within." (R, p. 178) The insight into the necessity for overcoming autonomous art arises from the reconstruction of what avant-garde art exposes about bourgeois art in transforming it.

- Finally, the decisive difference with Marcuse lies in Benjamin's conceiving the dissolution of autonomous art as the result of an upheaval in techniques of reproduction. In a comparison of the functions of painting and photography, Benjamin demonstrates in exemplary fashion the consequences of new techniques moving to the fore in the nineteenth century. In contrast with the traditional printing methods of pouring, casting, woodcarving, engraving, and lithography, these techniques represent a new developmental stage that may be comparable to the invention of the printing press. In his own day Benjamin could observe a development in phonograph records, films, and radio, which was accelerated by electronic media. The techniques of reproduction impinge on the internal structure of works of art. The work sacrifices its spatio-temporal individuality, on the one hand, but on the other hand it purchases more documentary authenticity. The temporal structure of ephemerality and repeatability, which replaces the uniqueness and duration typical of the temporal structure of the autonomous work of art, destroys the aura, "the unique appearance of a distance," and sharpens a "sense for sameness in the world." (*I*, pp. 222ff.) Things stripped of their aura move nearer the masses, as well, because the technical medium intervening between the selective organs of sense and the object copies the object more exactly and realistically. The authenticity of the subject matter, of course, requires the constructive use of means for realistic replication (that is, montage and captioning of photographs).

2

As these differences make clear, Benjamin does not let himself be guided by the concept of art based on ideology critique. With the dissolution of autonomous art, he has something else in mind than does Marcuse with his demand for the overcoming of culture. Whereas Marcuse confronts ideal and reality and highlights the unconscious content of bourgeois art that legitimates bourgeois reality while unintentionally denouncing it, Benjamin's analysis forsakes the form of self-reflection. Whereas Marcuse (by analytically disintegrating an objective illusion) would like to prepare the way for a transformation of the thus unmasked material relationships of life and to initiate an overcoming of the culture within which these relationships of life are stabilized, Benjamin cannot see his task to be an attack on an art that is already caught up in a process of dissolution. His art criticism behaves conservatively toward its objects, whether he is dealing with baroque tragic drama, with Goethe's *Elective Affinities,* with Baudelaire's *Fleurs du Mal,* or with the Soviet films of the early 1920s. It aims, to be sure, at the "mortification of the works," (O, p. 182), but the criticism practices this mortification of the art work only to transpose what is worth knowing from the medium of the beautiful into that of the true and thereby to rescue it.

Benjamin's peculiar conception of history explains the impulse toward rescuing: There reigns in history a mystical causality of the sort that "a secret agreement (comes about) between past generations and ours." "Like every generation that preceded us, we have been endowed with a *weak* messianic power, a power on which the past has a claim." ("Theses on the Philosophy of History," *I*, p. 254) This claim can only be redeemed by an ever-renewed critical exertion of historical vision toward a past in need of redemption; this effort is conservative in an eminent sense, for "every image of the past that is not recognized by the present as one of its own concerns threatens to disappear irretrievably." (*I*, p. 255) If this claim is not met, then danger threatens "both for the continuance of the tradition and for its recipients."

For Benjamin the continuum of history consists in the permanence of the unbearable and progress is the eternal return of catastrophe: "The concept of progress is to be founded within the idea of catastrophe." Benjamin notes in a draft of his work on Baudelaire that "the fact that 'everything just keeps on going' is the catastrophe." This is why "rescuing" has to cling "to the little crack within the catastrophe." (*GS*, I, p. 513) The concept of a present in which time stops and comes to rest belongs to Benjamin's oldest insights. In the "Theses on the Philosophy of History," written shortly before his death, the following statement is central: "History is the object of a construction whose site forms not homogeneous and empty time but time filled by the 'presence of the now' (*Jetztzeit; nunc stans*). Thus, to Robespierre ancient Rome was a past charged with the time of the now, which he blasted out of the continuum of history." (*I*, p. 261) One of Benjamin's earliest essays, "The Life of Students," starts off in a similar sense:

There is an apprehension of history that, trusting in the endlessness of time, discriminates only the different tempos of humans and ep-

ochs, which roll rapidly or slowly along the highway of progress. . . .
The following treatment, on the contrary, is concerned with a distinct condition in which history rests as if gathered into one burning
point, as has always been the case with the utopian images of thinkers. The elements of the final condition do not lie evident as shape-
less, progressive tendencies, but are embedded in *any* present time as
the most imperiled, scorned, and derided creations and ideas. (*GS II*,
p. 75)

To be sure, the interpretation of the rescuing intervention into
the past has shifted since the doctrine of ideas presented in Benjamin's book on baroque tragic drama. The retrospective gaze was
then supposed to gather the phenomenon rescued, inasmuch as it
escaped processes of becoming and passing away, into the fold of
the world of ideas; with its entry into the sphere of the eternal, the
primordial event was supposed to shed its pre- and post-history
(now become virtual) like a curtain of natural history. (*O*, pp. 45–
47) This constellation of natural history and eternity later gives way
to the constellation of history and the time of the now; the messianic cessation of the event takes over the place of the origin. But the
enemy that threatens the dead as much as the living when rescuing
criticism is missing and forgetting takes its place remained one and
the same: the dominance of mythic fate. Myth is the mark of a
human race hopelessly deprived of its vocation to a good and just
life and exiled into the cycle of sheer reproduction and survival.
The mythic fate can be brought to a standstill only for a transitory
moment. The fragments of experience that have been wrung at such
moments from fate (from the continuum of empty time) for the
relevance of the time of the now shape the duration of the endangered tradition. The history of art belongs to this tradition. Tiedemann quotes from the Paris Arcades project the following passage:
"In every true work of art there is a place where a cool breeze like
that of the approaching dawn breathes on whoever puts himself
there. It follows from this that art, which was often enough regarded as refractory toward any relationship with progress, can
serve its *authentic* distinctiveness. Progress is at home not in the
continuity of the flow of time, but in its interferences: wherever
something genuinely new makes itself felt for the first time with the
sobriety of dawn."
Benjamin's partially carried out plan for a primal history of modernity also belongs in this context. Baudelaire became central for
Benjamin because his poetry brings to light "the new within the

always-the-same, and the always-the-same within the new." (*GS, I*, p. 673)

Within the headlong processes of antiquation, which understands and misunderstands itself as progress, Benjamin's criticism uncovers the coincidence of time immemorial. It identifies within the modernization of forms of life propelled by the forces of production a compulsion toward repetition which is just as pervasive under capitalism—the always-the-same within the new. However, in doing this, Benjamin's criticism aims—and in this it is distinguished from critique of ideology—at rescuing a past charged with the *Jetztzeit.* It ascertains the moments in which the artistic sensibility puts a stop to fate draped as progress and enciphers the utopian experience in a dialectical image—the new within the always-the-same. The reversal of modernity into primal history has an ambiguous meaning for Benjamin. Myth belongs to primordial history, as does the content of the images. These alone can be broken away from myth. They have to be revived in another, as it were, awaited present and brought to "readability" for the sake of being preserved as tradition for authentic progress. Benjamin's antievolutionary conception of history, in accord with which the *Jetztzeit* runs perpendicular to the continuum of natural history, is not rendered utterly blind toward steps forward in the emancipation of the human race. However, it judges with a profound pessimism the chances that the punctual breakthroughs that undermine the always-the-same will combine into a tradition and not be forgotten.

Benjamin is acquainted with a continuity that, in its linear progress, breaks through the cycle of natural history and thereby menaces the lastingness of tradition. This is the continuity of demystification, whose final stage Benjamin diagnoses as the loss of aura: "In prehistoric times, because of the absolute emphasis on its cult value, the work of art was an instrument of magic. Only later did it come to be recognized as a work of art. In the same way today, because of the absolute emphasis on its exhibition value, the work of art becomes a structure with entirely new functions, among which the one we are conscious of, the artistic function, later may be recognized as incidental." (*I*, p.225) Benjamin does not explain this deritualization of art, yet it has to be understood as part of the world-historical process of rationalization that the developmental surge of the forces of production causes in social forms of life through revolutionizing the mode of production. Max Weber uses the term *disenchantment* too. Autonomous art became established only to the degree that, with the rise of civil society, the economic and political system was uncoupled from the cultural system and traditional-istic world views were undermined by the basic ideology of fair exchange, thus freeing the arts from the context of ritual. In the first place, art owes to its commodity character its liberation for the private enjoyment of the bourgeois reading, theater-going, exhibi-tion-going, and concert-going public that was coming into being in the seventeenth and eighteenth centuries. The advance of the pro-cess to which art owes its autonomy leads to its liquidation as well. In the nineteenth century the public made up of bourgeois private persons gave way to the laboring populace of large urban collec-tives. Thus, Benjamin concentrates on Paris as the large city *par excellence*. He also concentrates on mass art, since "photography and the film provide the most suitable means" to recognize the "de-ritualization of art." (*I*, p.225)

3

On no point did Adorno contradict Benjamin as vigorously as on this one. He regarded the mass art emerging with the new tech-niques of reproduction as a degeneration of art. The market that first made possible the autonomy of bourgeois art permitted the rise of a culture industry that penetrates the pores of the work of art itself and, along with art's commodity character, imposes on the spectator the attitudes of a consumer. Adorno first developed this critique in 1938, using jazz as an example, in his essay "The Fetish Character in Music and the Regression of Listening." He summa-rized and generalized the criticism—since carried out with regard to a number of different objects—in his volume on aesthetic theory under the title "Art Deprived of Its Artistic Character":

> Of the autonomy of works of art—which stirs the customers of cul-ture to indignation that one should consider it as something better—there is nothing left except the fetish character of the commodity. . . . The work of art is disqualified as the *tabula rasa* for subjective projections. The poles of its deprivation are that it becomes both just one thing among others and the vehicle for the psychology of the beholder. What reified works of art no longer say, the beholder re-places with the standardized echo of himself, which he receives from them. The culture industry sets this mechanism in motion and ex-ploits it. . . . (*ÄT*, p. 33)

The ingredient of historical experience in this critique of the cul-ture industry is disappointment, not so much about the history of the decline of art, religion, and philosophy as about the history of the parodies of their overcoming. The constellation of bourgeois culture in the age of its classical development was, to put it rather roughly, characterized by the dissolution of traditional images of the world, first by the retreat of religion into the sphere of privatized faith, then by the alliance of empiricist and relationalist philosophy with the new physics, and finally by an art which, having become autonomous, took up the complementary positions on behalf of the victims of bourgeois rationalization. Art was the preserve for a satisfaction, be it only virtual, of those needs that became, so to speak, illegal within the material process of life in bourgeois society: the need for a mimetic relation with external nature and the nature of one's own body, the need for life together in solidarity, and, in general, the need for the happiness of a communicative experience removed from the imperatives of purposive rationality and leaving room for fantasy and spontaneous behavior. This constellation of bourgeois culture was by no means stable; it lasted, as did liberalism itself, only a moment; then it fell prey to the dialectic of the enlightenment (or, rather, to capitalism as its irresistible vehicle).

Hegel announced the loss of aura in his *Lectures on Aesthetics.* In conceiving art and religion as restricted forms of absolute knowledge which philosophy as the free thinking of the absolute spirit penetrates, he set in motion the dialectic of a "sublation" [*Aufhebung*], which immediately transcended the limits of the Hegelian logic. Hegel's disciples achieved secular critiques of religion and then philosophy in order finally to allow the sublation of philosophy and its realization to come to term in the overcoming of political violence; this was the hour when Marxist ideology critique was born. What in the Hegelian construction was still veiled now came into the foreground: the special status assumed by art among the figures of the absolute spirit to the extent that it did not (like religion once it became subjectivized and philosophy once it became scientific) take over tasks in the economic and political system, but gathered residual needs that could not be satisfied in the "system of needs." Consequently, the sphere of art was spared from ideology critique right down to our century. When it finally fell subject to ideology critique, the ironic overcoming of religion and philosophy already stood in full view.

Today not even religion is a private matter, but with the atheism of the masses the utopian contents of the tradition have gone under as well. Philosophy has been stripped of its metaphysical claim, but within the dominant scientism even the constructions before which a wretched reality was supposed to justify itself have disintegrated. In the meantime, even a "sublation" of a science is at hand. This destroys the illusion of autonomy, but less for the sake of discursively guiding the scientific system than for the sake of functionalizing it for unreflected interests. Adorno's critique of a false elimination of art should also be seen in this context; it does destroy the aura, but along with the dominative organization of the work of art it liquidates its truth at the same time.

Disappointment with false overcoming, whether of religion, philosophy, or art, can evoke a reaction of restraint, if not of hesitancy, of the sort that one would rather be mistrustful of absolute spirit's becoming practical than consent to its liquidation. Connected with this is an option for the esoteric rescue of moments of truth. This distinguishes Adorno from Benjamin, who insists that the true moments of the tradition will be rescued for the messianic future either exoterically or not at all. In opposition to the false overcoming of religion, Adorno—like Benjamin an atheist, if not in the same way—proposes bringing in utopian contents as the ferment for an uncompromisingly critical thought, but precisely not in the form of a universalized secular illumination. In opposition to the false overcoming of philosophy, Adorno—an antipositivist, like Benjamin—proposes bringing a transcendent impetus into a critique that is in a certain way self-sufficient, but does not penetrate into the positive sciences in order to become universal in the form of a self-reflection of the sciences. In opposition to the false overcoming of autonomous art, Adorno presents Kafka and Schoenberg, the hermetic dimension of modernity, but precisely not the mass art that makes the auratically encapsulated experience public. After reading the manuscript of Benjamin's essay on the work of art, Adorno (in a letter dated March 18, 1936) objects to Benjamin that "the center of the autonomous work of art does not itself belong on the side of myth." He continues: ". . . Dialectical though your work may be, it is not so in the case of the autonomous work of art itself; it disregards the elementary experience which becomes more evident to me every day in my own musical experience—that precisely the utmost consistency in the technological law of autonomous art changes this art and, instead of rendering it into a taboo or a fetish, approximates it to the state of freedom, of something that can consciously be produced and made." After the destruction of the aura, only the formalist work of art, inaccessible to the masses, resists the pressures toward assimilation to the needs and attitudes of the consumer as determined by the market.

Adorno follows a strategy of hibernation, the obvious weakness of which lies in its defensive character. Interestingly, Adorno's thesis can be documented with examples from literature and music only insofar as these remain dependent on techniques of reproduction that prescribe isolated reading and contemplative listening (the royal road of bourgeois individuation). In contrast, for arts received collectively—architecture, theater, painting—just as for popular literature and music, which have become dependent on electronic media, there are indications of a development that points beyond more culture industry and does not *a fortiori* invalidate Benjamin's hope for a generalized secular illumination.

Of course, the deritualization of art has an ambiguous meaning for Benjamin too. It is as if Benjamin were afraid of myth's being eradicated without any intervening liberation—as if myth would have to be given up as beaten, but its content could be preserved for transposition into tradition, in order to triumph even in defeat. Now that myth is wearing the robes of progress, the images that tradition can find only within the innermost recesses of myth are in danger of toppling over and being forever lost to rescuing criticism. The myth nesting within modernity, which is expressed in positivism's faith in progress, is the enemy against which Benjamin sets the entire pathos of rescuing. Far from being a guarantee of liberation, deritualization menaces us with a specific loss of experience.

4

Benjamin was always ambivalent about the loss of aura. In the aura of a work of art is enclosed the historical experience of a past *Jetztzeit* in need of revitalization; the undialectical destruction of aura would be a loss of that experience. When Benjamin, as a student, still trusted himself to sketch "The Program of Coming Philosophy" (*GS II*, p. 159), the notion of an unmutilated experience already stood at the center of his reflections. At that time, Benjamin polemicized against "experience reduced to point zero, the minimum of significance," against the experience of physical objects with respect to which Kant had paradigmatically oriented his attempt at an analysis of the conditions of possible experience. Against this, Benjamin defended the more complex modes of experience of people living close to nature, madmen, seers, and artists. At that time he still had hopes of restoring a systematic continuum of experience through metaphysics. Later he assigned this task to art criticism, supposing that *it* would transpose the beautiful into the medium of the true, by which transposition "truth is not an unveiling, which annihilates the mystery, but a revelation and a manifestation that does it justice." (O, p. 31) The concept of aura ultimately takes the place of the beautiful illusion as the necessary outer covering, which, as it disintegrates, reveals the mystery of complex experience: "Experience of aura thus rests on the transposition of a response common in human relationships to the relationship between the inanimate or natural object and human beings. The person whom we look at, or who feels he is being looked at, looks at us in turn. To perceive the aura of an object means to invest it with the capacity to look at us in turn." (I, p. 298)

The auratic appearance can occur only in the intersubjective relationship of the I with its counterpart, the alter ego. Wherever nature gets so "invested" that it opens its eyes to look at us in return, the object is transformed into a counterpart. Universal animation of nature is the sign of magical world views in which the split between the sphere of the objectified, over which we have manipulative disposal, and the realm of the intersubjective, in which we encounter one another communicatively, has not yet been achieved. Instead, the world is organized according to analogies and correspondences for which totemistic classifications supply an example. A subjectivistic remainder of the perception of such correspondences are the synaesthetic associations.

In the light of the appearance of aura, Benjamin develops the emphatic notion of an experience that needs to be critically conserved and appropriated if the messianic promise of happiness is ever to be redeemed. On the other hand, he also treats the loss of aura in a positive way. This ambiguity is also expressed in Benjamin's emphasis on just those achievements in autonomous art that are also distinctive of the deritualized work of art. Art fully stripped of the cultic element—and surrealist art, whose proponents have once again taken up Baudelaire's notion of *correspondence*, is exemplary in this regard—has the same aim as autonomous art, namely to experience objects within the network of rediscovered correspondences as a counterpart that makes one happy: "The *correspondences* constitute the court of judgement before which the object of art is found to be one that forms a faithfully reproduced image—which, to be sure, makes it entirely problematic. If one attempted to reproduce even this aporia in the material of language, one would define beauty as the object of experience in the state of resemblance." (I, p. 99, n. 13) The ambiguity can be resolved only if we separate the cultic moment in the notion of the auratic appearance from the universal moments. With the overcoming of autonomous art and the collapse of aura, the esoteric access to the work of art and its cultic distance from the viewer disappear. Hence, the contemplation characteristic of the solitary enjoyment of art disappears too. However, the experience released by the shattered shell of aura, namely the transformation of the object into a counterpart, was already contained in the experience of aura as well. A field of surprising correspondences between animate and inanimate nature is thereby opened up wherein things, too, encounter us in the structure of vulnerable intersubjectivity. In such structures, the essence that appears escapes the grasp after immediacy without any distance at all; the proximity of the other refracted in the distance is the signature of a possible fulfillment and a mutual happiness. Benjamin's intention aims at a condition in which the esoteric experiences of happiness have become public and universal, for only in a context of communication into which nature is integrated in a brotherly fashion, as if it were set upright once again, can human subjects open up their eyes to look in return.

The deritualization of art conceals the risk that the work of art also sacrifices the experiential content along with its aura and becomes trivial. On the other hand, the collapse of aura opens up the chance of universalizing and stabilizing the experience of happiness. The absence of a protective shell around a happiness that has become exoteric and has dispensed with auratic refraction grounds an affinity with the experience of the mystic, who in the experience of rapture is more interested in the actuality of the nearness and sensible presence of God than in God himself. Only the mystic closes his eyes and is solitary; his experience as well as its transmission is esoteric. Exactly this moment separates the experience of happiness that Benjamin's rescuing criticism validates from religious experience. Benjamin therefore calls *secular* the illumination he elucidates in terms of the effect of surrealistic works that are no longer art in the sense of autonomous works but manifestation, slogan, document, bluff, and counterfeit. Such works bring us to the awareness that "we penetrate the mystery only to the degree that we recognize in it the everyday world, by virtue of a dialectical optic that knows the everyday as impenetrable, the impenetrable as everyday." (R, p. 190) This experience is secular because it is exoteric.

No interpretation—however insistent in wrestling for the soul of a friend, as is Scholem's contribution to the volume *Zur Aktualität Walter Benjamins*—can dismiss Benjamin's break with esotericism. In the face of the rise of fascism, political insight forced Benjamin to break with that esotericism of the true for which the young Benjamin had reserved the dogmatic concept of doctrine. Benjamin once wrote to Adorno that "speculation sets out upon its necessarily bold flight with some prospect of success only if, instead of donning the waxen wings of esotericism, it sees its source of power in construction alone." (*NLR*, p. 76) Benjamin turned against the esotericism of fulfillment and happiness just as decisively. His intention—and this sounds like a repudiation of Scholem—is "the true, creative *overcoming* of religious illumination. . . . a *secular* illumination, a materialist, anthropological inspiration" (*R*, p. 179), for which solitary ecstasy could at most serve as a primer.

If we look back at Benjamin's thesis about the overcoming of autonomous art from this point, we see why it cannot be a thesis of ideology critique: Benjamin's theory of art is a theory of experience (but not of the experience of reflection). In the forms of secular illumination, the experience of aura has burst the protective auratic shell and become exoteric. It does not derive from an analysis that sheds light on what has been suppressed and sets free what has been repressed. It is gained in a manner other than reflection would be capable of, namely by taking up again a semantics that is pried piece by piece from the interior of myth and released messianically (that is, for purposes of emancipation) into works of great art at the same time as it is preserved. What is unexplainable in this conception is the peculiar undertow that must be stemmed by rescuing criticism: Without its permanent exertion, it seems, the transmitted testimony of punctual liberations from myth and the semantic contents wrung from it would have to fall into a void; the contents of tradition would fall victim to forgetfulness without leaving a trace. Why? Benjamin was obviously of the opinion that meaning was not a good capable of being increased, and that experiences of an unimpaired interchange with nature, with other people, and with one's self cannot be engendered at will. Benjamin thought instead that the semantic potential on which human beings draw in order to invest the world with meaning and make it accessible to experience was first deposited in myth and needs to be released from it, and that this potential cannot be expanded but only transformed. Benjamin was afraid that semantic energies might escape during this transformation and be lost to humanity. His linguistic philosophy affords a foothold for this perspective of decline and fall; the theory of experience is found in it.

5

Throughout his life, Benjamin adhered to a mimetic theory of language. Even in the later works he comes back to the onomatopoetic character of single words and even of language as a whole. It is unimaginable to him that words are related to reality accidentally. Benjamin conceives words as names. In giving names to things, however, we can either hit their essence or miss the mark; naming is a kind of translation of the nameless into names, a translation from the incomplete language of nature into the language of humans. Benjamin did not consider the special property of language to lie in its syntactical organization (in which he had no interest) or in its representational function (which he regarded as subordinate to its expressive function). It is not the specifically human properties of language that interest Benjamin but the function that links it with animal languages. Expressive speech, he thinks, is only one form of the animal instinct that is manifested in expressive movements. Benjamin brings this together with the mimetic capacity to perceive and reproduce similarities. An example is dance, in which expression and mimesis are fused. He cites a statement by Mallarmé: "The dancer is not a woman but a metaphor that can bring to expression an aspect of the elementary forms of our existence: a sword, a drinking cup, a flower, or anything else." (*GS*, p. 478) The primordial mimesis is the representation of correspondences in images: "As is known, the sphere of life that formerly seemed to be governed by the law of similarity was comprehensive; it ruled both microcosm and macrocosm. But these natural correspondences acquire their real importance only if we recognize that they serve without exception to stimulate and awaken the mimetic capacity in the human being that responds to them." (*R*, p. 333) Whatever is expressed in linguistic physiognomy or in expressive gestures generally is not a mere subjective state but, by way of this, the as-yet-uninterrupted connection of the human organism with surrounding nature; expressive movements are systematically linked with the qualities of the environment that evoke them. As adventurous as this mimetic theory of language sounds, Benjamin is correct in supposing that the oldest semantic stratum is that of expression. The expressive richness of the language of primates is well researched, and, according to Ploog, "to the extent that language is entoned emotional expression, there is no basic difference from the vocal expressive capacity of the nonhuman family of primates."

One might speculate that a semantic basis from the subhuman forms of communication entered into human language and represents a potential in meanings that is incapable of being increased and with which humans interpret the world in light of their needs and thereby engender a network of correspondences. Be that as it may, Benjamin counts on such a mimetic capacity with which the species on the verge of becoming human was equipped before it entered upon the process of reproducing itself. It is one of Benjamin's fundamental (non-Marxist) convictions that meaning is not produced by labor, as value is, but can at most be transformed in dependence upon the process of production.[38] The historically changing interpretation of needs feeds from a potential with which the species has to economize, because although we can indeed transform it we cannot enrich it:

> It must be borne in mind that neither mimetic powers nor mimetic objects or referents (which, one could add, have stored away in them something of the releasing qualities of whatever is compelling and pregnant) remain the same in the course of thousands of years. Rather, we must suppose that the gift of producing similarities (for example, in dances, whose oldest function was this), and therefore also the gift of recognizing them, have changed with historical development. The direction of this change seems definable as the increasing decay of the mimetic faculty. (*R*, pp. 333–34)

This process has an ambiguous significance.

In the mimetic capacity, Benjamin sees not only the source of the wealth of meaning that human needs, released in the socio-cultural form of life, pour out in language over a world that is thereby humanized. He also sees in the gift of perceiving similarities the rudimentary form of the once-violent compulsion to become similar, to be forced into adaptation—the animal legacy. To this extent, the mimetic capacity is also the signature of a primordial dependence on the violent forces of nature; it is expressed in magical practices, lives on in the primal anxiety of animistic world views, and is preserved in myth. The vocation of the human species, then, is to liquidate that dependence without sealing off the powers of mimesis and the streams of semantic energies, for that would be to lose the poetic capacity to interpret the world in the light of human needs. This is the secular content of the messianic promise. Benjamin has conceived the history of art, from the cultic to the postauratic, as the history of the attempts to represent in images these insensible similarities or correspondences but at the same time to loose the spell that once rested on this mimesis. Benjamin called these attempts divine, because they break myth while preserving and setting free its richness.

If we follow Benjamin this far, the question arises what is the source of those divine forces that at once preserve and liberate.

Even the criticism whose conservative-revolutionary power Benjamin counts on has to be directed retrospectively toward past *Jetzt-zeiten*; it lights on structures in which contents recovered from the myth (that is, documents of past deeds of liberation) have been deposited. Who produces these documents? Who are their authors? Benjamin obviously did not want to rely, in an idealist way, on an underivable illumination of great authors, and thus on an utterly nonsecular source. Indeed he was close enough to the idealist answer to the question, for a theory of experience grounded in a mimetic theory of language permits no other response. Benjamin's political insights stood opposed to this, however. Benjamin, who uncovered the prehistoric world by way of Bachofen, knew Schuler, studied and appreciated Klages, and corresponded with Carl Schmitt—this Benjamin, as a Jewish intellectual in the Berlin of the 1920s could still not ignore where his (and our) enemies stood. This awareness compelled him to a materialist response.

This is the background to Benjamin's reception of historical materialism, which he naturally had to unite with the messianic conception of history developed on the model of rescuing criticism. This domesticated historical materialism was supposed to supply an answer to the open question about the subject of the history of art and culture, an answer at once materialist and yet compatible with Benjamin's own theory of experience. To have thought he had achieved this was Benjamin's mistake and the wish of his Marxist friends.

Ideology critique's concept of culture has the advantage of introducing the cultural tradition methodologically as a part of social evolution and making it accessible to a materialist explanation. Benjamin went behind this concept, because the kind of criticism that appropriates the history of art under the aspects of rescuing the messianic moments and preserving an endangered semantic potential has to comprehend itself not as reflection on a process of self-formation but as identification and *re-trieval* of emphatic experiences and utopian contents. Benjamin also conceived the philosophy of history as a theory of experience. Within this framework, however, a materialist explanation of the history of art—which Benjamin, for political reasons, does not want to give up—is not possible in any direct way. That is why he tries to integrate this doctrine with basic assumptions of historical materialism. He announces his intention in the first of his "Theses on the Philosophy of History": The hunchbacked dwarf theology is supposed to take the puppet historical materialism into its service. This attempt must fail, because the materialist theory of social development cannot simply be fitted into the anarchial conception of the *Jetztzeiten* that intermittently break through fate as if from above. Historical materialism, which reckons on progressive steps not only in the dimension of productive forces but in that of domination as well, cannot be covered over with an antievolutionary conception of history as with a monk's cowl. My thesis is that Benjamin did not succeed in his intention of uniting enlightenment and mysticism because the theologian in him could not bring himself to make the messianic theory of experience serviceable for historical materialism. That much, I believe, has to be conceded in Scholem's favor.

I would like now to take up two difficulties: the odd adaptation of Marxian critique of ideology and the idea of a politicized art.

6

In 1935, at the behest of the Institute for Social Research, Benjamin prepared an expose in which he presented for the first time some motifs of the Paris Arcades Project (*Paris, Capital of the Nineteenth Century*). Looking back on the lengthy history of its preparation, Benjamin writes in a letter to Adorno about a process of recasting that "has brought the entire mass of thought, which was metaphysically motivated at the start, to a state in which the universe of dialectical images has been secured against the objections provoked by metaphysics."(B2, p. 664) By this he is referring to "the new and incisive sociological perspectives that provide a secure framework for the span of interpretation." (B2, p. 665) Adorno's response to this expose and his critique of the first study on Baudelaire that Benjamin offered the *Zeitschrift für Sozialforschung* three years later reflect very exactly the way Benjamin makes original use of Marxist categories—and in terms of both what Adorno understands and what he misunderstands. Adorno's impression is that Benjamin does violence to himself in the Arcades Project in order to pay tribute to Marxism, and that this turns out for the good of neither. He warns against a procedure that "gives to conspicuous individual features from the realm of the superstructure a 'materialist' turn by relating them, without mediation and perhaps even causally, to corresponding features of the base." (NLR, p. 71) He refers particularly to the merely metaphorical use of the category of commodity fetishism, concerning which Benjamin had announced in a letter to Scholem that it stood at the center of the new work in the same way the concept of the tragic drama stood at the center of his book about the Baroque. Adorno lances the superficially materialist tendency to relate "the contents of Baudelaire's work immediately to adjacent features in the social history of his time, and, as much as possible, to those of an economic kind." (*NLR*, p. 70) In doing so, Benjamin gives Adorno the impression of a swimmer "who, covered with great goose pimples, plunges into cold water." (Ibid.) This sharpsighted judgment, which loses none of its trenchancy even when Adorno's rivalry with Brecht is taken into account, still contrasts oddly with the unintelligent insistence that his friend might wish to make good the "omitted theory" and the "lacking interpretation" so that the dialectical mediation between cultural properties and the overall social process would become visible. Adorno never noticeably hesitated to attribute to Benjamin the precise intention of ideology critique that he followed in his own work, and in this he was wrong. This error is shown in exemplary fashion by the objections that were supposed to have moved Benjamin to revise the notion of dialectical image that was central to his theory of experience so that "a purification of the theory itself might be achieved." (*NLR*, p. 54) Adorno does not see how legitimate it is to want to carry out the project for a primal history of modernity—which aims at decodifying a semantics that has been buried and is threatened with forgetfulness—by hermeneutical means, through the interpretation of dialectical images. For Benjamin, imaginal fantasies of the primal past are set loose under the impulse of the new, in which the continuity of the always the same is carried on; they "mingle with the new to give birth to utopias." (*R;* p. 148)

Benjamin's expose speaks of the collective unconscious as the storehouse of experiences. Adorno is rightly put off by this use of language; however, he is quite incorrect in thinking that disenchantment of the dialectical image has to lead back to an unbroken mythic thinking, for the archaic dimension of modernity—in which Adorno would see Hell instead of the golden age—contains just the potentialities for experience that point the way to the utopian condition of a liberated society. The model is the French Revolution's recourse to Roman antiquity. Here Benjamin uses a comparison with the realization of dream elements upon waking, which was developed into a technique in surrealism and which Benjamin misleadingly calls a classic instance of dialectical thinking. Adorno takes Benjamin too literally here. Transposing the dialectical image into consciousness as a dream seems to him to be naked subjectivism. The fetish character of commodities, he contends against Benjamin, is no mere fact of consciousness but is dialectical in the eminent sense that it produces consciousness—archaic images—within alienated bourgeois individuals. However, Benjamin has no need to take up this claim of ideology critique; he does not want to reach behind the formations of consciousness to the objectivity of an evaluation process by means of which the commodity as fetish gains power over the consciousness of individuals. Benjamin wants and needs to investigate only "the mode of apprehension of the fetish character in the collective consciousness," because dialectical images are phenomena of consciousness and not (as Adorno thought) transposed into consciousness.

Of course, Benjamin also deceived himself about the difference between his manner of proceeding and the Marxist critique of ideology. In the manuscripts for the Arcades Project he once put it as follows: "If the base determines the superstructure to a certain extent in regard to the material for thought and experience, and if this determination is, however, not that of a simple mirroring, how then is it to be characterized, quite apart from the cause behind emergence(!)? As its expression. The superstructure is the expression of the base. The economic conditions under which the society exists come to expression in the superstructure." (cited after Tiedemann, *Studien*, p. 106) Expression is a category of Benjamin's theory of experience; it is related to those insensible correspondences between animate and inanimate nature upon which the physiognomical gaze of the child and of the artist rests. Expression, for Benjamin, is a separate category that is more akin to what Kassner or even Klages intended than to the base-superstructure theorem. The same misunderstanding is shown in relation to the critique of ideology as practiced by Adorno, when Benjamin remarks about chapters of his later book on Wagner that "*one* tendency of this work interested (me) in particular: situating the physiognomical immediately, almost without psychological mediation, within the social realm." (*B2*, p. 741) In fact Benjamin did not have psychology in mind, but neither was he concerned with a critique of necessarily false consciousness. His criticism was concerned with doing justice to the collective fantasy images deposited in the expressive qualities of daily life as well as in literature and art. These images arise from the secret communication between the oldest semantic potentials of human needs and the conditions of life generated by capitalism.

In their correspondence concerning the Arcades Project, Adorno appeals to the goal "for the sake of which you sacrifice theology." (*NLR*, p. 54) Benjamin had surely made this sacrifice, inasmuch as he now accepted mystical illumination only as secular (i.e., universalizable) exoteric experience. However, Adorno, who in comparison with Benjamin was certainly the better Marxist, did not see that his friend was never prepared to give up the theological heritage, inasmuch as he always kept his mimetic theory of language, his messianic theory of history, and his conservative-revolutionary understanding of criticism immune against objections from historical materialism (to the degree that this puppet could not simply be brought under his direction). This can also be seen in Benjamin's assent to the instrumental politicization of art, where he confessed to being an engaged Communist. I understand this assent, which becomes clearest in the lecture "The Author as Producer" (*R*, pp. 220–38), as a perplexity resulting from the fact that an immanent relation to political praxis is by no means to be gained from rescuing critique, as it is from consciousness-raising critique.

When it uncovers within apparently universal interests the particular interest of the ruling class, ideology critique is a political force. Insofar as it shakes the normative structures that hold the consciousness of the oppressed captive and comes to term in political action, ideology critique aims to dismantle the structural violence invested in institutions. It is oriented toward the participatory eradication of the violence thus set loose. Structural violence can also be released preventatively or reactively from above; then it has the form of a fascist partial mobilization of the masses, who do not eradicate the violence unleashed but "act it out" in a diffuse manner.

I have shown that there is no room in this relational frame of reference of ideology critique for the type of criticism developed by Benjamin. A criticism that sets out to rescue semantic potential with a leap into past *Jetztzeiten* has a highly mediated position relative to political praxis. On this, Benjamin did not manage to achieve sufficient clarity.

In the early essay "Toward a Critique of Violence," Benjamin differentiates law-making violence from law-keeping violence. The latter is the legitimate violence exercised by the organs of the state; the former is the structural violence set loose in war and civil strife, which is present latently in all institutions. Law-making violence, unlike law-keeping violence, does not have an instrumental character; instead it "manifests itself." And, to be sure, the structural violence embodied in interpretations and institutions is manifested in the sphere that Benjamin, like Hegel, reserves for destiny or fate (the fates of wars and families). Of course, changes in the sphere of natural history change nothing: "A gaze directed only at what is close at hand can perceive at most a dialectical rising and falling in the law-making and law-preserving formations of violence. . . . This lasts until either new forces or those suppressed earlier triumph over the hitherto law-making violence and thus found a new law, which is destined in turn to decay." (*R*, p. 300) Here again we meet Benjamin's conception of fate, which affirms a natural historical continuum of the always the same and excludes cumulative changes in the structures of domination.

This is where the figure of rescuing criticism sets in. Benjamin then shapes the concept of revolutionary violence in accord with this figure; he invests with all the insights of praxis the act of interpretation that extracts from the past work of art the punctual breakthrough from the continuum of natural history and makes it relevant for the present. This is then the "pure" or "divine" violence that aims at "breaking the cycle under the spell of mythical forms of law." (Ibid.) Benjamin conceptualizes the "pure" violence in the framework of his theory of experience; hence, he has to divest it of the attributes of purposive rational action: Revolutionary violence, like mythical violence, manifests itself—it is the "highest manifestation of unalloyed violence in humans." (Ibid.) In a consistent way, Benjamin refers to Sorel's myth of the general strike and to an anarchistic praxis characterized by the way it bans the instrumental character of action from the realm of political praxis and negates purposive rationality in favor of a "politics of pure means": "The violence (of such a praxis) may be assessed no more from its effects than from its goals, but only from the law of its means." (*R*, p. 292)

That was in 1920. Nine years later Benjamin wrote his famous essay on the surrealist movement, in which Baudelaire's idea of an intimate connection between dream and deed had in the meantime gained ascendancy. What Benjamin had conceived as pure violence had, in the surrealist provocation, surprisingly taken shape: In the nonsensical acts of the surrealist, art was translated into expressive activity; the separation between poetic and political action had been overcome. Thus, Benjamin could see in surrealism the confirmation of his theory of art. Nonetheless, the illustrations of pure violence offered by surrealism found in Benjamin an ambivalent spectator. Politics as show, or even poeticizing politics—when Benjamin saw these realizations, he did not want after all to close his mind to the difference in principle between political action and manifestation: "This would mean the complete subordination of the methodical and disciplinary preparation for revolution to a

praxis oscillating between training for it and celebrating its immi-
nent onset." (R, p. 199) Encouraged by his contact with Brecht,
Benjamin thus parted with his earlier anarchist inclinations; he then
regarded the relationship of art and political praxis primarily from
the viewpoint of the organizational and propagandistic utility of
art for the class struggle. The resolute politicizing of art was a concept that he found ready at hand. He may have had good reasons
for taking up this notion, but it did not have a systematic relation to
his own theory of art and history. Inasmuch as Benjamin accepted it
without any bother, he mutely admitted that an immanent relation
to praxis cannot be gained from his theory of experience: The experience of shock is not an action, and secular illumination is not a
revolutionary deed.

Benjamin's intention was to "enlist the services" of historical
materialism for the theory of experience, but that intention had to
lead to an identification of ecstasy and politics that Benjamin could
not have wanted. The liberation from cultural tradition of semantic
potentials that must not be lost to the messianic condition is not
the same as the liberation of political domination from structural
violence. Benjamin's relevance does not lie in a theology of revolution. His relevance can be seen if we attempt now, conversely, to
"enlist the services" of Benjamin's theory of experience for historical materialism.

7

A dialectical theory of progress, which historical materialism claims
to be, is on its guard; what presents itself as progress can quickly
show itself to be the perpetuation of what was supposedly overcome. More and more theorems of counter-enlightenment have
therefore been incorporated into the dialectic of the enlightenment,
and more and more elements of a critique of progress have been
incorporated into the theory of progress—all for the sake of an idea
of progress that is subtle and relentless enough not to let itself be
blinded by the mere illusion of emancipation. Of course, this dialectical theory of progress has to contradict the thesis that emancipation itself mystifies.

In the concept of exploitation that was determinative for Marx's
critique, poverty and domination were still one. The development
of capitalism has taught us in the meantime to differentiate between
hunger and oppression. The deprivations that can be provided
against by an increase in the standard of living are different from
those that can be helped, not by the growth of social wealth, but

by that of freedom. In *Natural Right and Human Dignity* Bloch introduced into the concept of progress distinctions that were made necessary by the success of the forces of production developed under capitalism. The more the possibility grows in developed societies of uniting repression with prosperity (that is, satisfying demands directed to the economic system without necessarily having to redeem the genuinely political exigencies), the more the accent shifts from the elimination of hunger to emancipation.

In the tradition that reaches back to Marx, Benjamin was one of the first to emphasize a further moment in the concepts of exploitation and progress: besides hunger and repression, failure; besides prosperity and liberty, happiness. Benjamin regarded the experience of happiness he named secular illumination as bound up with the rescuing of tradition. The claim to happiness can be made good only if the sources of that semantic potential we need for interpreting the world in the light of our needs are not exhausted. Cultural goods are spoils that the ruling elite carries in its triumphal parade, and so the process of tradition has to be disentangled from myth. The liberation of culture is certainly not possible without the overcoming of the repression anchored in institutions. Yet, for a moment the suspicion cannot help but arise that an emancipation without happiness and lacking in fulfillment might not be just as possible as relative prosperity without the elimination of repression. This question is not without risks; however, on the verge of *posthistoire*, where symbolic structures are exhausted, worn thin, and stripped of their imperative functions, neither is it entirely idle.

Benjamin would not have posed this question. He insisted on a happiness at once most spiritual and most sensual as an experience for the masses. Indeed, he was almost terrified by the prospect of the possibility of the definitive loss of this experience, because, with his gaze fixed on the messianic condition, he observed how progress was successively cheated for the sake of its fulfillment by progress itself. The critique of the Kautskian way of viewing progress is therefore the political context of the "Theses on the Philosophy of History." Even if one does not argue with respect to each of the three dimensions discussed above that progress in the increase of prosperity, the expansion of liberty, and the promotion of happiness does not represent real progress as long as prosperity, liberty, and happiness have not become universal, it still can plausibly be argued with respect to the hierarchy of the three components that prosperity without liberty is not prosperity and that liberty without happiness is not liberty. Benjamin was profoundly imbued by this:

We cannot be sure about even partial progress before the Last Judgment. Naturally, Benjamin wove this emphatic insight into his conception of fate, according to which historical changes effect no change unless they are reflected in the orders of happiness: "The order of the secular should be erected upon the idea of happiness." (R, p. 312) In this totalizing perspective, the cumulative development of the productive forces and the directional change of the structures of interaction are wound down into an undifferentiated reproduction of the always-the-same. Before Benjamin's Manichean gaze, progress can be perceived only at the solar prominences of happiness; history spreads out like the orbiting of a dead planet upon which, now and then, lightning flashes down. This forces us to construe the economic and political systems in concepts that would really only be adequate to cultural processes: Within the ubiquity of the context of guilt, revolutions are submerged beyond recognition—revolutions that, for all their questionable partiality, take place not only in the dimensions of the forces of production and of social wealth but even in the dimension in which distinctions are infinitely difficult to make in the face of the weight of repression. (I mean progress, which is certainly precarious and permanently threatened by reversal, in the products of legality if not in the formal structures of morality.) In the melancholy of remembering what has been missed and in conjuring up moments of happiness that are in the process of being extinguished, the historical sense for secular progress is in danger of atrophy. No doubt these advances generate their regressions, but this is where political action starts.

Benjamin's critique of empty progress is directed against a joyless reformism whose sensorium has long since been stunted as regards the difference between an improved reproduction of life and a fulfilled life (or, better, a life that is not a failure). But this criticism becomes sharp only when it succeeds in making this difference visible in connection with the uncontemptible improvements of life. These improvements create no new memories, but they dissolve old and dangerous ones. The step-by-step negations of poverty and even repression are, it has to be conceded, oddly without traces; they make things easier, but they do not fulfill, for only alleviation that was remembered would be a preparatory stage for fulfillment. In the face of this situation, there are in the meantime two overworked positions. The counter-enlightenment based on a pessimistic anthropology would have us realize that utopian images of fulfillment are the life-serving fictions of a finite creature that will never be able to transcend its mere life to reach the good life. On the other side, the dialectical theory of progress is quite sure of its prognosis that successful emancipation also means fulfillment. Benjamin's theory of experience could—if it were not the monk's cowl but the core of historical materialism—oppose to the one position a grounded hope and to the other a prophylactic doubt.

Here we are talking only about the doubt that Benjamin's semantic materialism suggests: Can we preclude the possibility of a meaningless emancipation? In complex societies, emancipation means the participatory transformation of administrative decision structures. Is it possible that one day an emancipated human race could encounter itself within an expanded space of discursive formation of will and yet be robbed of the light in which it is capable of interpreting its life as something good? The revenge of a culture exploited over millennia for the legitimation of domination would then take this form: Right at the moment of overcoming age-old repressions, it would harbor no violence but it would have no content either. Without the influx of those semantic energies with which Benjamin's rescuing criticism was concerned, the structures of practical discourse—finally well established—would necessarily become desolate.

Benjamin comes close to wresting the reproach of empty reflection from the counter-enlightenment and appropriating it for a theory of progress. Whoever looks for Benjamin's relevance in this direction is of course open to the objection that emancipatory efforts, in the face of an unshaken political reality, should not be encumbered so light-heartedly with further mortgages, however sublime they might be—first things first. I of course think that a differentiated concept of progress opens a perspective that does not simply obstruct courage but can make political action more sure of hitting its mark, for under historical circumstances that prohibit the thought of revolution and give one reason to expect revolutionary processes of long duration, the idea of the revolution as the process of forming a new subjectivity must also be transformed. Benjamin's conservative-revolutionary hermeneutics, which deciphers the history of culture with a view to rescuing it for the upheaval, may point out one path to take.

A theory of linguistic communication that wanted to bring Benjamin's insights back into a materialist theory of social evolution would need to conceive two of Benjamin's theses together. I am thinking of the assertion that "there is a sphere of human agreement that is nonviolent to the extent that it is wholly inaccessible to violence: the proper sphere of 'mutual understanding,' language." (*R*, p. 289) And I am thinking of the warning that belongs with this: ". . . pessimism all along the line. Absolutely . . . , but above all mistrust, mistrust, and again mistrust in all reciprocal understanding between classes, between nations, between individuals. And unconditional trust only in I.G. Farben and the peaceful perfection of the Luftwaffe."(*R*, p. 191)

Translated by Frederick G. Lawrence

Abbreviations

W. Benjamin, *Schriften*, 2 vols., T. W. and Gretel Adorno, eds. (Frankfurt am Main, 1955). Citations and references in the text use available English translations where possible. Abbreviations to the editions used are:

T. W. Adorno, *Ästhetik Theorie (ÄT)*. *Gesammelte Schriften 7*. Adorno and Rolf Thiedemann, eds. (Frankfurt am Main, 1970).

Briefe (B), Gershom Scholem and T. W. Adorno, eds. (Frankfurt, 1966).

"Correspondence with Benjamin" *(NLR)*, *New Left Review* 81 (1972): 55–80.

"Edward Fuchs, Collector and Historian" *(F)*, *New German Critique* 5 (1975): 27–58.

Gesammelte Schriften I±V (GS), Rolf Tiedemann and Hermann Schweppenhäuser, eds. (Frankfurt am Main, 1972–   ).

Illuminations (I), Hannah Arendt, ed. (New York, 1969).

H. Marcuse, *Negations (Ng)*. J. J. Shapiro, trans. Boston: Beacon, 1968.

The Origins of German Tragic Drama (O) (London, 1977).

Refections (R), Peter Demetz, ed. (New York, 1978).

MARCUSE–PSYCHIC THERMIDOR AND THE REBIRTH OF REBELLIOUS SUBJECTIVITY

1

We all remember what Herbert Marcuse kept denouncing as the evils of our age: the blind struggle for existence, relentless competition, wasteful productivity, deceitful repression, false virility, and cynical brutality. Whenever he felt that he should speak as a teacher and philosopher he encouraged the negation of the performance principle, of possessive individualism, of alienation in labor—as well as in love relations. But the negation of suffering was for him only a start. No doubt, Herbert Marcuse claimed negation to be the very essence of thinking—as did Adorno and Horkheimer; but the driving force of criticism, of contradiction and contest carried him well beyond the limits of an accusation of unnecessary mischief. Marcuse moved further ahead. He did not hesitate to advocate, in an affirmative mood, the fulfillment of human needs, of the need for undeserved happiness, of the need for beauty, of the need for peace, calm, and privacy. Although, certainly, Marcuse was not an affirmative thinker, he was nevertheless the most affirmative among those who praised negativity. With him negative thinking retained the dialectical trust in determinate negation, in the disclosure of positive alternatives. Marcuse did not, in contrast to Adorno, only encircle the ineffable; he made appeals to future alternatives. I am interested in this affirmative feature of Herbert Marcuse's negative thinking. Let me illustrate what I mean by "affirmative feature" with reference to a rather personal reminiscence. I have just reread the two lectures which Marcuse gave when I first met him. For us it was a surprisingly new tone when we heard the following sentences: "The order of values of a nonrepressive principle of progress can be determined on almost all levels in opposition to that of its repressive counterpart. Men's basic experience would be no longer that of life as a struggle for existence but rather that of the enjoyment of life. Alienated labor would be transformed into the free play of human faculties and forces. In consequence all contentless transcendence would come to a close, and freedom would no longer be an eternally failing project. . . . Time would not seem linear . . . , but cyclical, as the return contained in Nietzsche's idea of 'the perpetuity of pleasure.' "

This is not quoted from the Marcuse of 1967, who came to Berlin for intense discussions on violence and the expected end of utopia and who, at that time, was hailed by the protesting students as their inspirational intellectual leader. Neither is that quote from the Marcuse of 1964, who came to the Max Weber centennial in Heidelberg, made his professional appearance as an important emigre social theorist and immediately aroused excited discussions. I am speaking of the Marcuse of 1956, who came to Frankfurt for another centennial: the commemoration on the occasion of Freud's one hundredth birthday was the date of Marcuse's first academic return to Germany. I should mention that the international conference of *Freud in der Gegenwart*, where Marcuse lectured side by side with famous analysts such as Alexander, Balint, Erikson, and Spitz, was the first opportunity for young German academics to learn about the simple fact that Sigmund Freud was the founding father of a living scientific and intellectual tradition. In this context Marcuse opened his first lecture with sentences which, at a time when Freud and Marx were "dead dogs" and practically unknown at German universities, sounded strange and radical: "The psyche appears more and more immediately to be a piece of social totality, so that individuation is almost synonymous with apathy and even with guilt, but also with the principle of negation, of possible revolution. Moreover, the totality of which the psyche is a part becomes to an increasing extent less 'society' than 'politics.' That is, society has fallen prey to and becomes identified with domination."

For us, the research assistants at the Institute of Horkheimer and Adorno, this was the moment when we first faced an embodiment and vivid expression of the political spirit of the old Frankfurt School. As a school it had been alive only during a few years of American exile. If there ever has been a Frankfurt School, it did not exist in Frankfurt, neither before nor after the Nazi period, but during the 1930s, in New York. I was reminded of this fact when Herbert, before his death in Starnberg, while he was, after a stroke, already somewhat inhibited in his verbal fluency, did not speak his mother tongue: the language of his last days was English. But let me return to our first encounter. What, in 1956, made a stunning impression was the forthright style of Marcuse's thought and presentation. You know better than I that Herbert Marcuse's spoken English never quite lost the mark of a Berlin accent, that his written English was never completely stripped of the clumsiness of the German grammar underneath. But with his German it was the other way round. By the standards of the jargon of German philosophers Marcuse spoke a straight, affirmative language, easy to understand and without the rhetorical loopholes where the more shocking consequences of a dialectical argument might have found a hiding place. Although rather a shy person, Marcuse was never afraid of being outspoken and for taking the responsibility for what he said, even for taking the risk of oversimplification, if there seemed to be no other way to address an important issue. In the following years, when I became closer to Herbert Marcuse and learned more about the first generation of critical theorists, that affirmative feature which struck me from the very beginning became even more obvious. Compared with Horkheimer, Löwenthal, and Adorno, with whom he had formed the inner circle, Marcuse represented a singular combination.

Since he first joined the Institute, Marcuse had made the most "orthodox" contributions to critical theory. This is true of his essays in the *Zeitschrift* where Marcuse was chosen to write the article "Philosophy and Critical Theory," counterpart to Horkheimer's famous position paper on "Traditional and Critical Theory." But it is also true of his later writings including the very last: in *Reason and Revolution*, in *One-Dimensional Man*, and in *The Aesthetic Dimension*, Marcuse elaborated themes and arguments, pursued lines of reasoning that were more or less shared by the whole group. This orthodoxy is, however, only one side of Marcuse's work. His work reflects, on the other side, quite distinct features which set it apart from the background tradition. Marcuse received his philosophical training in Freiburg with Heidegger, and he never lost contact with existential phenomenology. Marcuse was, among his colleagues, the most professional in attitude; his major works, *Reason and Revolution, Soviet Marxism*, and *Eros and Civilization* are all well placed in the context of related disciplines and exemplify an almost conventional type of systematic academic presentation.

Marcuse's personal history followed, as compared to the biographies of those next to him, including Neumann and Kirchheimer, an almost opposite trend; he, who started from a rather conservative theoretical position, became in the course of his life more and more radicalized—he was, moreover, the only one who assumed a direct political role; supported by his wife Inge, he deliberately took this role and played it at times with a considerable sense for the imponderables of political activism.

Take one example: when Marcuse was in Berlin in 1967, he was asked about his relation to the heroes of the Third World and, in his inimitable manner, gave the answer: "I would not have mentioned Fanon and Guevara as much as a small item that I read in a report about North Vietnam and that had a tremendous effect on me, since I am an absolutely incurable and sentimental romantic. It was a very detailed report, which showed . . . that in the parks in Hanoi the benches are made only big enough for two and *only two* people to sit on, so that another person would not even have the technical possibility of disturbing.''

Here, again, we encounter something very affirmative. Imagine, for the moment, that Adorno in a similar situation would have wanted to express a similar intention! He probably would have made a cautious appeal to a poem of Eichendorff while anticipating what all of us today, after the Vietnamese invasion into Cambodia, do think: that the facts will reveal as an incurable romantic one who tries to affirmatively spell out utopia in terms of particular examples, as Herbert did. What I have called the affirmative feature is documented by a type of self-confessed romanticism which is lacking in Adorno and Horkheimer, and even in Benjamin.

The question which I would like to pursue is whether this peculiar feature should just count as a trait of Herbert Marcuse's personality or whether it is due to a theoretical position which separates him from his close friends. Since there is a good deal of manifest agreement among the members of the inner circle, we tend to think that the affirmative feature of Marcuse's negative thinking indicates a difference rather in style and character than in theory. How otherwise could we explain the fact that the author of the deeply pessimistic *One-Dimensional Man*—a book which ends with the quote from Benjamin that it is only for the sake of those without hope that hope is given to us—that this man, less than one year later, inspired the student movement with his hope? I think there is another explanation. In Marcuse's version of critical theory we find a twist on an argument which well can explain why Marcuse was different. In order to identify this twist I will briefly outline the main stages of the thought of Herbert Marcuse.

2

I will start with (A) the transition from Heidegger to Horkheimer, and then (B) indicate the classical position of critical theory in the mid-1930s, with a subsequent shift marked by Horkheimer and Adorno's *Dialectic of Enlightenment*. From this perspective we will see (C) the route that Marcuse took as his way out of the dilemma posed by the alleged totalization of instrumental reason. He discovered this way with *Eros and Civilization*, the book that appeared

in 1955 and the substance of which was contained in the two Freud
lectures given at Frankfort one year later.

(A) *Hegels Ontologie und die Grundlegung einer Theorie der
Geschichtlichkeit*, published in 1932, was planned as *Habilitations-
Schrift*. The aspired *Habilitation* did not work out—Heidegger was
soon to become one of the Nazi Rectors of the first hour. That
Hegel book was written by one of the brightest students of Heidegger; it is the document of an attempt to interpret dialectical thinking
from a peculiar Heideggerian point of view. Hegel is here presented
as another ontologist who conceived being as the essence of becoming—*Sein als Bewegtheit*. Heidegger had a lasting impact on Herbert Marcuse—as much in terms of personal loyalty, bridging the
political abyss, as in terms of certain philosophical motivations. For
Marcuse, Heidegger remained the one of *Being and Time*, moreover that Heidegger whose analysis of *Dasein* was received as a
radicalized transcendental approach. Of course, after the period of
Being and Time, both Heidegger and Marcuse moved in opposite
directions. While Heidegger made *Dasein*, the abstract structures
of the human world, dependent on some metahistorical fate, of an
even more abstract *Sein* or fateful being, Marcuse, on the other
hand, tried to link the ontological structures of the life world to the
ontic, that is, to the contingent and concrete processes of society
and history; he looked out for the differentiation of the ontological
difference. It was no accident that Marcuse, in this transitional period, did not move away from Heidegger by way of a critique of
Heidegger. For the preparation of this lecture, Leö Lowenthal lent
me his copy of *Hegels Ontologie*, and in this old copy I found a
yellowed cutout from the feuilleton of the *Vossische Zeitung* with
a long and intense review of the three volumes of Karl Jaspers's
Philosophie, written by somebody with the initials H.M., dated December 14, 1933. It is in this context of a criticism of Jaspers that
we find a passage which indicates, still guarded by clauses, Marcuse's detachment from Heidegger. Here, Marcuse insists that the
formal properties of historicity conceal rather than disclose the substance of history. He raises the question, "Whether it is not the case
that particular and contingent situations can destroy the authenticity of human existence, can abolish freedom or transform it into
sheer illusion." Any talk about historicity, he continues, "must remain abstract and uncommitted until the analysis focuses on the
concrete, 'material' situation." (*Vossische Zeitung*, 339, December
14, 1933.)

The term *material* is printed in quotes, thereby inconspicuously referring to an earlier article of the same author on the recently discovered Paris Manuscripts, not by Karl Jaspers but by Karl Marx. This article shows how young Marcuse appropriated young Marx from the viewpoint of existential phenomenology, taking the very notions of *Praxis* and *Lebenswelt* as guidelines for the liberation from alienated labor. Marcuse was the first Heideggerian-Marxist, anticipating the later phenomenological Marxism of Jean-Paul Sartre, Karl Kosik, Enzo Paci, and the Yugoslav *Praxis* philosophers.

(B) In the meantime, Marcuse had joined the Frankfurt Institute on its way to the United States. In his famous essay on "Philosophy and Critical Theory," published in 1937, Marcuse presents himself at the center of the Frankfurt School's theory. The vacant place of *Dasein* and *Geschichtlichkeit*, of the abstract structures of the human world, is not filled with ahistorically situated reason: "Reason is the fundamental category of philosophical thought, the only one by means of which it has bound itself to human destiny." The abstract and ahistorical concept of reason which is at the heart of idealistic philosophy lends itself to all forms of ideology, but the bourgeois ideals, of cognitive and moral universalism on the one hand, of expressive subjectivism on the other, carry also a utopian content which transcends the limits of false consciousness. For critical theory those ideals "are exclusively potentialities of the concrete social situation. They become relevant only as economic and political questions and as such bear on human relations in the productive process, the distribution of the product of social labor, and men's active participation in the economic and political administration of the whole." The demand for reason simply means, resonating indeed to an ancient truth, a demand for "the creation of a social organization in which individuals can collectively regulate their lives in accordance with their needs."

At the time when he wrote this, Marcuse was already aware of, and explicitly referring to the fact that, with fascism and, moreover, with Stalinism, history had taken a course quite contrary to the predictions of Marxist theory. He therefore stressed the constructive as against the descriptive and explanatory role of theory, admitting that critical theory "must concern itself to a hitherto unknown extent with the past." But Marcuse did not yet question the revolutionary dynamic of the productive forces developing in the womb of capitalism. The stifling of the proletariat, its lack of revolutionary consciousness, is still explained in the old vein: "Fettering the productive forces and keeping down the standard of life is characteristic of even the economically most developed countries."

In the following years Marcuse elaborated the classical position of critical theory in careful studies on Hegel and the rise of social theory. At the same time, Horkheimer and Adorno, who had moved to Santa Monica, had already taken a somewhat different line. With *Dialectic of Enlightenment* they definitely lost their trust in the revolutionary dynamic of the productive forces, and in the practical impact of negative thinking. Both the productive forces and critical thought were seen in the perspective of merging with their opposite, with the forces of domination. As they develop they become regressive, more and more subordinated to the imperatives of an instrumental reason which is no longer instrumental for the satisfaction of human needs, but gaining the autonomy of an end in itself. The totality of instrumental reason finds its expression in totalitarian society. I will not go into the subtleties of this gloomy exposition which Marcuse soon adopted. In the foreword to an English translation of his old essays, published three decades ago in the *Zeitschrift*, Marcuse declared the break in his thinking: "That . . . this was written before Auschwitz deeply separates it from the present. What was correct in it has since become, perhaps not false, but a thing of the past . . . : remembrance of something that at some point had lost its reality and had to be taken up again . . . The end of a historical period and the horror of the one to come were announced in the simultaneity of the civil war in Spain and the trials in Moscow."

Marcuse described this new period as a totalization of instrumental reason, that is, in the light of his own analysis in *One-Dimensional Man:* "Productivity and prosperity in league with a technology in the service of monopolistic politics seem to immunize advancing industrial society in its established structure." He then asks the central question: "Is this concept of immunity still dialectical?"

Adorno answered this question with a qualified "No"; he explained this reaction in terms of his "Negative Dialectics." Marcuse, on the contrary, still stuck to an affirmative answer. According to Marcuse, the earlier theory, with its concept of a free and rational society, made only one mistake—it did not promise too much but rather too little.

* * *

(C) The reasons why Herbert Marcuse could both accept Hork-heimer's and Adorno's analysis of the eclipse of reason and yet re-main faithful to the political intention of early Critical Theory are laid out in *Eros and Civilization*, among Marcuse's books the most Marcusian one.

Let me first state the question at issue. Marcuse agreed with Horkheimer and Adorno in their assumption that with the expan-sion of capitalism the project of instrumental reason would shape the entire universe of discourse and action, intellectual and material culture: "In the medium of technology, culture, politics, and the economy merge into an omnipresent system which swallows up or repulses all alternatives." On the other hand, Marcuse still main-tained that the same project does undermine the stability of domi-nation which fuses technology with practical rationality, since "[t]he progressive reduction of physical labor power in the produc-tion process . . . suggests possible liberation from alienated labor." If these objective possibilities are at all suggestive, we must, how-ever, rely on a subjectivity which is still sensitive to a utopian hori-zon. This is the question then: how could Marcuse believe in the rebirth of rebellious subjectivity if he accepted the first of the two arguments, in fact the core argument of *Dialectic of Enlightenment*, that with each conquest over external nature the internal nature of those who gain ever new triumphs is more deeply enslaved?

It is at this point that Marcuse shows reservations based on his distinctive reading of Freud's theory of instincts. To put the argu-ment in a nutshell: even if the individual, the sole bearer of reason, is more and more swallowed up by a totalitarian society, and even if this shrinkage of the ego is without any limits, we still may hope for the rebirth of rebellious subjectivity from a nature which is older than, and arises from below the level of, individuation and rationality. Marcuse has a chiliastic trust in a revitalizing dynamic of instincts which works through history, finally breaks with his-tory and leaves it behind as what then will appear as prehistory. Let us recall how he interprets Freud's theory of patricide:

> This dynamic of domination, which begins with the institution of despotism, leads to revolution and ends after the first attempt at lib-eration with the reestablishment of the father in internalized and generalized, i.e. rational form, repeats itself . . . during the entire history of culture and civilization, although in diluted form. It does so as the rebellion of all sons against all fathers in puberty . . . and . . . in the ever recurring dynamic of revolutions in the past. . . .

Insurrection succeeds and certain forces attempt to drive the revolution to its extreme point, from which the transition to new, not only quantitatively but qualitatively different conditions could perhaps proceed. At this point the revolution is usually vanquished and domination is internalized, reestablished, and continued at a higher level. . . . we can raise the question whether alongside the sociohistorical Thermidor . . . there is not also a *psychic* Thermidor. Are revolutions perhaps not only vanquished, reversed, and unmade from the outside, is there perhaps in individuals themselves already a dynamic at work that *internally* negates possible liberation and gratification and that supports external forces of denial?

At a first glance, this consideration is nothing but a translation, of what the dialectic of instrumental reason means, into Freudian language. On a careful reading, the difference however comes to the fore—the difference is in the move to keep separate the internal or instinctual from the external or social forces of domination. If the psychic as compared with the socio-historic thermidor gains a dynamic of its own, it is no longer social theory alone, but the theory of instincts which also provides the key. The question, whether the psychic thermidor must be repeated again and again, gains an almost existentialist dignity, since the answer to this question no longer depends on whether or not late capitalism, as an economic and a political system, can contain its inner conflicts.

From the metahistory of instincts Marcuse defends two related propositions. (1) There is no final opposition between Eros and Thanatos; in spite of their antagonism both are conservative in nature, both strive for pacification, and both are unproductive and similarly directed against a relentless struggle for existence. (2) As soon as the progress of civilization, which is based on the repressive modification of the instincts, increases, the existence of a surplus product not leading to individual gratification provokes a reaction from both Eros and Thanatos. Once instinctual repression loses its function for necessary self-preservation, the two conservative powers behind the scenes of civilization form a coalition and demand the recalling of energies from alienated labor.

3

This theory has the weakness that it cannot consistently account for its own possibility. If rebellious subjectivity had to owe its rebirth to something that is beyond—a too deeply corrupted—reason, it is hard to explain why some of us should at all be in a position to recognize this fact and to give reasons in defense of it. In this respect, Adorno was the more consistent thinker. However implausible the argument may seem, it had the function to preserve in Herbert Marcuse one of his most admirable features—not to give in to defeatism. But there is more to the search for an "instinctive" base of socialism. This effort is, after all, the result of a true philosophical intention. Marcuse did not want to fall back into existentialism, he did not want just to appeal to the vital needs of freedom or merely to evoke the pathos of emancipation. He felt the obligation to give theoretical explanations and thereby to ground action in reason.

Moreover, Marcuse was one of the few philosophers who were severely and chronically rebuked for the seriousness of their philosophical attitude. In summer 1967, at the Free University, Marcuse was exposed to a situation where he knew that any single word could have irrevocable consequences. He was invited to talk about the use of violence, and he had just declared the unity of moral, sexual, and political rebellion, when he found himself confronted with questions about the doubtful nature of moral justifications. Some of the questions indicated a then-widespread inclination, on the side of the students, to free political activism from the painful hesitations of moral-practical reasoning. One student complained about difficulties he had experienced in discussions with a worker: "What does this worker care about the terror in Vietnam? Humanitarian arguments wouldn't do, since humanity itself gave rise to terror." The student apparently referred, although in an elliptic and misleading form, to the core of the analysis of the eclipse of reason. But Marcuse was not irritated at all. "As to your suspicion about humanitarian arguments . . . We must finally relearn what we forgot during the fascist period, or what you, who were not even born . . . have not fully become conscious of: that humanitarian and moral arguments are not merely deceitful ideology. Rather, they can and must become central social forces." Another student countered this straight answer with a moral skepticism which in my country often reveals the strong influence of Carl Schmitt even on the left: "On the right of resistance: in your essay on tolerance you put this right in quotation marks, but now you have interpreted it as an ancient principle. What is this right based on? Is it a romantic relic of natural law, or is it a self-posited right and, if so, how can the opposition invoke a right which it must first generate?" In this moment, Marcuse decided to be inconsistent rather than irresponsible. He swept aside his own doubts on a corrupted practical reason which supposedly had been absorbed into a totality of instrumental reason. His answer was clear, without the slightest ambiguity: ". . . appealing to the right of resistance is an appeal to a higher law, which has universal validity, that is, which goes beyond the self-defined right and privilege of a particular group. And there really is a close connection between the right of resistance and natural law. Now you will say that such a universal higher law simply does not exist. I believe that it does exist. Today we no longer call it Natural Law . . . If we appeal to humanity's right to peace, to the right to abolish exploitation and oppression, we are not talking about self-defined, special, group interests, but rather and, in fact, interests demonstrable as universal rights."

Before his eightieth birthday, and in preparation for an interview on that occasion, Marcuse and I had a long discussion on how we could and should explain the normative base of Critical Theory. Last summer, when I saw him for the first time since that discussion, Herbert was under intensive care in a hospital in Frankfurt, all types of controlling apparatuses on his left and on his right. None of us knew that this was the beginning of the end. On this occasion, indeed our last philosophical encounter, Herbert made the connection with our controversy two years ago, telling me: Look, I know wherein our most basic value judgments are rooted—in compassion, in our sense for the suffering of others.

Translated by Frederick G. Lawrence

The Authors

THEODOR WIESENGRUND ADORNO (b. Frankfurt am Main 1903; d. Visp, Wallis 1969), was the leading philosopher of the Frankfurt School and a composer. His mother was an opera singer, and at the beginning of his career he took the name *Adorno* from her side of the family (father's name Wiesengrund). An extremely gifted student, he studied music with Alban Berg in Vienna, and philosophy at the University of Frankfurt. Music editor of "Anbruch" (Vienna) 1928–31. Received his Ph.D. 1924 and his habilitation 1931 at the University of Frankfurt. Since 1931, member of the Institute for Social Research. Emigrated 1934, postdoctoral studies at Oxford, moved to New York in 1938, and on to Los Angeles in 1941. He was co-director of the Research Project on Social Discrimination at the University of California, Berkeley, until he returned to Frankfurt in 1949. Finally in 1956 appointed Professor of Philosophy and Sociology at the University of Frankfurt, he was director of the Institute for Social Research 1959–69, and his work became an inspiration for the 1968 student rebellion in Germany. Publications (latest editions): *Dialectic of Enlightenment* (1972, 1994), *Minima Moralia* (1978), *Against Epistemology* (1982), *Prisms* (1983), *Negative Dialectics* (1983), *Aesthetic Theory* (1983), *Kierkegaard: Construction of the Aesthetic* (1989), *The Culture Industry* (1991), *Mahler: A Musical Physiognomy* (1992), *Critical Models* (1998).

WALTER BENJAMIN (b. 1892 Berlin; d. Portbou, Spain 1940) was a groundbreaking philosopher of art and language as well as an accomplished writer. Studied German literature and philosophy in Freiburg, Berlin, Munich, and Bern 1912–18. Received Ph.D. with a dissertation on "The Concept of Art Criticism in German Romanticism" at the University of Bern 1919. The son of a banker, he lived in postwar Berlin and became friends with Ernst Bloch, Martin Buber, Bertolt Brecht, and Theodor W. Adorno. The poet Hugo von Hofmannsthal published Benjamin's essay on "Goethe's *Elective Affinities*" (1925). After a habilitation attempt with the book *Origin of German Tragic Drama* (1928) at the University of Frankfurt failed, he formed close ties with the Frankfurt School and discovered an interest in Marxism. When the Nazis took over, he emigrated to Paris where he did research work at the National Library for his Arcades-Project. Benjamin became acquainted with the circle of Georges Bataille. After the German occupation of France in 1940, Benjamin fled to the unoccupied

South. His friends Adorno and Horkheimer finally secured a visa for him to come to New York, and Benjamin crossed the border to Spain in September attempting to reach Lisbon. After a strenuous hike over the Pyrenees, the Spanish authorities threatened to send him back the next day; bereft of hope, Benjamin committed suicide in Portbou. The manuscript of the "Arcades" that he carried with him was lost and has never been recovered. Publications: *Illuminations* (1968), *Reflections* (1978), *The Correspondence of Walter Benjamin and Gershom Scholem* (1992), *One-Way Street and Other Writings* (1997), *Charles Baudelaire: A Lyric Poet in the Era of High Capitalism* (1997).

NORBERT ELIAS (b. Breslau 1897; d. Amsterdam 1990) was one of the founders of process sociology and figurational studies. Studied medicine, psychology, and philosophy in Breslau, Heidelberg (with Karl Jaspers) and Freiburg (with Edmund Husserl). Ph.D. on "Idee und Individuum" at University of Breslau 1925. Assistant to Alfred Weber in Heidelberg, he followed Karl Mannheim, the author of *Ideology and Utopia,* to the University of Frankfurt. Member of the discussion circle of the Institute for Social Research, he emigrated in 1933 to Paris, a few years later to London. Held adjunct positions at the London School of Economics, appointed lecturer at the University of Leicester 1954. Beginning 1969, he was guest lecturer in Ghana, Germany, France, and the United States. Elias received the Adorno Prize in 1977 and had become permanent resident of Amsterdam in 1984. Publications: *The Established and the Outsiders* (1966), *The Civilizing Process* (1978), *The Court Society* (1983), *The Loneliness of Dying* (1985), *Involvement and Detachment* (1987), *The Symbol Theory* (1991), *The Society of Individuals* (1991), *Reflections on a Life* (1994).

JÜRGEN HABERMAS (b. 1929) grew up in Gummersbach, a small town east of Cologne. After his studies in philosophy at the University of Bonn, he became an assistant to Theodor W. Adorno at the Institute for Social Research, eventually becoming identified with the Frankfurt School as one of its most prominent thinkers. At the end of the 1950s, he left the Institute to become associated with the Universities of Marburg and Heidelberg. His first influential book, *Structural Transformation of the Public Sphere* (1962), related its topic to the political philosophy of the Enlightenment whereas his first collection of essays was clearly indebted to Marx's idea that praxis was not to denounce theory (particularly social theory, 1963). In 1964, he returned to Frankfurt as Professor of Philosophy and Sociology, where he became a sympathetic supporter of the student movement until it turned violent, when he became its ardent critic. During this period, he concentrated on social theory and the methodology of the social sciences, publishing, among other books and articles, *Logic of the Social Sciences,* 1967, and *Knowledge and Human Interest,* 1968. In 1971, he became one of the two directors of the *Max Planck Institute for the Study of the Conditions of Life in a Scientific-Technical World* (the other director being Carl-Friedrich von Weizsäcker, a nuclear physicist). He held this post until 1981. He returned to a chair in Philosophy at the University of Frankfurt in 1983, two years after the publication of his monumental *Theory of Communicative Action*. Major philosophical treatises on legal and political theory followed. Among his further publications are: *Toward a Rational Society* (1971), *Legitimation Crisis* (1975), *Communication and the Evolution of Society* (1979), *The Philosophical Discourse of Modernity* (1987), *Moral Consciousness and Communicative Action* (1990), *Postmetaphysical Thinking* (1992), *Justification and Application* (1993), *Between Facts and Norms* (1996), and *The Inclusion of the Other* (1996).

MAX HORKHEIMER (b. Zuffenhausen near Stuttgart 1895; d. Nürnberg 1973) was the visionary director of the Frankfurt Institute for Social Research 1930–59. Worked for years in his father's textile business. Studied psychology, philosophy, and economics in Munich, Frankfurt, and Freiburg 1919–22. Ph.D. 1922, habilitation 1925, professor of philosophy 1930 at the University of Frankfurt. Emigrated 1933 with the Institute to Geneva and 1934 to New York where the Institute operated in association with Columbia University and served as lifeline for many exiled German scholars. Lived in Pacific Palisades, California, where the climate was more beneficial to his health. Returned to Frankfurt in 1949 where he resumed his professorship and restored the Institute. Appointed rector of Frankfurt University 1951–53. Visiting professor University of Chicago 1954–59. Emeritus following 1958, Horkheimer lived in Montagnola, Switzerland. Publications (latest editions): *Eclipse of Reason* (1947), *Dawn and Decline: Notes* (1978), *Dialectic of Enlightenment* (1972, 1994), *Between Philosophy and Social Science* (1995), *Critical Theory* (1995).

LEO LÖWENTHAL (b. Frankfurt 1900; d. Berkeley 1993) was one of the founders of communication studies and sociology of literature. Studied literature, history, philosophy, and sociology in Frankfurt, Heidelberg, and Gießen. Ph.D. with a study on the social philosophy of Franz von Baader at the University of Frankfurt 1923. Since 1926, member of the Institute for Social Research and managing editor of *Journal for Social Research* (from 1932). Emigration with the Institute to New York, investigated German propaganda, and in 1949 became research director of the *Voice of America*. Since 1959, professor of sociology (with emphasis on literature) at the University of California, Berkeley, he received the Adorno Prize 1989. Publications: *Prophets of Deceit* (1949), *The Image of Man* (1970), *Literature and Mass Culture* (1984), *Literature, Popular Culture, Society* (1985), *Critical Theory and Frankfurt Theorists* (1989).

HERBERT MARCUSE (b. Berlin 1898; d. Starnberg 1979) was a noted philosopher of technology and the most widely known member of the Frankfurt School. A leading theorist of the New Left and outspoken opponent of the Vietnam War, he became the mentor of the worldwide student movement. Studied German literature and philosophy in Berlin and Freiburg, did his Ph.D. on "The German Artist Novel" (1922), and became assistant to Martin Heidegger at the University of Freiburg in 1928. Member of the Frankfurt Institute for Social Research since 1931. Emigrated with the Institute to Geneva 1933, and New York 1934. Worked for the American State Department 1942–50. Professor of political science at Brandeis University 1954–65, he was appointed professor of philosophy at the University of California at San Diego, 1965. Visiting professor Berkeley, Berlin, Paris. Publications: *Reason and Revolution* (1941), *Eros and Civilization* (1955), *Soviet Marxism: A Critical Analysis* (1961), *The One-Dimensional Man* (1964), *Repressive Tolerance* (1965), *An Essay on Liberation* (1969), *Counter-Revolution and Revolt* (1972), *The Aesthetic Dimension* (1978), *Technology, War, and Fascism* (1998).

Bibliography

Ben Agger. *The Discourse of Domination: From the Frankfurt School to Postmodernism*. Evanston: Northwestern University Press, 1994.

Fred Alford. *Science and the Revenge of Nature: Marcuse and Habermas*. Gainesville: University of Florida Press, 1985.

Joan Alway. *Critical Theory and Political Possibilities: Concepts of Emancipatory Politics in the Works of Horkheimer, Adorno, Marcuse, and Habermas*. Westport: Greenwood, 1995.

Seyla Benhabib, Wolfgang Bonss, and John McCole. *On Max Horkheimer*. Cambridge: MIT Press, 1993.

Momme Brodersen. *Walter Benjamin. A Biography*. New York: Norton, 1997.

Susan Buck-Morss. *Dialectics of Seeing: Benjamin and the Arcades Projects*. Cambridge: MIT Press, 1991.

Howard Caygill. *Walter Benjamin: The Color of Experience*. London: Routledge, 1997.

Margaret Cohen. *Profane Illumination: Walter Benjamin and the Paris of Surrealist Revolution*. Berkeley: University of California Press, 1993.

Peter Dews. *Logic of Disintegration: Post-Structuralist Thought and the Claims of Critical Theory*. London: Verso, 1987.

Jonathan Fletcher. *Violence and Civilization: An Introduction to the Work of Norbert Elias*. Cambridge, UK: Polity Press, 1997.

David Held. *Introduction to Critical Theory: From Horkheimer to Habermas*. Berkeley: University of California Press, 1990.

Peter Uwe Hohendahl. *Reappraisals: Shifting Alignments in Postwar Critical Theory*. Ithaca: Cornell University Press, 1994.

Tom Huhn and Lambert Zuidervaart. *The Semblance of Subjectivity: Essays in Adorno's Aesthetic Theory*. Cambridge: MIT Press, 1997.

Martin Jay. *The Dialectical Imagination: A History of the Frankfurt School and the Institute of Social Research*. Berkeley: University of California Press, 1996.

Douglas Kellner. *Critical Theory, Marxism, and Modernity*. Baltimore: Johns Hopkins University Press, 1989.

Douglas Kellner. *Herbert Marcuse and the Crisis of Marxism*. Berkeley: University of California Press, 1984.

Robert van Krieken. *Norbert Elias*. London: Routledge, 1998.

John McCole. *Walter Benjamin and the Antinomies of Tradition.* Ithaca: Cornell University Press, 1993.

Christoph Menke. *The Sovereignty of Art: Aesthetic Negativity in Adorno and Derrida.* Cambridge: MIT Press, 1999.

Charles Reitz. *Art, Alienation, and the Humanities. A Critical Engagement with Herbert Marcuse.* Albany: SUNY Press, 2000.

Gary Smith (ed.). *On Walter Benjamin.* Cambridge: MIT Press, 1988.

Judith Stamps. *Unthinking Modernity: Innis, McLuhan, and the Frankfurt School.* Montreal: McGill-Queens University Press, 1995.

Sigrid Weigel. *Body and Image Space: Re-reading Walter Benjamin.* London: Routledge, 1996.

Rolf Wiggershaus. *Frankfurt School: Its History, Theories, and Political SigniÆcance.* Cambridge: MIT Press, 1995.

John Witebook. *Perversion and Utopia: A Study in Psychoanalysis and Critical Theory.* Cambridge: MIT Press, 1996.

Robert W. Witkin. *Adorno on Music.* London: Routledge, 1998.

Richard Wolin. *The Terms of Cultural Critics: The Frankfurt School, Existentialism, Poststructuralism.* New York: Columbia University Press, 1995.

Lambert Zuidervaart. *Adorno's Aesthetic Theory.* Cambridge: MIT Press, 1991.

Acknowledgments

Every reasonable effort has been made to locate the owners of rights to previously published works and translations printed here. We gratefully acknowledge permission to reprint the following material:

"Theses on the Philosophy of History" from ILLUMINATIONS by Walter Benjamin, copyright © 1955 by Suhrkamp Verlag, Frankfurt a.M., English translation by Harry Zohn copyright © 1968 and renewed 1996 by Harcourt Brace & Company, reprinted by permission of Harcourt Brace & Company. This essay will be included in the forthcoming collected works of Walter Benjamin to be published by Harvard University Press.

Reprinted by permission of Transaction Publishers. Chapter 11 of *False Prophets: Studies on Authoritarianism* by Leo Löwenthal. Copyright © 1987. All rights reserved.

Jürgen Habermas, Frederick G. Lawrence, translator, *Philosophical Political Profiles,* pages 67–77, 99–109, 129–59. Courtesy the MIT Press.

"On Hedonism" from *Negations* by Herbert Marcuse. Translations from German © 1969 by Beacon Press. Reprinted by permission of Beacon Press, Boston. "Solidarity" from *An Essay on Liberation* by Herbert Marcuse. Copyright © 1969 by Herbert Marcuse. Reprinted by permission of Beacon Press, Boston. "The Catastrophe of Liberation" from *One-Dimensional Man* by Herbert Marcuse. Copyright © 1964 by Herbert Marcuse. Reprinted by permission of Beacon Press, Boston.

From *Dialectic of Enlightenment* by Max Horkheimer and Theodor W. Adorno, English translation © 1972 by Herder and Herder, Inc.

Titles Available in
The German Library

*All titles available from Continuum International
370 Lexington Avenue, New York, NY 10017
www.continuum-books.com*

Titles Available in The German Library

Titles Available in The German Library

Titles Available in The German Library

Titles Available in The German Library

Complete Author Listing
in The German Library
by Volume Number